ORWELL IN CUBA

ORWELL IN CUBA

How **1984** Came to Be Published in Castro's Twilight

FRÉDÉRICK LAVOIE

TRANSLATED BY DONALD WINKLER

TALONBOOKS

Talonbooks
9259 Shaughnessy Street, Vancouver, British Columbia, Canada V6P 6R4
talonbooks.com

Talonbooks is located on xʷməθkʷəy̓əm, Sḵwx̱wú7mesh, and səl̓ilwətaʔɬ Lands.

Second printing: February 2020

Typeset in Arno
Printed and bound in Canada on 100% post-consumer recycled paper

Cover design by Typesmith
Cover illustration by andrea bennett
Interior design by Chloë Filson

Talonbooks acknowledges the financial support of the Canada Council for the Arts, the Government of Canada through the Canada Book Fund, and the Province of British Columbia through the British Columbia Arts Council and the Book Publishing Tax Credit.

This work was originally published in French as *Avant l'après: Voyages à Cuba avec George Orwell* by La Peuplade, Saguenay, Québec, in 2018. We acknowledge the financial support of the Government of Canada through the National Translation Program for Book Publishing, an initiative of the *Roadmap for Canada's Official Languages 2013–2018: Education, Immigration, Communities,* for our translation activities.

LIBRARY AND ARCHIVES CANADA CATALOGUING IN PUBLICATION

Title: Orwell in Cuba : how 1984 came to be published in Castro's twilight / Frédérick Lavoie ; translated by Donald Winkler.
Other titles: Avant l'après. English

Names: Lavoie, Frédérick, 1983– author. | Winkler, Donald, translator.
Description: Translation of: Avant l'après: voyages à Cuba avec George Orwell. | Includes bibliographical references.
Identifiers: Canadiana 20200160222 | ISBN 9781772012453 (softcover)
Subjects: LCSH: Lavoie, Frédérick, 1983––Travel—Cuba. | LCSH: Orwell, George, 1903–1950. Nineteen eighty-four. | LCSH: Freedom of speech—Cuba—History—20th century. | LCSH: Cuba—Politics and government—20th century. | LCSH: Cuba—Social conditions—21st century.
Classification: LCC F1788 .L3813 2020 | DDC 972.9106/4—dc23

Revolution is the sense of the historical moment; it is changing everything that must be changed; it is full equality and freedom.

—Fidel Castro

Freedom is the freedom to say that two plus two makes four. If that is granted, all else follows.

—George Orwell

TABLE OF CONTENTS

PROLOGUE

BEFORE

The news was buried in the next-to-last paragraph of a routine article outlining the Arte y Literatura Editions' new releases, to be launched in the course of Havana's twenty-fifth International Book Fair.

> We might regard as wise the decision to publish the iconic novel *1984* by the English writer George Orwell, deemed controversial and thought-provoking, given the fact that it portrays life in a society where information is controlled, and where mass surveillance and social and political repression are the order of the day.[1]

The news was certainly surprising. Somewhere in the opaque hierarchy of a dictatorship where, indeed, news was managed while mass surveillance and political and social repression were standard operating procedure, someone had hatched the curious idea, to say the least, of authorizing the publication of the most notorious antitotalitarian novel of the twentieth century. And Radio Enciclopedia, a media organization controlled by the regime, was characterizing this decision as "wise."

When I came across this article online, I was in Miami. I was paying a visit to the capital city of exiled Cubans in order to meet some members of the diaspora in anticipation of my first trip to the island, which would coincide with the book fair, and so with the unveiling of *1984*. For a rare moment in my career, I found myself with a small international scoop. Only the rarely consulted website for Radio Enciclopedia had relayed this news to the outside world, and no media outlet outside of Cuba had yet got wind of it. But what could I do with this privileged information? I was a freelance francophone journalist with no regular outlet where I

---

1   Miguel Darío García Porto, "Propuestas para la Feria Internacional del Libro de La Habana 2016," Radioenciclopedia.cu, January 20, 2016. As in this quote, this book will generally opt to employ the common alternative *1984* to refer to Orwell's *Nineteen Eighty-Four*.

could publish this sort of item, which in any case was too specialized for the publications to which I contributed. What is more, I was preparing to spend a month in Cuba, ostensibly as a tourist. It was no time to attract the authorities' attention and to risk having myself refused entry into the country when I disembarked from the plane.

The day of my discovery, I had an appointment with a Cuban American journalist at a Starbucks in Coral Gables, a ritzy municipality in Miami-Dade County. I passed on the information, which surprised her as much as it had me, and after the usual verifications she published an article on the subject on Café Fuerte, a Cuban diaspora news site.[2] The news was quickly picked up by almost all the media outlets keeping an eye on Cuba. Each had its own interpretation. Should it be perceived as a sign of more openness on the part of the regime, thirteen months after the re-establishment of diplomatic relations between Cuba and the United States? Or on the contrary, was it not just another ruse on the part of the Castro brothers to make people feel there had been an opening, while behind the scenes they continued to discourage dissidence? Unless it was just a bad joke and at the last minute the book's appearance would be delayed indefinitely? The commentators' theories, coloured by a virulent hatred of the regime, or conversely by an optimism bordering on naïveté, were of course pure speculation. None of them were confidants of the gods, and the gods were keeping their counsel.

What was going on across the Florida Strait for 1984 to be suddenly published in 2016? What impact would the release of this novel have on a society where, as in the Oceania imagined by Orwell, although with less ferocity, a single party maintained strict control over the lives of its citizens and the news to which they had access?

In these early days of 2016, it was said that Cuba was "in transition." It had been ten years since Raúl Castro had succeeded his brother Fidel. Since that time, he had embarked on a redefinition of the "economic

---

2   Ivette Leyva Martínez, "Publican en Cuba la novela '1984' de George Orwell," Café Fuerte, January 26, 2016.

and social model for socialist development," a process that, in reality, consisted of the dismantling of that model and a gradual drift toward a market economy.

Since December 17, 2014, the date when the warming of relations between Cuba and the United States was proclaimed, hardly a month had passed without the Obama administration announcing yet another relaxation of its commercial embargo upon the island, put in place by John F. Kennedy in the wake of the 1962 Cuban missile crisis. Barack Obama did not hide his desire to lift it definitively before the end of his mandate, but that was impossible without the consent of the two houses of Congress, controlled by the Republicans, who were opposed to the measure.

Despite that, each new breach in the *bloqueo*, as the Cubans called the embargo, encouraged businessmen and women from the United States and around the world to converge on the island. They all wanted to position themselves in anticipation of the day when the market would be open for good. Tourists also flocked to Cuba more frequently than ever. For a first or last time they wanted to photograph Havana in its period costume, before it was totally overtaken by the twenty-first century: the American cars out of the 1950s, the vintage façades of the state stores, the faded revolutionary slogans on the walls, Hemingway's Havana, Fidel's Cuba with no McDonald's or Starbucks, the ruins of the Communist utopia. They came from everywhere to see Cuba "before it all changed."

Simultaneously, this same race against time was inciting a horde of Cubans to swim against the tide of the American tourists and businessmen. By the thousands, they fled the island, hoping to set foot on American soil "before things changed," in other words before the repeal of the Cuban Adjustment Act, a law that guaranteed them automatic asylum and a green card a year after their arrival. In 2015, 40,139 individuals were successful, an increase of 78 percent over the previous year. Many had begun their journey by flying to Ecuador, one of the only countries in the Americas that, until December 2015, did not require visas from Cubans. From there, they spent many months making their way up the entire continent with no legal status and under difficult conditions, to the Mexican–American border. Others, on board clandestine vessels, crossed the 150 kilometres of ocean waters that separated their island from the Florida coast. Thousands failed to reach the promised land, intercepted by the American coast guard or forced to turn back before sinking. Many also remained stuck in Costa Rica after the sudden tightening of security at the Nicaraguan border, ordered by President Ortega, a long-time ally of the Cuban Revolution. An indeterminate number of risk-takers met their death in the shark-infested waters of the Florida Strait, or on the violent roadways of Central America.

Cuba, *before* it changes. Cuba, before what comes *after*. It was this period of flux between two eras that I wanted to capture on travelling there; this period caught between a past at the end of its tether but stubbornly refusing to yield, and a future whose profile was still undetermined. Of course, the future still had the right to refute any speculations as to its nature, as it had so often done in the past. My goal in any case was not to predict the island's future, but to create a time capsule for future reference.

*

In *1984*, Winston Smith is a bureaucrat in the Ministry of Truth, a ministry that, in truth, is responsible for lies. Winston's work consists of tirelessly rewriting yesterday's newspapers in order to expurgate individuals and facts that no longer jibe with today's official version. If, for example, the production goals for the third trimester of 1983 are not achieved by the end of that period, they have to be retroactively matched with the results actually obtained in order for the achievement to have taken place. If in April the weekly ration of chocolate is suddenly reduced from thirty to twenty grams, the firm promise made by the Party in February not to do so must be replaced in the same February issue of the *Times* by a warning that it will very shortly be decreased. If Party officials are disgraced, they must vanish from all the archives in order never to have existed. "He who controls the past controls the future. He who controls the present controls the past," goes the Party's slogan. In doing away with any dissonance between the past and the present, the Party can declare itself infallible. It has always been right, is always right, and will always be right.

Despite years of conditioning, Winston is still unable to believe in the infallibility of the Party and its leader, Big Brother. Worse, he realizes that far from loving Big Brother as a Party member ought to, he hates him. Instinctively, he knows that the society in which he lives is not the ideal entity it pretends to be. However, unable to compare it with any other, he can find no proof. Oceania's citizens have no contact with foreigners. Their archived past is but a web of lies. Winston knows this better than anyone, finding himself on the front line of falsification. To sustain the impression that life was better before the revolution, he has only his dim childhood memories.

One day, Winston starts writing a personal diary. Before even dipping his pen in ink, he knows that this act will lead to his undoing. Sooner or later the Party will expose him and punish him. Sooner or later Winston will fall back into line, or if not, will be fated never to have existed. Despite this certainty, he cannot stop himself from writing. He wants, at any price, "to transfer to paper the interminable restless monologue that had been running inside his head, literally for years."[3] In documenting his life in a totalitarian society, Winston is offering his unlikely future readers an alternate account of the past.

> During his first writing session, when he has barely set down the date he thinks to be accurate, without being certain – April 4, 1984 – he pauses. For whom, it suddenly occurred to him to wonder, was he writing this diary? For

---

3 All excerpts from George Orwell's *Nineteen Eighty-Four* are taken from the 1977 American edition of the book, published by Houghton Mifflin Harcourt.

the future, for the unborn … For the first time the magnitude of what he had undertaken came home to him. How could you communicate with the future? It was of its nature impossible. Either the future would resemble the present, in which case it would not listen to him: or it would be different from it, and his predicament would be meaningless.

In the dystopic world imagined by Orwell, the future bears out Winston's defeatism: he is arrested and re-educated by the Party, he betrays the woman he loves, and in the end comes to love Big Brother. As for his version of history, it is obliterated, never to be read, never to be seen.

In the real world, the fate of Winston's narrative was very different. Since the first appearance of *1984* in June 1949, it has been read by millions of people around the world. The account of his life in Oceania has been used both to denounce existing totalitarian regimes – be they fascist, communist, or other – and to alert democracies to the danger of totalitarian drift.

Winston has been heard: his "predicament" is now iconic. Prisoner of a totalitarian world, the main character of *1984* writes with no hope that his words will change a thing in the course of events. Neither in the present or in the future. Except that he cannot help writing. Winston is deeply pessimistic, but he wants at least to have tried to resist, even if it's in vain and at the risk of his life.

As for Orwell, he was writing his novel in a democratic country, three years after the Second World War. Unlike his character, he knew that his words might be read, even if he could not conceive of the extraordinary impact they would have. He set his story in the future. Basing it on the worst things he had seen in the course of his life, he imagined the bleakest future possible, doubtless in hopes of inciting his readers to stand in the way of such a dystopia.

Eric Arthur Blair, alias George Orwell, died of tuberculosis on January 21, 1950, at the age of forty-six, seven months after the release of his novel. He never saw the future he had tried to foretell.

*

On January 1, 1959, nine and a half years after the initial appearance of *1984*, Fidel Castro and his bearded followers overthrew the dictator Fulgencio Batista, vowing to put power back into the hands of the Cuban people. On that first day of the year and of a new Cuba, a huge majority of Cubans was united behind the revolutionaries. This unity was rooted both in the opposition to the deposed despot, in hopes of a better and more democratic future, and in the charismatic personality of the chief revolutionary.

But it soon became clear that Fidel Castro had thought much more deeply about his plan to *take* power than to *exercise* it. For many months the Revolution's aims remained vague. Castro and his band were improvising. For Cuba, it was a period of uncertainty. The present was clearly tending toward a future different from the past, but no one could define this future, not even those who had the popular mandate to forge it.

In the beginning, in order to calm the fears of his powerful American neighbour, Fidel Castro swore that his Revolution was "not communist" but "humanist." He even issued a stamp to that effect, in English, destined for *yanqui* mailboxes. Four months after coming to power, he visited the United States and Canada to persuade the world of his neutrality. But in the midst of a cold war, for an island state a stone's throw from one of the great world powers, non-alignment was not a viable option.

For Dwight D. Eisenhower, then President of the United States, it made little difference whether Castro was a democratic humanist or a bloodthirsty dictator. As long as he was not a communist. If the American president had resigned himself to abandoning Batista at the last minute, it was not out of admiration for the *barbudos*, but because he thought that the overthrow of the dictator would put an end to the civil war, and so to a period of instability on this island he saw as a backyard where his citizens could invest and amuse themselves. And so, six days after the "triumph of the Revolution," the United States was the first country to recognize the legitimacy of the new government.

As for the First Secretary of the Communist Party of the Soviet Union, Nikita Khrushchev, he didn't care if Castro was not initially a communist. If the Cuban leader sought protection and support from his empire, Khrushchev would be happy to provide them. When the United States halted their purchases of Cuban sugar at an inflated price in July 1960, the Soviets were quick to take the place of their great rival.

On January 3, 1961, with the revolutionary government edging ever closer to Moscow and its antagonism toward Washington becoming more and more evident, Eisenhower broke off diplomatic relations with Cuba. That same January, three months before Castro proclaimed the "socialist character" of his revolution and a few hours before anti-Castro mercenaries botched their landing at the Bay of Pigs, the independent publishing house Librerías Unidas S.A. published a first Cuban edition of *1984*.

*

I spent a good part of the last decade travelling in the former Soviet Union. In Russia, in Turkmenistan, in Georgia, in Belarus, and elsewhere, I observed post-communist societies longing for a future.

Between 1985 and 1991, Mikhail Gorbachev had tried to renew the Soviet socio-economic model by introducing his policy of perestroika, or "reconstruction." But the gangrene ran too deep. Years of lies and hypocrisy had carved out an unbridgeable gulf between official discourse and reality. Far from rescuing the model, as the regime had hoped, the opening up to small-scale entrepreneurship and greater freedom of speech for citizens demonstrated, rather, that it was beyond repair. After six years of drifting, the reforms had to be abandoned. The fifteen states that emerged when the USSR was dismantled all officially rejected

Marxist-Leninist ideology and embraced – enthusiastically or by default – capitalism. Now, a quarter of a century later, it has to be acknowledged that those states are at best flawed democracies, and for the most part find themselves under the yoke of regimes just as authoritarian, if not more so, than that of the old Soviet Union. Only a handful of oligarchs have profited from the unbridled capitalism that followed the demise of communism, while millions of people have seen the collapse of the social safety net that guaranteed them minimal protection.

In shifting from communism to a market economy, most of the former Soviet republics drew on the worst of both systems. The transition failed.

Today, therefore, it's no surprise that a high proportion of these states' citizens look back with nostalgia to the past and that some even dream of turning back the clock, from *after* to *before*. In those days you could certainly stand in line for hours for a piece of sausage, and wait years for an apartment or a car. But what people remember today is that their salaries, however meager, were guaranteed, and that education and healthcare, however mediocre, were free. With the fall of the USSR, many thought the market economy was going to solve everything. The illusion did not last.

The future betrayed them.

Will Cubans find a way to avoid the pitfalls that ensnared those who made the transition before them? Or will the future leave them in the lurch as well?

*

When I was living in Moscow, in winter I used to play hockey on an outdoor skating rink with a bunch of neighbourhood Russians. Every time I said I was going out of the country, my friend Vova invariably told me the same Soviet joke from the time of scarcity and of poor-quality local products. "Bring us back a T-shirt and some chewing gum!"

On my first trip to Cuba, along with my personal effects, I brought the following items from the continent: two bottles of medicine for treating the chronic migraines of the mother of a Cuban friend exiled in Chicago; analog photo equipment for an artist, the friend of an acquaintance; and chocolate bars, "preferably with hazelnuts," for the Cuban translator of 1984.

FEBRUARY 14 TO MARCH 16, 2016

FIRST TRIP

A LEAKY BOAT

The almost-empty Air China Boeing 777 from Beijing with a stop in Montréal is starting its descent into Havana's night sky. I think again of how improbable it must have seemed, on December 2, 1956, that the twenty-two survivors of a yacht's botched landing and the subsequent battle on a beach more than eight hundred kilometres from the capital could in two years conquer the entire island and proclaim the triumph of their revolution. All it would have taken for the course of Cuban history to have been radically changed was for the expedition's leader to have been killed, like sixty of his comrades, as he walked across the Las Coloradas beach, or that he die on one of the hundreds of other occasions when he ought to have perished before and after this fiasco. But he survived, on that occasion and others. And he is still surviving, against all odds, at eighty-nine-and-a-half years of age, despite his increasingly frail health. Unkillable, just like his revolution, which has been given up for dead as often as he has.

On the tarmac of José Martí Airport, an Eastern Air Lines airplane, an American flag painted on the side of its nose, is at rest between two flights. Early in 2016, air traffic between Florida and Cuba is limited to a few very expensive charter trips: between four and five hundred dollars, return, for an hour and a quarter in the air. For a year now, the American government has been allowing its citizens to travel to Cuba without having to obtain prior authorization. But they cannot go just as tourists. The purpose of their trip must fall into one of the twelve categories of approved exemptions: a family visit; educational, religious, or journalistic activities; a humanitarian project; a sports competition; scientific research; a professional meeting; and other justifications of the sort. In theory, if the Treasury Department learned that one of its citizens had spent the week on a Cuban beach sipping mojitos, it could still exact a penalty. In practice, no American has been punished since the swearing-in of Barack Obama in January 2009. Hundreds had been punished under his predecessor, George W.

Bush. Given the price of tickets and the restrictions, many American tourists still prefer to travel through a third country such as Mexico, Canada, or Panama. The clientele of Eastern Air Lines is mainly made up of Americans of Cuban origin who are going to visit their families, and, above all, to bring them supplies. Which explains why, in the baggage pickup hall, dozens of enormous suitcases, electrical appliances, cartons of medicine, and other cardboard colossi wrapped in blue plastic block the way to the carousels.

When Miami lands in Havana, Terminal 2 is bedlam in spades.

*

During my first days in Cuba I stay with Armando, an artist in his thirties. During our online conversations, we'd agreed to barter. For every night I spend in his home he deducts fifteen convertible pesos (CUC) from the 150 or so he owes me for the boxes of photo paper, the acetate film, the fixer, and the developer I have brought from Canada. Thanks to our deal, he can now mount the photo exhibition he is planning without spending a cent on the materials, which are unfindable in Cuba. The arrangement also helps me save money. The Playa neighbourhood is out of the way, but it would have been hard to find a room at such a low price in Havana.

According to Cuban law, my staying with him is totally illegal. Aside from hotels, foreigners are only allowed to sleep in authorized *casas particulares*. The owners of those guest houses have to inform the authorities of the presence of new visitors on the day of their arrival, and to pay a tax on the rental of the room. Armando does neither.

During my stay he gives me his room and goes to sleep with a woman he met a couple of days before my arrival, on the Malecón, the wide promenade by the sea, the capital's favourite spot for strolling, flirting, and prostitution. He leaves me in the good hands of his mother Sonia, a retired meteorologist.

During the period of friendship between the Cuban and Soviet people, Sonia studied at the Academy of Sciences in Moscow. Her Russian is rusty, but we manage to communicate. She also speaks English, and for several months has been studying French for her own pleasure at the Alliance française. Sonia was seven years old when the *barbudos* took power. Looking back on her middle-class childhood – her father was also a meteorologist – she recalls that under the old regime, "the poor were really poor." The Revolution did away with these inequities, and introduced health and education systems that were free for all and sundry. Like many Cubans Sonia is very proud of those achievements and tries to do her part in bettering the Revolution. She is a member of the Communist Party, and regularly attends, along with her former colleagues, all the massive workers' demonstrations. But these days she's thinking of turning in her party card. "The problem," she says, "is that the Revolution has got bogged down in its ideals." Ideologically blinded, the Party and its leaders have made decisions that were certainly noble, but that turned out to be counterproductive. "The young people get free education in Cuba, then go abroad to make money. We ought to make them stay here long enough to repay what they owe to our system," she says. "The Revolution is a leaky boat."

The day after my arrival, Sonia tells me how to get around on Havana's public transport. By the side of 31st Avenue, we hail the *almendrones*, the "big almonds," the American cars from before the Revolution that serve as collective taxis. But at nine in the morning the competition is fierce. Several prospective passengers are mounting the avenue, hoping to be the first in line for the next free space heading to the old town. It's pointless to try the *guaguas*. The public buses are full to bursting. At each stop, the doors close on the last bold passengers daring to embark despite the obvious lack of space. The more cautious and less aggressive are left behind on the road, hoping that the next *guagua* will be the good one. As for the *taxis ruteros*, the private buses twenty-five times as expensive as the public ones, they take on no waiting passengers, and all of them pass us by, already full.

After waiting forty-five minutes, we resign ourselves to giving up on the 31st, and continue our quest on the 41st. Lucky for us, in less than two minutes an empty *almendron*, just beginning its day, stops. The old wreck's insides are full of anachronisms. Built into the dashboard is a mini-screen showing reggaetón videoclips. Stuck onto the glove compartment is a homemade sign informing clients that if they pay in convertible pesos, they'll receive their money in Cuban pesos at a rate of one for twenty-four, instead of the official rate of one for twenty-five. The segregation that once existed between the CUC (pronounced "cooc" by some, "say-oo-say" by others), the tourist industry's currency pegged to the American dollar, and the CUP ("coop"), the *moneda nacional* in which the Cubans receive their salaries, has almost disappeared. The two currencies are exchanged with almost no distinction. As long as the government does not decide to do away with one or other of the currencies, the monetary bipolarity on the island serves only to confuse tourists and make it easier for them to be swindled. But I won't be fooled. Neither on the conversion nor on the going rate. Alejandro has already filled me in on the *colectivos'* pricing. Between Playa and Vieja, I'll pass through the neighbourhoods of Vedado and Centro. The trip between the two costs ten Cuban pesos. For two neighbourhoods or more, it's a maximum of twenty pesos. I do the calculation. If workers make a return trip between work and home each day in a collective taxi, and if the two are situated in adjacent neighbourhoods, and they earn the official average salary of 687 pesos per month, they will spend almost all their money just on transport. If they have no other source of revenue, they are condemned, like most people, to cramming themselves into the *guaguas* every morning for forty centavos per ride.

The car fills up quickly. The driver reminds every new client to go *suave* with the wonky door. How many times has this door been opened and closed over the last sixty years? How many times has it been mended? And how many more times will it open and close before the long-awaited economic transformation of the island or the lifting of the embargo allows it to be sent to its final resting place?

*

Armando and I are waiting in line before the offices of the state telecommunication company ETECSA. My first *cola*. After about half an hour, we're asked to present ourselves at a window. I need a SIM card for my phone. To facilitate the process, Armando has offered to get it for me under his name. He presents his identity card. An unhelpful cycle in the washing machine has rendered it almost illegible. The information on it was inscribed by hand. The clerk makes a face. The document is not acceptable, she says. Too damaged. Armando tries to sweet talk her. "If you'd accept it," he replies, "I'd be very grateful." His charm, and especially his veiled promise of a recompense, have their effect. She agrees to go on with the procedure, not without warning him to get a new identity card "for next time." I slip the money to Armando for him to pay. Forty convertible pesos, including ten for usage credits. At thirty cents for a minute of conversation and fifteen cents for sending an SMS, the cell rates in Cuba are among the highest in the world. Cubans with cellphones use them as little as possible.

The clerk gives Armando the change. He extracts three CUC coins and returns them to her with a smile, not even trying to disguise what he is doing. She drops them into a bribes jar under the counter, where they go to join other tokens of gratitude for bending the rules.

My first *regalito*. My first crack in the Revolution.

LITERATURE IS NOT DANGEROUS

He enters the café, spots me, comes over, takes his earphones out of his ears, letting them hang down between two shirt buttons, shakes my hand without looking me in the eye, without smiling, lifting his chin slightly as his only greeting, as if we were old friends who had just seen each other the day before. He sits down, declares that he doesn't like coffee and won't be drinking anything, then begins to talk.

In English his accent has certain British intonations that don't entirely mask those of his Spanish mother tongue. His vocabulary is rich, that of a wide-ranging reader. To support his arguments, he cites from memory a host of authors. He makes occasional errors in grammar, but I only notice them because they're different from mine in the same language. He talks and talks, passing from the trivial to the philosophical, from literature to women, from Cuba to Spain. Almost everything he says is interesting. But I have to interrupt him, or he'll never stop and I'll never know how he came to be the translator of the second Cuban edition of *1984*.

Fabricio González Neira was born on February 6, 1973, in Havana. If I learned his identity before even holding a copy of the book in my hands, it was thanks to his excessive rigour.

Two weeks before my departure, doing research on the internet using key words – "1984 Orwell Cuba Arte y Literatura" – I came across a translators' forum in which a certain gabrielsyme73 stated that a Cuban publishing house had asked him to translate *1984*. The message was dated March 11, 2015. The person behind the avatar was asking his colleagues to help him translate an expression used by Orwell in the third chapter of the novel's first section. In this passage, Winston is imagining a "Golden Country," far from the dark world in which he was living.

Suddenly he was standing on short springy turf, on a summer evening when the slanting rays of the sun gilded the ground. The landscape that he was looking at recurred so often in his dreams that he was never fully certain whether or not he had seen it in the real world. In his waking thoughts he called it the Golden Country. **It was an old, rabbit-bitten pasture**, with a foot-track wandering across it and a molehill here and there. In the ragged hedge on the opposite side of the field the boughs of the elm trees were swaying very faintly in the breeze, their leaves just stirring in dense masses like women's hair. Somewhere near at hand, though out of sight, there was a clear, slow-moving stream where dace were swimming in the pools under the willow trees.

What exactly did Orwell mean by saying that the old pasture was "rabbit-bitten"? "Is it that the pasture ought to have been giving off light differently than another eaten by cows, horses, giraffes, or elephants?" asked gabrielsyme73. For the translator, the problem dwelled in the fact that Orwell was not the sort of writer to be carried away by lyric descriptions only for their beauty. If he used an expression so precise, it must have had a meaning that was just as precise. Perhaps he was referring to a particularity of the English countryside with which a Cuban could not possibly be familiar? No responses offered by the other members of the forum were able to satisfy gabrielsyme73's appetite for a deeper meaning to the phrase. To his great disappointment, he had to resign himself to the same literal translation that his predecessors had employed.

Era un campo viejo cuya hierba estaba mordida por conejos ...

Barely a few hours after I sent a private message to gabrielsyme73 on the forum, Fabricio González replied. We embarked on a correspondence wherein he told me about his life. His beginnings: the only child of a Havana correspondent for the Spanish daily *El Mundo* and of an ex-bureaucrat for the Cuban Ministry of Foreign Affairs, long divorced. His current status: a bachelor living with his mother and a nameless cat. His years outside the island: eight in all, less than one in London and the rest in Spain. His tastes: "Music, books, chocolate, and women." His convictions: from the religious point of view, an atheist; philosophically, a pessimist; and politically, a leftist, "but not fanatic." And his current employ: as an English instructor for college teachers, an editor for the state publisher Letras Cubanas, and a freelance translator.

In his emails, Fabricio gave me advice on what to read, and offered to introduce me to people in Havana who, in his opinion, could provide me with insights on today's Cuba. Before even waiting for me to express interest, he'd already contacted some of them.

Throughout our exchanges, I'd never posed the question that made me want to write him in the first place: How did he become the translator of *1984*?

Now that I was face to face with him in the café on Obispo Street, I was able to ask.

"So how did this all come about?"

It all began in April 2014, with a call from the director of Arte y Literatura Editions. They were seeking a translator for *1984*, and his name had come up. At first Fabricio told himself that someone must have had too much to drink the night before and would call the next day to withdraw this curious offer to translate an antitotalitarian literary classic. Still, he accepted. No one called him the following day. In fact, the second call came almost a year later, and its purpose was not to withdraw the project, but on the contrary to put pressure on him to complete it. Arte y Literatura was preparing its catalogue for the 2016 book fair, and wanted at all costs to include *1984*. Now, since he had first been given this assignment, Fabricio had provided no update on the progress he was making. His silence was not hard to explain: during the year that had passed, he had barely touched the manuscript. Instead, he had been concentrating on contracts from Spain that were much more lucrative. Financially speaking, his procrastination made sense. For the hundreds of hours of work required to translate the 88,942 words of one of the landmark works of the twentieth century, he would receive only six thousand Cuban pesos, barely three hundred Canadian dollars. That was a decent amount of money in Cuba, the equivalent of ten or so months of salary in a publishing house, but it was still starvation wages compared to the smallest translation contracts Fabricio received from foreign sources.

A few months after the second call, Fabricio finally sent off the translation. It was given a rudimentary edit, a preface by a prominent historian was tacked on, the layout was hastily done, and it was dispatched to the printer.

Translating 1984 inevitably threw Fabricio back into Orwell's world. Reading the novel for the first time in the early 1990s, he had been overwhelmed by its power. It was his friend José Miguel – who would later become one of the most prolific science-fiction writers on the island – who had passed him a copy. Back then, they had made a pact along with a third collaborator: whichever one of them was able to lay his hands on a book had to lend it to the two others before reading it. The cover of José Miguel's copy of 1984 was hidden behind thick paper. In theory, it was not stated anywhere that the book was banned in Cuba. But everyone knew that any book that was not explicitly permitted by the regime was implicitly forbidden. Books being rare, it was common practice to cover them and protect them from wear. You could just as easily, in a park or on a bus, be reading a collection of Fidel's speeches, a romantic novel, or a work that could be condemned as counter-revolutionary, without arousing any suspicions.

Rereading 1984 before embarking on the translation, Fabricio was much less impressed than during his adolescence. In the intervening time he had combed through the world's great literary works, and many more obscure books. His eye had sharpened. Like many critics, Fabricio judged that 1984's narrative line and its characters were not especially well-developed, and there was nothing in Orwell's prose to impress a practised reader. On the other hand, he still admired the qualities that had made the book a classic. Orwell was extremely insightful when it came to many aspects of life under a dictatorship. That is why in translating him, Fabricio often asked himself whether those who had authorized the project had truly gauged the import of their decision. Political repression in the Castro brothers' Cuba had certainly never approached the extremes of Big Brother's Oceania, but every Cuban reader would certainly see parallels between the two societies. For example, in the passage where Orwell describes the generational gulf that separates Winston, thirty-nine years old, from his lover Julia, ten to fifteen years younger and born well after the revolution, Fabricio felt that in Julia's attitude he could recognize his own generation.

> She hated the Party, and said so in the crudest words, but she made no general criticism of it. Except where it touched her own life ... Any kind of organized revolt against the Party, which was bound to be a failure, struck her as stupid. The clever thing was to break the rules and stay alive all the same ... He wondered vaguely how many others like her there might be in the younger generation, people who had grown up in the world of the Revolution, knowing nothing else, accepting the Party as something unalterable, like the sky, not rebelling against its authority but simply evading it as a rabbit dodges a dog.

Fabricio, like Julia, never embraced the Party's ideals. Unlike the generation that preceded his, he never knew disillusionment. He has no intention of rebelling against the powers that be. He only wants to limit the Party's influence on his life. To direct confrontation, he prefers serene disobedience, only breaking the rules he knows he can transgress without consequences.

In the café where we're talking, when Fabricio mentions the Castro brothers, he takes no particular precautions. Rather than miming a beard to invoke Fidel or slanted eyes to mimic Raúl, as some more fearful

Cubans still do today, he utters their names without even lowering his voice. He would not take to a microphone to express his contempt for them, but he does not shy away from criticizing them during a private conversation in a public space. He knows that indiscreet ears might be listening in. But in 2016, how many informers would still take the trouble to denounce someone who says out loud what the majority are thinking to themselves?

Fabricio believes that this state of apathy, as widespread among the regime's supporters as its detractors, explains in part why the authorities thought it possible to authorize the publication of *1984*. "They've understood that literature is not dangerous, that a book won't change anything." All the more so given that the Cubans who really wanted to read Orwell's dystopia did so long ago. Like Fabricio, they'd been able to lay their hands on one of the clandestine copies in circulation, or had more recently accessed its pirated digital version, either online or on a USB drive. The virtualization of information has robbed the regime of its monopoly on the distribution of literature, in the past compromised only by a few books brought in from outside. Fabricio made that clear to me even before my leaving for Cuba. Thinking I was doing him a big favour, I'd proposed bringing to him from North America a book in English of his choosing. He replied that he already downloaded many more titles than he was able to read, but that, on the other hand, he'd be most grateful if I could buy him some chocolate, as he found the taste of what was produced in Cuba to be "so to speak, naive."

Given all that, it was most improbable that the publication of a new version of *1984* would suddenly upset the established order and put the regime's survival in jeopardy. But why risk publishing it, however small the threat, when one could easily not do so? Why have everyone asking why you're bringing out *this* book at *this* time when all the queries could be avoided?

Why *this* rather than *nothing*?

Fabricio has no answer. He doesn't know who initiated the publication or who authorized it. What he has been led to suspect, between the lines, is that the request came "from a level higher than the publishing house." But how much farther up in the hierarchy? As high as the Cuban Book Institute, the Ministry of Culture, or even Raúl Castro? Fabricio is not the sort to be beguiled by facile scenarios. The Castro option seems very dubious to him. But beyond that, who knows?

He does, however, speculate that the authorities' motivation was basically a pragmatic one. For a number of years, the Cuban Book Institute, which oversees most of the country's publishing houses, has attributed a "business" status to some of them. That means that they continue to receive grants from the state, but that they must pay for certain operational expenses out of the revenue from their sales. Arte y Literatura is one of the companies that is now a business. Its print run for 1984 was seven thousand copies, which is huge for Cuba. "They knew the book was going to sell," Fabricio concludes.

To summarize: according to this theory, the wide distribution, in a communist, single-party regime, of one of the antitotalitarian literary classics, would have been authorized in order to contribute to the financial well-being of one of the system's institutions. If that were true, the irony would be enormous. But if one thinks about it, however cynical it seems, the theory holds water. If the regime felt that 1984 could become a bestseller without inspiring the book's readers to rise up, why not take advantage of the opportunity? Why not itself slake their thirst for subversive reading material while pocketing the profits deriving from their gratification? After all, as the capitalists say, money has no smell.

*

Once I've finished my coffee, Fabricio and I take the *guagua* to San Carlos de la Cabaña. The fortress, built in the eighteenth century by Spanish colonizers, is the book fair's main site every year. Under Batista, la Cabaña was a prison. During the Revolution's first months, summary trials and executions of presumed counter-revolutionaries took place there, under Che Guevara's supervision.

It's very fitting to call this a fair. To reach the fortress's entrance from the main street where the bus has left us, we have to walk a few hundred metres through a dense crowd massed in front of dozens of temporary food and amusement kiosks. Along the way, we can amuse ourselves with inflatable games or bounce on a trampoline, buy a hat, try a plate of roast chicken, *ropa vieja*, or hamburger, but there are no books in sight.

At three Cuban pesos, the entry ticket to the fair is very affordable. *Leer es crecer*, said José Martí, the writer and revolutionary regarded as the father of the Cuban nation. *To read is to grow.* The Revolution made it a slogan, and saw it as its duty to make literature accessible to the greatest number. If it had not at the same time locked the literary world up in an ideological straitjacket that hampered its growth and inventiveness, that bias in favour of culture would have been much to its credit.

Inside the fortress the event's popularity is clear to see, even if most of the visitors seem less interested in the books than in wandering about and meeting people. Posters of sports heroes and cartoon characters are much in demand with the younger crowd.

Passing by the stands of different publishing houses, Fabricio notes that many books whose releases have been announced are impossible to find. As so often, the printers have not met their production deadlines in time for the fair, and have given priority to works by authors from the invited country, which this year is Uruguay. At the Arte y Literatura kiosk, we see that, happily, *1984* has not fallen victim to this problem. A copy of the new edition has pride of place in its display. Its black, yellow, and orange cover shows silhouettes walking in all directions under the huge nebulous eye of Big Brother. Fabricio is seeing the design for the first time. He finds it terrible. What's more, he remarks, one of the passersby is in a wheelchair. "That's ridiculous. In Orwell's Oceania, a handicapped person would have been eliminated in short order." I buy a copy for fifteen Cuban pesos. It's 3:30 p.m., and the saleswoman informs us that it's her last. She had a hundred that morning. She'll be getting more the next day. "It's one of our bestsellers," she says. "Why? Because it's a classic!" Fabricio leafs through the inferior object that contains the fruits of his work. He is credited for the translation on page four, just before the prologue. He doesn't boast to the bookseller. In any case, the publisher didn't even invite him to participate in the formal launch, scheduled for the next day. He'll attend anyway. We'll go together.

A BANAL ACCIDENT

On July 22, 2012, at 1:50 p.m., on a deserted road in the east of the island of Cuba, a blue Hyundai rental car veered away and slammed into a tree by the side of the road. Two of the passengers died on the spot. The victims were Oswaldo Payá, sixty years old, a well-known dissident, founder of the Christian Liberation Movement, and Harold Cepero, thirty-two years old, one of his militants. The driver and the other passenger, both foreigners, escaped with minor injuries. The first, Ángel Carromero, was an official in the youth wing of the Spanish People's Party. The second, Jens Aron Modig, was president of the Swedish Young Christian Democrats. The four men were on their way to Bayamo, in the province of Granma, to meet partisans of the Christian Liberation Movement.

After the accident, Carromero was arrested. In a video filmed by the Cuban police, the Spanish politician claimed to have lost control of the vehicle because of the poor road conditions, while he was driving at high speed. At the end of the trial that lasted just a single day, he was condemned to four years in prison for involuntary homicide. Still, he only served two months in a Cuban jail before Spanish diplomats were able to arrange his repatriation.

Once back on Spanish soil, Carromero altered his account of the events. He now claimed that the Cuban security services had tailed the group from when it left Havana the morning of the accident. Near Bayamo, a car with a government licence plate deliberately struck the rear of their vehicle, forcing it off the road. Carromero said he'd lost consciousness when the car struck the tree, and woke up on a stretcher in the hospital, surrounded by soldiers and agents from the Ministry of the Interior. He was drugged by medical personnel and threatened by the police, who forced him to sign a statement in which he incriminated himself. He said he was not tortured, but received some slaps.

During the press conference in Havana shortly after the accident, Modig, for his part, claimed to have no memory of the moment preceding the impact, nor of that which followed. He also confessed to having lied to Cuban immigration officials when he entered the country. He had not, in fact, come to Cuba on vacation as he had declared, but to present four thousand euros in cash to Cuban dissidents in the name of his political party. Once back in Sweden, he stuck to that story.

Oswaldo Payá's family did not believe the official version of the accident. From the very first day, they asked that the accusations against Carromero be withdrawn, and that he be released. For them, there was no doubt that Payá had been assassinated by the regime because of his political convictions.

In Spain, before the accident, Ángel Carromero had been about to lose his driver's licence. The twenty-six-year-old politician had exhausted his demerit points due to forty-two parking fines and three speeding tickets that he had accumulated over the last year and a half. In his own country, Carromero had the reputation of being a bad driver. The day of the accident, the four men had left Havana at about six in the morning – that is, less than eight hours before the catastrophe. To cross almost the entire island in so little time, their car must have been travelling at high speed. That does not, however, constitute incontrovertible evidence that Ángel Carromero was responsible for the accident that cost the lives of the two dissidents.

During the early years of the Revolution, several hundred counter-revolutionaries were shot on the orders of the new government. Each new execution was reported in the newspapers. The regime staunchly defended its right to proceed in this way, in order to defend the budding Revolution, even if it meant alienating some foreign supporters from the early days. Once firmly in the saddle, Fidel Castro halted this practice. Since that time, he and his brother have been content to imprison their opponents, to force them into exile, or to have them roughed up by the government's supporters. At the time of the accident in which Payá and Cepero perished, the killing of dissidents was no longer common practice for the Cuban regime. But this does not exclude the possibility of political murders on the island.

What, then, happened on that deserted road on July 22, 2012, at 1:30 p.m.?

It is clearly hard to swallow the authorities' official version without calling it into question. Not that it's unbelievable, but because its source is a regime that over the decades has showed itself ready to lie in order to protect its grip on power. If this version does reflect reality, it makes for a felicitous concordance between the regime's interests and the facts. On the other hand, it would be just as risky to trust only the accounts of the two survivors, which have their own shadowy zones and incoherencies. For fear of reprisals or to protect their reputations, it was in the interests of Carromero and Modig – especially the former – not to reveal everything.

Instinctively, I would tend to think that the real cause of the blue Hyundai's leaving the road was a combination of the two conflicting versions: the dangerous driving of a young Spanish politician on a bad road, combined with his tailing by Cuban agents who were themselves imprudent.

But what do I know? I wasn't there.

*

On February 16, 2016, at around 1:40 p.m., in Havana's Vedado neighbourhood, a sea-blue Toyota Corolla approached the O Street intersection along 17th Avenue, with no intention, clearly, of stopping. It was only at the last instant that the fearful cries of two of the passengers wrenched the driver out of his stupor and made him hastily slam on the brakes. The group was on its way to la Cabaña, where in a few minutes the new Cuban edition of George Orwell's novel 1984 was to be presented to the public. In a moment of distraction to which he'd been increasingly prone in recent days, the driver, Ángel Tomás González Ramos, sixty-nine years old, a correspondent in Cuba for the Spanish newspaper *El Mundo*, had not noticed the yield sign that gave priority to the cars coming along O Street. Only the presence of mind of his ex-wife, María de la Encarnacíon Neira Robaina, sixty-six years old, a retired civil servant with the Cuban Ministry of Foreign Affairs, and their son, Fabricio González Neira, forty-three years old, the translator of *1984*, an editor and teacher of English, brought the vehicle to a halt. As for the fourth passenger in the car, a Québécois journalist and writer who had arrived in Cuba the day before with the intention of clarifying the circumstances surrounding the appearance of Orwell's landmark novel, he only realized two seconds after the braking, when a Daewoo Tico came across the intersection, that an accident had narrowly been avoided.

What would people have thought if some or all of the occupants of the Toyota Corolla had died in that collision? The Cuban correspondent of a Spanish daily paper who was very critical of the Castro regime, a foreign journalist with a tourist visa, a Cuban ex-civil servant, and the translator of *1984*, dead or injured on the roads of a Communist dictatorship, on their way to the launch of a book denouncing the repression of dissidence in a totalitarian state. Who would have believed in an accidental collision? Even if the passengers of the Corolla had survived and supported this version, would their testimony have seemed credible or would people have assumed that they must have been pressured by the authorities to tell that story?

And yet, I know, it would unquestionably have been nothing more than a banal accident.

BITS AND PIECES OF
A LAUNCHING

It's 2 p.m. on the dot in la Cabaña fortress's Alejo Carpentier Room. Arriving a few minutes ago, I was able to find an empty seat in the fourth row, one of the few that were left. Since then, people have continued to stream in. Many are skeptical. They've come to find out if what they've read in the program is really true: if today, February 16, 2016, at 2 p.m., the novel *1984* will in fact be offered to the Cuban people with the blessing of the communist regime. They won't believe it until they see it with their own eyes. Two video cameras, a few stills cameras, telephones, tablets, and sound recorders are poised to capture the event. All that's missing is the presenter, who is now officially late.

As we wait, Fabricio introduces me to a writer sitting just behind me. In one sentence, he makes it clear why he might be of interest to me. "Daniel published an excerpt from *1984* in a literary journal a few years ago, and he speaks very good English." Daniel and I exchange a few words, and agree to meet another day to talk further at his Unión Editions office, where he is the poetry editor.

2:08 p.m. The historian Pedro Pablo Rodríguez arrives. He is the author of the prologue to *1984*'s new edition, and is here to present the book. I just read his introduction the day before. He writes that in publishing this novel, Arte y Literatura is embarking upon "an enterprise that will certainly provoke controversy in today's Cuban society." In his opinion, it is sure to "spark an intellectual debate" on the island. He also hopes that the debate will be public, but that if not, "each reader will be able to have one with him or herself." Nowhere in the text, however, does he explain what there is in the novel that might be considered controversial in the Cuban context. Rather, he diverts the readers' attention toward the disturbing increase in mass surveillance in the capitalist empires. If there is a connection to be made between Orwell's dystopic world and that in which we live today, it is to be found in "the subordination of people to the market, and in the control of all aspects of life and of the mind by this same market."

The historian installs himself behind a melamine table. There are displays on each side of him. On one there is a copy of *1984*, and on the other, one of the well-known photos of George Orwell, facing a BBC microphone. Rodríguez has barely sat down when Fabricio takes the vacant seat at his right, on the side of Orwell. His name does not appear in the official program, but seeing him arrive, the organizers have politely asked him to participate.

Pedro Pablo Rodríguez begins to speak.

"... Cuban readers ... thank you very much ... this book ... we have been waiting for this translation ..."

The sound is terrible. I only catch a few bits and pieces. Even the Spanish speakers have to concentrate to pick out words overlaid one on top of the other by the echo. The Alejo Carpentier Room is deep. Its walls are concrete and its ceiling is semi-cylindrical. It would have been hard to find a more inappropriate space for this sort of presentation. And yet it's in rooms like this that, for years, most of the fair's events have taken place. And no one has thought to deal with the obvious acoustic problems.

"Orwell shows ... the consequences of the state control of a society by a totalitarian regime that, superficially, resembles German Nazism and Soviet Communism, but ... differently ..."

The historian shifts between his own notes, quotations from anonymous readers' comments he's found on the internet, and improvised digressions.

"Some believed that this book contained ideologically unacceptable material ..."

In the row in front of me, a young woman taps alternately on her phone and her computer. Looking over her shoulder I see that, in the Sent box of the Mail application on her iPhone, a message is awaiting an internet connection to be sent to the email address of the well-known opposition blogger Yoani Sánchez. I deduce that the woman must contribute to the news site 14ymedio, launched by Sánchez.

"As you know, the United States is able to control all the planet's news and all its computers ..."

Overall, the historian is in the process of repeating his prologue's argument. The presentation drags on; the audience tunes out. To add to the confusion, Adèle is singing "Hello" from the other side of the door.

"... he is speaking of the capitalist world, of the Catholic Church ..."

All at once a woman in the first row starts applauding with vigour. I haven't caught what has inspired her enthusiasm. Either the audience doesn't share it, or it's no longer listening. Only one or two other people follow her lead, possibly as a reflex. The applause soon dies down.

"Here we can see an instance of the crisis of civilization that we are currently experiencing ..."

After thirty minutes, Rodríguez announces that to conclude his presentation, he will read the last paragraph of his prologue: "The Cuban reader is privileged to have access to a translation created specifically for this publishing house. Let us hope that in being read, it will widen our vision of the world, of our present day in particular, and of our destiny as a nation, a destiny that we are still in the process of shaping. *Muchas gracias.*"

The room applauds politely. The weary spectators start to rise and chat as Fabricio approaches the microphone on his side of the table.

"One moment, one moment ..."

A woman comes to his aid.

"If you please! Just a minute, we're not finished! This is a literary event, not a potato stand, for God's sake!"

She is able to impose silence. The hasty exiters sit back down. Fabricio is free to speak.

"Just one moment, so I may clarify a few things ..."

Fabricio tells the public about his first crucial encounter with *1984*, then his disappointment in rereading it and discovering the novel's weaknesses. He assures the readers that his translation is complete, unlike other pre-existing Spanish versions, which are missing several paragraphs from the original.

"The best way to deal with obstacles when you're a translator is to skip the difficult passages."

There is a brief burst of laughter in the room.

One of the main challenges in translating *1984*, Fabricio explains, is doing justice to Big Brother's Newspeak, a good part of whose vocabulary derives from the fusion of two English words. In most cases he could not find a better combination than that devised by his predecessors. His contribution to the Newspeak lexicon in Spanish is therefore a very minor one.

"That's all. *Muchas gracias.*"

Fabricio's talk has lasted only three minutes.

Fabricio and I leave the room. I tell him that I laughed a lot inside, hearing him assert that his translation was complete. That was a subtle message letting people know that this edition was not censored by the regime, no?

"No."

He just wanted to make it clear, so people would be aware of it.

Thus it was that the second Cuban edition of *1984* saw the light, and was presented to the Cuban people.

THE AMERICANS
ARE COMING

They've arrived with their PowerPoint presentations, their smiles, and their sales pitches. They're here to test the waters, to network, and to seduce their Cuban counterparts. One day, if all goes well, their gamble will pay off. They'll be able to flood the Cuban market with their books. It's the first time in sixty years that a delegation of American publishers has visited Cuba. Their country's Treasury Department still forbids them from discussing copyright and cultural products with the communist regime, but it's rumoured behind the scenes in Washington that this ban might soon be lifted. If the American government gives them the okay at last, the publishers could take the next step: to convince the Cuban regime to make room for them on the shelves of the island's bookstores.

When I enter the conference room in the Memories Miramar Hotel this Tuesday morning, the Americans are having their say. "The book industry in Cuba tends to be dominated by women. In the United States, it's the same thing." Armed with words, graphics, and statistics, Tina Jordan, vice-president of the Association of American Publishers, is seeking common ground with her audience. Many are listening through a simultaneous translation earpiece, noting almost all her remarks as if they were attending a Party meeting. "With this opening, there is a huge interest in discovering new Cuban authors," she adds.

After the panel I collar Larry Downs, the Senior Vice President and Publisher of HarperCollins Español. For him, Cuba means "100 percent literacy." Ten million readers, and therefore ten million potential clients. "We're here for a dialogue, to get some sense of our authors' impact, to ask questions in order to figure out how we might have some success in this kind of market. We're trying to imagine what sort of business model would work best. We want to be ready for when the opportunity presents itself," he says. Downs knows that nothing is guaranteed. But his investment for the moment is minimal. A plane ticket, a few nights in a hotel, some handshakes and chit-chat. The Americans have much to gain, little to lose.

As for the Cuban publishers, it's hard to see how they might profit from future exchanges. With their poorly printed books, their recurring production problems and the censorship that has already driven many of their best writers to be published outside the island, they don't have much to offer the Americans.

Still, Jesús David Curbelo, director of the Dulce María Loynaz Cultural Centre, which promotes Cuban writers, insists "I think both parties can benefit from this relationship." Certainly, the market would be disrupted by all the titles flooding in from the United States, and Cuban publishers would be adversely affected, but readers would at last have much more to choose from. "Those books are not currently available, and we need them."

Jesús David Curbelo is an important player in the Cuban literary world. The institution he heads operates under the umbrella of the Cuban Book Institute. Perhaps, then, he can tell me why 1984's publication has just now been permitted? "Before, there was no consensus on whether this book was a classic. It was also possible to claim that it was speaking to the Cuban reality, but that is not the case," he replies, without elaborating on the erroneous connections, in his opinion, that some people may have made between the island and Orwell's world. "This book was demonized here for a long time, but it circulated all the same. Some people in the opposition saw its re-release as a sign of change. But in fact, it's just a coincidence. The decision to publish it was made before December 17, 2014," the date when diplomatic relations with the United States were re-established.

Jesús David Curbelo seems quite well informed as to the circumstances of 1984's publication. Perhaps he was even present when the title was proposed and approved by the literary authorities. If that was the case, he gives no sign of it. On the other hand, he does not hide the fact that he's delighted by the relaxation of censorship. "We must not be afraid of the classics. We must not be afraid of books."

Whether the monuments of world literature are published in dribs and drabs by Cuban publishers or whether they arrive by the hundreds from the United States, the important thing for him, in the long run, is that Cubans may one day have access to them.

*

Obama is coming. He's announced it on Twitter. It's only a partial surprise. After having worked so hard to bring the two countries together, it was obvious that he would want to visit Cuba before the end of his second term. He had planned a trip to Latin America in March. All he had to do was to tack on a stopover in Havana. Now it's done.

In the American press, they're talking about a "historic" visit. For once, the use of this word is not an exaggeration. The last American president to visit Cuba was Calvin Coolidge in 1928. At the time, Cuba was ruled by another dictator, Gerardo Machado, who would be overthrown by the populace five years later. A bilateral treaty gave the United States "the right to intervene in order to preserve Cuba's independence." Meaning: the right to intervene in order to preserve its dependence on the United States. For rich Americans, the island was a haven of debauchery. Especially during prohibition. During Coolidge's visit, as soon as the taciturn president was in bed, the reporters accompanying him seized the opportunity to swarm Havana's bars and bordellos. To their great delight, the day before their return, it was announced that they wouldn't need to have their baggage inspected at customs. Thirty years later, a *Saturday Evening Post* reporter remembered having brought back six half-gallons of Bacardi from the trip.[4]

During Obama's visit, the reporters will not have much time to savour Havana's night life. The president will be there for fewer than three days, and they will be very busy ones. According to his planned

---

4   Beverly Smith Jr., "To Cuba with Cal," *Saturday Evening Post*, February 1, 1958.

itinerary, Obama is to meet Raúl, members of civil society, small business people, and perhaps dissidents (certainly dissidents). He will give a public speech and participate in many other activities. Unless there is a change, he will not, however, sit down with Fidel. That would constitute too strong a symbol. The Cuban Americans would be enraged to see Obama shaking the hand of the person they hold responsible for their exile. As for the Cubans who still support the regime, they can understand the pragmatic Raúl meeting with the head *yanqui*-in-chief. But Fidel, the embodiment of their ideals, ought never to stoop to that as long as the embargo has not been lifted.

The American president will be arriving in a country very different from the one Coolidge visited eighty-eight years ago. Rather than imposing his wishes on the dictator in power, as his predecessor was able to do, he will have to negotiate with the Cubans and try to seduce them without angering dissidents in Miami.

On February 19, the day after the announcement, *Granma*, the Communist Party's official newspaper, features on its front page the presidential tweet and the White House communiqué. Its headline:

**IN CUBA, PRESIDENT OBAMA WILL BE TREATED
WITH RESPECT AND CONSIDERATION.**

*

Almost all Cuban Americans are critical of Castro's regime. If Barack Obama has not succeeded in lifting the embargo, it's largely because the Republican members of Congress and the senators of Cuban origin fiercely oppose any reconciliation with the communist regime, and they influence their party's caucus in this regard. All the 2016 candidates for the Republican Party's presidential nomination have made it known that they will maintain a hard line where Havana is concerned, except for the erratic Donald Trump, who has stated that he finds Obama's overture "correct," even if he would have preferred "a better deal." His sixteen opponents have promised to repeal all the decrees the Democratic president has adopted, aimed at circumventing the embargo.

Of course, politicians no longer really reflect the spirit of the times. In the Cuban diaspora, the wind is turning. The original exiles still swear that they will never set foot on the island as long as the Castro brothers are in power, but they are increasingly older and fewer in number. Their descendants, like the recent immigrants who have come over for reasons that are more economic than political, are less adamant than their elders. Recent polls indicate that, for the first time, a small majority of Cuban Americans are in favour of lifting the embargo.

Recent immigrants have every reason to hope for a complete normalization of relations. In 2013, the Cuban government announced that its citizens could henceforth travel freely outside the country. It also extended from eleven months to two years the amount of time they could remain outside without losing the rights to their property. If they go to the United States, they can obtain permanent residence there after twelve months, and then return to Cuba for at least a few days every two years in order to hold onto their possessions. Their departure from the island no longer has to be definitive.

Among the old exiles, some are also beginning to put aside their hatred and to again interest themselves in their country of origin. During my stop in Miami a few weeks before leaving for Cuba, I met a Cuban American billionaire who was trying to overcome his ancient enmities.

Miguel Fernández prefers to be called Mike. He was born in Cuba in 1952, but it's the United States that made him the man he is. "Here, I have seven residences, my five children, my relatives, my businesses. Behind my house on Biscayne Boulevard, there's only one flag flying: that of the United States," he tells me in the chic offices of MBF Healthcare Partners, his private investment firm.

You only have to listen to Mike for a few minutes to see how American he is. He is the very incarnation of the dream that drives his adopted country: an immigrant become a billionaire who, once rich, gives back to his community. Thanks to the fiscal laws that favour the well-to-do, Mike can play the big-hearted philanthropist without having to compromise the value of his fortune. His name is inscribed on a dozen Miami buildings as a donor, and he has four times made the pilgrimage to Santiago de Compostela in order to benefit sick children. Every Christmas he gives the Miami police cheques to distribute to families in need. The process is a bit peculiar: the officers locate cars seeming to belong to poor people, and order the drivers to pull over. Instead of giving them a fine, they hand them a two-hundred-dollar cheque, while wishing them a merry Christmas.

A great friend of the Bush family, Mike is also one of the most generous donors to the Republican Party. But he opposes the Party's policies where Cuba is concerned. "There are two areas where I agree with Barack Obama: getting rid of Osama bin Laden, and his openness toward Cuba." What stops him from being a Democrat is that party's tendency to create social programs he feels are too lavish. "It destroys people's will to accomplish anything at all," he says, clearly not realizing – or not wanting to realize – that it is the very absence of those programs that allows him to appear so generous to the sick and deprived.

His contempt for any policies that hint at socialism is certainly not foreign to the fact that just before Christmas 1964, he and his family fled an island that was becoming a bit more communist every day. "My father owned a little sandwich stand. He was not political, but if you were in business, you were automatically considered a counter-revolutionary."

It took Mike a long time to make his peace with Cuba. He returned for the first time only in the year 2000. "I don't forget, but I forgive and I look to the future." That is, in fact, the message he's trying to send to the members of the diaspora in Miami, still clinging to their antipathy toward the Castros. "Many of them want the Cuban government to say it's sorry, that it made a mistake, that it failed, but if they wait for that day, they'll die in exile. Governments rarely apologize. And dictatorships, never."

Since the re-establishment of diplomatic relations, Mike regularly goes to Cuba, where he accompanies representatives of American companies who want to explore the Cuban market. Surprisingly, he has no intention of investing his own funds. For two reasons. First, he doesn't want to give ammunition to those who criticize his endeavours to promote reconciliation on the pretext that there's a profit motive behind them. It's true that if ever the embargo is lifted, medical tourism, already a thriving industry in Cuba, risks attracting thousands of Americans looking for low-priced healthcare. But Mike swears that he's ready to forgo this business opportunity to show how irreproachable are his intentions. The other reason that holds him back is much more down to earth and has nothing to do with a pure heart: for him, the risks are still too high. "There's no recognition of private property in Cuba. There are many other places in the world where I can invest my money, so why risk doing it there? When someone asks me if they should invest in Cuba today, I tell them that if they're prepared to lose everything, as that's what could happen, then they can go ahead and take their chances."

Mike's readiness to help out the country of his birth stops where a risk to his capital begins.

Even if he makes a case for more bilateral exchanges, Mike's wariness of the Cuban authorities endures. Every time he travels to Havana in his private plane, he immediately sends the aircraft back to the other side of the Florida Strait. There's no question of leaving it on the tarmac overnight. The last nationalizations of American assets by the revolutionary government date back half a century, but, he says, you never know what some official might try to do.

Beyond his commercial missions, Mike says he wants above all to help ordinary Cubans to prepare themselves for the market economy. Through the Catholic Church, he has founded an organization that gives free training in entrepreneurship to Cubans on the island. The first forty hours of the course are designed to enhance the participants' self-esteem. "If you live in a country where they tell you what to do, where on the day of your birth you receive a ration card that tells you what you'll be eating for the next five years, you don't develop much self-respect," Mike believes. The second phase of the training aims to educate the participants in basic entrepreneurship. "Knowing how to build a business, no longer relying on the government and on money sent to them by their families abroad."

Mike wants to help propagate in Cuba the basic principle taught to him by the United States: pride in private property. He dreams that together, Cuban Americans and Cubans on the island might in the future build a capitalist country where everyone would have their place. And for that, he believes that all options are on the table. "If they want to maintain a single party in power, perhaps it's a compromise the United States must make. In due course, when the Cubans will want more than one party, they can decide to change the system."

Leaving Mike's office on this January afternoon, I'm of two minds. On the one hand, I tell myself that the help he'd like to provide to small business owners is exactly what Cubans need to prepare themselves for an eventual opening up of the economy and the invasion of foreign interests that will go along with it. On the other hand, I remember that before being Cuban, before being American, Mike and his fellows are businessmen. He even said to me, "Money doesn't care where it's being invested."

The massive amount of capital that will perhaps, one day, cross the Florida Strait, will not do so out of disinterested love for the Cubans, but because a country in tatters offers great opportunities for doing business.

*

The economist Ricardo Torres meets me at one of the best restaurants in Havana, at the edge of Vedado, near the Almendares River. El Cocinero shares a former edible oil factory with another popular destination for tourists and trendy Havana dwellers: the Fábrica de Arte Cubano (FAC), a multidisciplinary arts centre that also includes several bars and music rooms. Entry to both places is controlled. On opening nights, there is a long line in front of the Fábrica, and the doormen give priority to VIPs.

At El Cocinero, you have to furnish the name associated with your reservation if you hope to get through the door. So much for egalitarianism. Had I known the place was so fancy, I would at least have worn a nice shirt and long pants. My foreign accent, however, is more than enough to persuade them that I'll be able to pay the tab.

While I'm waiting for Ricardo, I listen in on the English being spoken at the tables around me. The clientele is mostly American. On the menu, the main courses are pegged at between ten and fifteen CUCs.

Ricardo arrives. A good-looking man in his thirties, whose clean dress shirt stands out next to my sweat-stained T-shirt. He's used to meeting delegations of businessmen like those Mike Fernández accompanies to Cuba. He's often invited to the United States to give lectures. "You can't imagine how many companies have sent representatives to Cuba since the announcement on December 17, 2014," Ricardo says, right off the bat. "Some come from countries I didn't even know existed!" Once in Cuba, however, their bubbling enthusiasm has to contend with reality. Because on the Cuban side, the process takes a lot of time. The offers of partnership are studied with no sense of urgency, because of the bureaucratic machine's overall slowness on the one hand, "but also because the authorities want to remind the Americans and others that they are in control and they'll decide who can do business here, and when. They want to show that we're not desperate." In that way the regime can maintain its power of negotiation. "If that power is wielded intelligently, I believe it's not a bad thing," adds Ricardo.

The economist believes in "a gradual transition toward a new equilibrium," both economic and political. "People are very poor here, and they're afraid to lose the little they have. They saw what happened in Eastern Europe, and they tell themselves that radical change is perhaps not a good idea." If they are celebrating the re-establishment of relations with the United States, they still believe that Cubans have to be on their guard. "We can't be naive. Part of the American elite still sees Cuba as its backyard. And the Cubans hate that idea. Even those who detest the Castro government do not want the Americans, the International

Monetary Fund, and the World Bank to come here and tell them what to do."

Beyond opening itself up to the outside world, what awaits Cuba in the coming years is a major restructuring of its system, according to Ricardo. "For five decades we've worked to build an egalitarian society. This system is still in large part intact. Now, the reality is changing. Some people have forgotten where they put their ration card, while others dream of possessing two or three. Everything has been conceived with a society in mind where everyone earns approximately the same salary. That's no longer the case."

We receive our food. We've each ordered an extra helping of vegetables. They arrive on the same plate. "That's socialism!" jokes Ricardo.

"In an economy like this," he goes on, "it would be fair to give more to the most vulnerable than the same thing to everyone. Yes, we must conserve our systems of free education and healthcare, but we can't go on subsidizing prices for all services." He cites El Cocinero as an example. "In Cuba, electricity is cheaply available for everyone. When you reach a certain limit in your consumption, you must, on the other hand, buy the surplus at the market price. That means that the owners of this restaurant pay for part of their electricity at the same price as I do. And it's the same for water, which is almost free. Businesses like this consume a lot. Ought they not to be paying the full price when they sell their services at market value?"

If ever the government, however, embarks on such a reorganization of social benefits, Ricardo observes, it risks being faced with a serious problem: since a good part of the economy is informal, it would be hard to calculate the true revenue of the citizens, so as to determine which ones ought to have a right to those benefits, and from whom they ought to be withdrawn.

I share with Ricardo my fears of seeing Havana transformed into a second Miami. If the transition is sudden, many in Havana might be tempted to sell their property to the first speculator who comes along, Cuban or foreign. As in Russia after the fall of the USSR, those close to the regime might in a few months transform themselves into ultra-rich, ultra-powerful oligarchs. Pulling the strings of the reforms, they could certainly find a way to lay their hands on state properties for a pittance. For Ricardo, it's "inevitable and even desirable" that property laws be liberalized if the government wants to hasten, somewhat, the country's development. He's also confident that Havana dwellers will want to preserve their patrimony and will refuse to see hundred-year-old buildings destroyed and replaced by big luxury hotels. Still, he admits, "it won't be easy to stop. There's a lot of pressure, and a lot of money at stake."

What could save Cuba and help it to integrate into the world economy more successfully than other poor countries, Ricardo believes, is the high educational level of the people, and its geographic location, a stone's throw from the American market. "One thing is sure: we'll never go back to 1958. Because Cuba is not the illiterate country it was then."

Given the implacability of market forces, his confidence still comes across as more a wish than a prediction.

THE PRECEDENT

In its June 2013 edition, the literary journal *La Letra del Escriba* ("the scribe's letter") included an excerpt from *1984*'s first chapter, along with a short biography of Orwell. It was Daniel Díaz Mantilla, to whom Fabricio had introduced me at the launch of *1984*, who was responsible for its publication.

It would be almost impossible to make an exhaustive survey of everything published in Cuba over the last six decades; it is, however, very likely that this was the first appearance of a text by Orwell in an official publication since the early days of the Revolution. In fact, probably since a fragment of *Homage to Catalonia* was included in the July 18, 1960, edition of *Lunes de Revolución* ("Mondays of the revolution"), devoted to the Spanish Civil War. The editors of the cultural supplement to the newspaper *Revolución*, the official organ of Fidel Castro's 26th of July Movement, wanted to share with its readers the first paragraphs of what they described as "an honest man's homage to the valour of a people." In joining an anarchist militia to oppose the fascists, the English writer reaffirmed his commitment to fighting tyranny in the cause of freedom. As did the Cubans in rising up against the dictator Batista.

A year and a half later, *Lunes de Revolución* ceased to exist, though the magazine was extremely popular on the island and even beyond. It published some of the finest Cuban writers, and certain editions had runs of 250,000 copies. In intellectual circles, *Lunes* was admired for its daring and creativity. But now that the ideological profile of the Revolution was more clearly defined – it was officially socialist and had been aligned with the Soviet Union for seven months – those features that had made for the magazine's success became problematic for the regime. Its director Guillermo Cabrera Infante and his collaborators had supported the Revolution from the beginning and did so still. But what would these free spirits write the day that it let them down?

"Within the Revolution, everything. Outside the Revolution, nothing," Castro proclaimed in his famous "Speech to the Intellectuals," in June

1961, six months before *Lunes* disappeared. With a few words inserted into a very long speech, he defined the limits of expression that would henceforth hold sway over Cuba's intellectual life. Before expressing themselves, before publishing or distributing anything at all, every artist, writer, editor, or film director had to ask themselves the following question: does my song, my poem, my book, my film, have a place in the context of the Revolution? Short of being able to enter Fidel Castro's head in order to be certain, they could only hope that the *Comandante* or some official would not decide that their work had gone too far.

At the beginning of 2013, when Daniel Díaz Mantilla suggested to the editorial committee of *La Letra del Escriba* that they publish an excerpt from *1984*, the Revolution's leadership was no longer as rigid and narrow-minded as it had once been. Determining its limits, however, was still a delicate exercise in deduction. During the meeting, Daniel, as the journal's editor, reminded his colleagues that June would mark the 110th anniversary of Eric Arthur Blair's birth. In his opinion, Orwell was an "important writer" of the twentieth century whom the Cuban readers ought to know. Why not capitalize on this event to publish a fragment of his most famous novel? To his great surprise, the assistant editor of the publication made no objection. Usually she was the one who tried to head off his most daring suggestions, with what were essentially ideological arguments. The two of them could debate at length the acceptability of a text, sometimes arguing over a single word that, for her, violated the boundaries of the Revolution. In the end it was often the third member of the committee, the journal's director, who had to intervene, rarely in Daniel's favour.

About a month after this editorial meeting, the director paid Daniel another visit to ask him to choose a passage from *1984* that they might publish in the June edition. Daniel's first reaction was to ask him if this was a joke. "My proposal was first and foremost a provocation. I didn't expect it to be accepted. But he told me, no, this isn't a joke. There was an awkward moment. He seemed astonished by my question, as if nothing had ever stood in the way of Orwell's publication in Cuba."

Most often, in order to publish a controversial author, Daniel has to launch an offensive more than once, and space out his initiatives over several months or years. That is how, for example, he earlier succeeded in publishing a poem and photo of Heberto Padilla, one of the greatest Cuban poets. In 1971, this former contributor to *Lunes de Revolución* had been imprisoned for his writings, judged counter-revolutionary. He died in exile in the United States in the year 2000. The short poem that Daniel was able to insert into the September 2012 edition was taken from *Fuera del juego* ("out of the game"), the collection that, after having been praised by the critics and awarded a national prize, led to his imprisonment. The few lines from "Poética" ("Poetica") seem to foreshadow his falling out of favour:

> Say the truth.
> Say, at the very least, your truth.
> And later
> let anything happen:
> let them tear your cherished page,
> let them stone your door down,
> let the people
> gather before your body
> as if you were a prodigy or a dead man.[5]

Daniel remembers that after the publication of this poem, some dissidents were very angry. "They said that we were trying to make people believe that freedom exists in Cuba. But it does exist. And you can take advantage of it up to a certain point. Except that there are risks associated with it. If I push too hard, especially where politics is concerned, I might lose my job. *They* are not so naive."

---

5   Ramón Mestre's translation of Heberto Padilla's "Poética." Mestre's translation appeared in the Spring issue of the magazine *Dissent* in 1973; the original poem appeared in the collection *Fuera del juego* (Havana: Casa de las Américas, 1968).

There is no official list of banned authors in Cuba that one can consult for the revolutionary authorities' latest updates. Or if it exists, the cultural workers at Daniel's level have no access to it. To know whether the limits have shifted, you have to dare to submit for publication what was – or seemed to be – unacceptable up to that point. If he had proposed Orwell a few years earlier, he would probably have been turned down.

Daniel does not know the exact process by which fragments of works by Orwell, Padilla, and other writers, once deemed counter-revolutionary, have found themselves published in *La Letra del Escriba*. As he understands it, the journal's director, who despite their ideological differences remains a friend, has extensive decision-making powers. "But he's not totally autonomous. And in some instances, he can feel the need to ask for authorization."

Daniel thinks that if the director has any doubts, he will turn to the president of the Cuban Book Institute, which oversees the revue. And if, in her turn, she's not certain of a writer's acceptability or that of a particular text, she'll probably appeal to the Ministry of Culture. "But that's just a supposition. I've never tried to find out who makes the final decision, because that could lead to a discussion of ideological censorship that's too explicit. We all know it exists, but we usually behave as if it didn't."

It's amid this atmosphere of widespread simulated naïveté that Daniel, who is also a poet, essayist, short story writer, and poetry editor at Unión Editions, tries to publish texts and books that seem important to him. "I push, I push, but not too hard. And sometimes there are openings that appear in the walls of censorship; inconstant openings that let in light for a brief period before shutting back down."

Daniel does not at all give the appearance or resort to the methods of a sabre-rattling combatant for publishing freedom: he is forty-six years old, long-haired but balding, skinny, his voice soft and monotone. His English is slow but precise, giving me the time to transcribe almost word for word each of his sentences. He doesn't talk much faster in Spanish. His words never crowd each other on their way out of his mouth. He lets them ripen between two puffs on his cigarette, and frees up only those that make sense to him. I admire his economy of language, his composure during silences, his concern for exactness. Perhaps I should also take up smoking.

Daniel is not a great fan of Orwell as a novelist. Like Fabricio, it's Orwell the essayist whom he admires. Recently, the editorial committee of *La Letra del Escriba* accepted Daniel's proposal to publish in a future issue a translation of "Why I Write," one of Orwell's best-known short essays, first published in 1946.

Even if, in Daniel's opinion, *1984* is not a masterpiece from a strictly literary point of view, the novel is an invaluable source of insights into totalitarianism and the way it works. "And that's important. Literature ought not to be only a matter of beautiful texts. It must also contain ideas." By exposing the mechanisms used by the Party to control the citizens of Oceania, Orwell makes his readers aware of how they themselves are being manipulated. And by imagining a new language whose very purpose is to limit citizens' ability to express their feelings and opinions, the writer reminds us of the importance of words and their meaning so that we might apprehend, understand, and call into question the world in which we live.

When Daniel first read *1984* at the age of eighteen, the similarities between Cuba and Orwell's world were much more abundant than they are today. Like the novel's Winston, he was then convinced that the merest ideological indiscretion would be punished. "Now, I feel that it's up to *them* to explain to me why they think I'm wrong." He no longer feels the need to censor himself when he's talking on the phone, in the street, or elsewhere in public. "If *they* are listening to me, so much the better. Maybe *they* will find that what I'm saying is interesting, and that I'm right. You can't live your whole life thinking that you're being observed. You have to be free."

In 1988, in lending him his copy of *1984*, Daniel's friend had warned him not to be stopped by the police with the novel in his possession. The next year the Berlin Wall came down, then two years later the USSR fell apart. Cuba found itself alone, with no ally, no backer, and no resources. As its material situation deteriorated from day to day, the regime had to resign itself to easing its grip on its citizens' lives in order to avoid social collapse. "There was still a strong leader, but ideologically, *they* were no longer so demanding."

Twenty-five years later, culture is no longer a priority for the regime, in Daniel's opinion. "Today, *they* are primarily interested in business. If *they* have an opportunity to prove that we are living in a free society, *they* will allow polemical texts to be published." That is probably one of the explanations for Orwell's novel being published by Arte y Literatura. "If *1984* had come out in the 1990s, it would have landed like a bomb. But now *they* have stepped back from communism and almost no one remembers what life was like in the 1960s, '70s, and '80s. This book is still potentially dangerous of course, even very dangerous. But only if you allow people to freely debate it."

Which is clearly not the case.

Reading Pedro Pablo Rodríguez's preface, Daniel was deeply irritated. The historian wrote that he hoped for a public debate over the publication of the novel. But he knew perfectly well that there was no chance that the state media, the only outlet where such a debate could take place, would magically transform itself into an open forum.

I try out a theory on Daniel: might it have been the reading of the *1984* excerpt in *La Letra del Escriba* in June 2013 that gave someone the idea a few months later of publishing the entire novel with Arte y Literatura? Had not the publication in *La Letra* proven that Orwell was now an acceptable author? Daniel doubts that any link can be established between the two appearances. Or rather, with no proof, he prefers not to jump to conclusions. In 2013, he notes, many people in Cuba and beyond were already comparing Orwell's novel to the surveillance programs of the American and British secret services. Edward Snowden's revelations concerning them appeared in that same month of June in 2013. "That was a very seductive view of the novel for the Cuban cultural police. Perhaps my proposal was just one more drop in an already brimming cup." Rodríguez's preface, like the historian's speech at the book's launch, also was trying to tilt Cuban readers in the direction of another interpretation.

In any case, Daniel is less interested in the exact identity of the person or persons behind the re-release of *1984*, than in the reasons for the regime's rehabilitation of Orwell and his work. He also remembers another Englishman long demonized by the Cuban authorities, who was later lionized by them: John Lennon.

For decades, like all rock musicians, Lennon and the Beatles were perceived as prime representatives of the "enemy culture," a culture regarded as inferior and degrading by revolutionary institutions. Then, during the 1990s, Lennon quietly became an acceptable figure. In December 2000, to commemorate the twentieth anniversary of his assassination, a Havana park was renamed in his honour, and a bronze statue of him was installed there. Why? Because it seemed a good way to ingratiate the government with young Cuban rockers, according to Daniel. "The decision was taken at a time when Lennon was no longer the source of any ideological problems, when it was more advantageous to authorize him than to ban him. Who made the calculation? I don't know. But what I find most interesting is to analyze the calculation itself, the process of rehabilitation."

Like the regime, Daniel tends to calculate. If he does not overtly denounce every obvious instance of censorship, it's because he knows that if he were excluded from the system, he would be unable to change things from the inside. To subtly widen the scope of what is acceptable, he has to live with frustrations, show patience, know how to take advantage of opportunities, and sometimes, to take risks.

Daniel Díaz Mantilla had nothing to do, directly, with *1984*'s appearance with Arte y Literatura. Still, in finding a way to publish an excerpt from the novel in *La Letra del Escriba* three years earlier, he established a precedent. Thanks to him, after years of tacit prohibition, Orwell's work, like that of Padilla and other authors long beyond the pale, now has one foot inside the Revolution's cultural domain.

THE USEFUL IDIOT

It's April 26, 1959. Jean-Guy Allard is eleven years old. He's a boarder at Montréal's Jean-de-Brébeuf College. At the end of the afternoon, while he's playing on the grass with his friends, he sees a long cavalcade of cars surging onto Côte-Sainte-Catherine, heading toward Sainte-Justine Hospital, just in front of the college. Sitting in the front of a black limousine, on the passenger side, is a large bearded man in olive-green military garb waving to his admirers from the window. Excited by this unexpected event that has come to break the monotony of an ordinary day, Jean-Guy and his companions work their way through the crowd. They still don't know what this man represents, who the media are calling "the most romantic figure of the hour." With all those cars following along, they just assume that it must be someone important. Like many other onlookers, Jean-Guy holds out his hand toward the limousine. For a second, perhaps less, his little child's hand finds itself in the grip of the revolutionary's giant one.

Later the same day, Fidel Castro gives a press conference at the Queen Elizabeth Hotel. He's in Montréal for less than twenty-four hours at the invitation of the Jeune chambre de commerce (the Junior Chamber of Commerce), which has organized a collection of toys for Cuban children.[6] The Queen Elizabeth, affiliated with the Hilton chain, has agreed to lodge the delegation for free. Since they took power in Havana on January 1, Castro's guerrilleros have made the Havana Hilton their headquarters. While the new government is starting to talk about nationalization, the hotel chain wants to be sure of remaining in its good graces so as to hang onto its Havana establishment, inaugurated a year earlier.

---

6   On his blog, Claude Dupras, the then-president of Montréal's Jeune Chambre de commerce, gives a detailed account of the circumstances surrounding Castro's visit, and the events of the day: claude.dupras.com/category/fidel-castro-a-montreal/.

To the journalists assembled at the Queen Elizabeth, Castro declares:

> Power, for us, is an unending succession of struggles and sacrifices, of sleepless nights: it is not, believe me, a matter of vainglory, ambition, personal satisfaction. You have to know what immense, acute problems we must resolve before we can offer Cubans a modicum of well-being. That is why we are in power, for that and to restore true democracy to the country. You understand that we will not get there in one day, but we will surely get there.[7]

Québec, like the rest of the world, is charmed. Castro, it's said, will not only revolutionize Cuba, but will make revolution respectable again. A few years will pass before little Jean-Guy becomes aware of politics and starts admiring Fidel Castro not only for his impressive stature, but for his ideas and accomplishments. In the instant when he is shaking his hand, he still does not know that forty years later he will be serving Castro's regime.

*

When Jean-Guy Allard opens his Havana apartment door to me after a long wait, I'm taken aback to find him in a wheelchair. His face and body are emaciated, his hands are frail, his hair is thin, and his legs are covered in sores. He's only sixty-seven years old, but he seems much older. Arthritis, he explains, has caused him suffering for years.

On a wall near his work desk, a photo shows him with the Colombian writer Gabriel García Márquez. His diplomas commend him on

---

7   Jean-Marc Léger, "Castro: éliminer la misère et l'ignorance et créer une démocratie humaniste; Une révolution qui n'est pas une illusion," *Le Devoir*, April 27, 1959. Now available at collections .banq.qc.ca/ark:/52327/2792218.

the quality of his revolutionary journalism. Over a row of books, a historical photo shows Lenin reading *Pravda*, the official newspaper of the Communist Party of the Soviet Union.

Jean-Guy's apartment is on the seventh floor of a building in Vedado, whose greatest luxury is a relatively recent elevator that works well. The living room window offers a splendid view of Havana, with the Florida Strait in the distance. From here you can see many of the city's grand hotels, including the Habana Libre, the former Hilton that the revolutionaries finally nationalized in October 1960. Jean-Guy has only lived here for three months. He's coming out of a difficult divorce. Despite the bitter end to his marriage and his delicate health, he doesn't regret a second of his life on the island. "I've had wonderful years here, my friend," he tells me.

On December 17, 2000, just retired from the *Journal de Québec*, where he was a reporter and then a news editor, Jean-Guy Allard came to live "for a while" in Havana. He hoped to spend his old age in a warm country, and for some time had felt "politically sympathetic" to Cuba. He had no definite plan. Nothing awaited him on the island, except for a woman. During his last active years, along with his job at the *Journal de Québec*, he'd organized economic missions to Cuba for the Québec government. It was during one of those trips that he met his future wife, confirming his decision to retire there.

Jean-Guy's first trip to Cuba goes back much further, to "1967 or 1968." At that time, he was dreaming of a worldwide revolution. For him, as for millions of other young people the world over, Cuba was then a model. The elections Castro promised during his visit to Montréal had long since been set aside, but the revolutionary fervour on the island remained intense. Unlike in Western democracies, the regime's supporters insisted, "the people's power" was being exerted in different ways from that of inserting a ballot into a box. The literacy campaign enabled hundreds of thousands of illiterate Cubans to learn to read and write, the lands of the great property owners had been redistributed to poor peasants, and a vast network of public services had been put in place. The future seemed radiant for this Caribbean utopia.

In Québec, after the Quiet Revolution, a new revolutionary wind was blowing, this time with a nationalist flavour. Jean-Guy was not a Front de libération du Québec follower, but he associated freely with the Marxists. Before going to Cuba he passed through Mexico and Guatemala, where he met militants on the far left. A few months after coming to the island, he flew off to communist China. During his travels, when he went broke, he asked his businessman father to send him money. And so it was in large part thanks to his capitalist progenitor's wealth that he was able to further his revolutionary education, and to nurture his idealism in the cause of a more egalitarian society.

Back in Québec, he became a journalist. In his thirty years in the profession, he recalls that he was "very well paid" and "led a good life." During that period, he considered himself a simple "newsman." He set his revolutionary convictions aside. It was his settling in Cuba that gave them a second life.

Three months after arriving in Havana, he met, by chance, in the Hotel Nacional parking lot, the editor of *Granma Internacional*, with whom he had friends in common. Two of the translators in the francophone section had just gone back to France. The editor was looking for replacements. "It was the fastest hiring in my life," Jean-Guy remembers. For a year, he spent most of his time translating, which enabled him to perfect his Spanish. Then, in Panama, there began the trial of Luis Posada Carriles. This most notorious anti-Castro terrorist – a CIA collaborator – boasted of several assassination attempts on Cuban soil over the years, as well as being suspected of orchestrating the explosion of Cubana Flight 455, which took seventy-three victims in 1976. Now he was being accused of trying to kill Fidel Castro in Panama itself. With his Canadian passport, Jean-Guy was the only one of *Granma*'s newsroom employees who could enter Panama "like strolling into a shopping centre," without a visa. He was sent to cover the trial and wrote a number of articles, in addition to a book. One thing led to another, and he became known in Cuba as an expert on Luis Posada Carriles, on the "Miami mafia," and on anti-Castro terrorism. "I was invited over and over onto *Mesa Redonda*, the most widely viewed Cuban television program. Almost every time they wanted to talk about terrorism, they called on me. Once, I found myself on the set with a specialist and two generals from the Cuban Security Service. Can you believe it? Me, a guy from Montréal!"

The Revolution had made him a star.

And so it's not surprising that Jean-Guy defends it with passion, and that he's full of paradoxes. He admires the Cuban Revolution for having "thrown out the Anglo-Saxons," but praises Fidel for maintaining a friendship with Pierre Elliott Trudeau, a figure who, as a Québec sovereigntist, he can't stand. He accuses Canada of all sorts of anti-democratic evils, but justifies Cuba's restrictions on freedom of expression and its absence of free elections on the grounds that "people would win them by lying and deceiving the public."

Someone rings the doorbell. Two of Jean-Guy's Québec friends are paying him a visit. They've brought their tablet and laptop computer. Despite his illness, Jean-Guy is still officially employed by *Granma* and possesses something very rare in Cuba: a free and limitless wireless internet connection.

As I'm getting ready to say goodbye to Jean-Guy, he asks me if I've registered with the foreign press office. I admit to having entered the country on a simple tourist's visa, given the complicated accreditation procedures. He warns me that in the past some foreign reporters have been arrested for the same reason. "They pull out their fingernails," he says as a joke. Because he can allow himself to joke.

*

When I go back to see Jean-Guy three weeks later, his health has hardly improved. As on my first visit, the television is tuned to teleSUR, the only foreign channel authorized in Cuba, founded by the late Venezuelan president, Hugo Chávez. I've come to talk to Jean-Guy about a documentary project I'm planning with a director friend born in communist

Romania. The project is still at an embryonic stage, but if ever it works out, we might want to shoot part of it in Cuba. We would in particular like to interview someone from a capitalist country who has settled on the island out of an ideological affinity with the Revolution. I confess to Jean-Guy that so far I've found no one else but him. He admits that foreigners living in Cuba for political reasons are less numerous than in past times. But according to him, those who leave after a few years do not do so out of distaste for or disappointment with the Revolution. "It's because they want their beefsteak back." When he settled in Cuba, the situation was much more difficult than it is today, Jean-Guy remembers. "It was like going camping." Since then, things have changed for the better. "In any case, I've adapted." According to him, almost all the current problems with the Cuban system are due to the American embargo. "Every time a socialist society has appeared, the capitalist world has rushed in to destroy it. We're seeing that now in Brazil, in Venezuela, in Bolivia. Look at all the actions taken by the Americans and the local capitalist class. There are no limits to the attacks that can be made in order to destroy socialism." In his opinion, that's why the Castro government has had to resort to authoritarian measures in order to stay in power all this time. "Normally, communism is not there to suppress anything at all. It's the circumstances that force it to do so."

I ask Jean-Guy if he still, today, considers himself a communist. "I'll tell you frankly, at my age, with the years I've lived, I don't give myself any labels. That would be absurd. The Soviet Union has been defunct for ages. Many things have vanished, others have been born, like Chavez's socialism. In times past, communists championed values. Cooperation, solidarity, those were real concepts. Today's young Cubans have grown up in a socialist society. But that's not the same as having known a revolution, having risked one's life to change society, like their parents did." Jean-Guy admits, up to a point, that the Cuban Revolution does not excite people the way it once did for young generations in Cuba and beyond. But out of pride or allegiance, he is still not prepared to dissect his youthful ideals. And even less to put them on trial.

*

On July 15, 1954, the newspaper *Libération* summarized on its front page the impressions Jean-Paul Sartre brought back from his trip to the Soviet Union. "Freedom to criticize is total in the US and the Soviet citizen is constantly bettering his condition at the heart of a society that is making progress day by day." It took tanks invading Hungary two years later for the French philosopher to become disenchanted with the Soviet system.

In 1960, Jean-Paul Sartre returned from a month in Cuba, just as enthusiastic. During the trip, he and his companion Simone de Beauvoir spent forty-eight hours with Fidel Castro. In a series of articles titled "Ouragan sur le sucre" ("hurricane over sugar"), published in the newspaper *France-Soir*, Sartre rejoiced at Castro's ambition – when he was not yet officially communist – to redefine the democratic ideal. He looked favourably on the revolutionary leader's wish to offer an alternative to the Americans' brand of democracy, those "puritans of the north." In Cuba, Sartre noted, the economy would defer to politics, and not the opposite.

His illusions regarding the "New Man" in Cuba suffered a blow in 1971, when the regime locked up the poet Heberto Padilla. Along with other writers, "supporters of the principles and objectives of the Cuban revolution," Sartre signed an open letter to Fidel, asking him to free Padilla. Castro took this request as an affront. Furious, he responded to the signatories, calling them "liberal bourgeois gentlemen" and "agents of colonialism, of the CIA, and of imperialism's security services."

During the Cold War, the tendency of Sartre and other Western intellectuals to support communist regimes and downplay their crimes on the pretext that you mustn't "discourage" the workers seeking a better future, merited them the moniker of "useful idiots." It was said of these intellectuals that they were naive, even if they were acting in good faith. If they were denying reality, it was supposedly in the cause of a greater truth.

Well before the beginning of the Cold War, George Orwell, two years older than Sartre, came to the conclusion that totalitarianism ought to be defied, whatever its hue or the ideological affinities one shared with a regime. He allied himself with social democracy and always refused to sacrifice democracy on the altar of socialism. During the Spanish Civil War he condemned the local communists under the USSR's thumb for their totalitarian tactics in crushing other leftist movements fighting alongside them against the fascists. During the Second World War he systematically denounced many British intellectuals and journalists, both on the left and the right, for their complacency where Stalin was concerned. They justified their silence in the face of the dictator's crimes by claiming that they had to avoid bruising his ego so as not to compromise the war effort against Hitler. In 1944, several English and American publishers refused the manuscript of *Animal Farm*, a satire of the 1917 Russian Revolution and its aftermath, making more or less the same argument. "Nothing has contributed so much to the corruption of the original idea of socialism as the belief that Russia is a socialist country and that every act of its rulers must be excused, if not imitated," Orwell wrote three years later in the preface to the Ukrainian edition of that same book. All his life, Orwell refused to stay quiet about the truths that disturbed him, including those that incriminated his own ideological camp. For him, the end never justified the means, because abusive means inevitably corrupted the goal being sought. During his lifetime, his independent spirit brought him few friends and even fewer honours and benefits.

In Cuba, as in the USSR, the regime in power rolled out its most attractive red carpet for Sartre and de Beauvoir. They were listened to, all doors were opened to them, they were shown everything they wanted to see and were allowed to meet whoever they wanted to meet. They were charmed.

When Jean-Guy Allard moved to Havana, he had just ended a respectable career as a journalist in Québec. His name was not, however, going to pass into history. That had, in any case, probably never been his ambition. Once in Cuba, thanks to Luis Posada Carriles's trial, he became one of the most prominent journalists on the island. For a

Cuban regime longing for foreign support, Jean-Guy was a godsend. As a Canadian journalist ready to defend tooth and nail the Revolution and the government's positions in all forums and by any intellectual means, he was showered with praise, awards, and privileges. The Revolution offered him a pedestal.

In Cuba, Jean-Guy became a somebody.

Even today he doesn't seem to realize that if life on the island is more bearable for him than for the average Cuban, it's because of the VIP treatment he receives from the regime, and above all because of the two pensions deposited in his account at the beginning of every month by the governments of his home country. Certainly, Jean-Guy is not completely immune from the shortages and other inconveniences of daily life in Cuba. In fact, aside from the Caribbean climate being more agreeable than the Québec winter, he would probably be living more comfortably in Montréal than in Havana.

Except that there, he would be nobody.

I don't know how deep Jean-Guy's revolutionary convictions run, just as I do not know the exact cause of his blindness. But naive or not, of good faith or not, one has to conclude that he is behaving like a useful idiot of the Cuban revolution.

Before leaving him, I thank him for his welcome. A nice guy, despite everything. Generous with his time, his stories, and his Wi-Fi. If my documentary project materializes, I tell him, I'll contact him again. Before crossing the threshold, glancing back at his frail silhouette, I can't help thinking that if that day does arrive, even soon, Jean-Guy will perhaps not be of this world.

LOOKING FOR THE EXIT

On November 5, 2002, two very different men, both very influential in their respective fields, came together on the stage of the Karl Marx Theatre in Havana: Fidel Castro and Steven Spielberg.

The American director had travelled to Cuba to present his most recent film, *Minority Report*, an adaptation of a short story by Philip K. Dick. The story takes place in Washington, DC, in the year 2054. The American government is testing a pilot project called "PreCrime." Thanks to human mutants who can predict crimes, police can arrive and arrest bandits even before they've done their deed. "PreCrime" – a portmanteau that could easily be at home in a Newspeak dictionary in Orwell's Oceania – is a huge success. The felony rate in the capital has gone down by 99.8 percent, and the authorities hope to extend the program to the rest of the country.

Presenting his film in Cuba, Spielberg probably did not know that, as in his dystopic Washington, the Cuban authorities, while not endowed with the prescient gift of *Minority Report*'s mutant officers, could arrest citizens on the grounds of a simple suspicion. The law in fact authorizes them to imprison, as a preventive measure, any individual who might have a "special propensity" to commit a crime "in manifest contradiction with socialist norms."[8]

In agreeing to make this trip – which angered Castro's critics in the United States – Spielberg gained the right to the warmest of welcomes and the greatest honours. Fidel spent eight hours in conversation with him, and even if in terms of revolutionary cultural politics most of his films would have been regarded as "pseudoculture," a festival devoted entirely to his work had been organized. A good guest, Spielberg did not fail to denounce in the international media his country's embargo against Cuba, a policy based, according to him, on "old grievances" that were no longer relevant in the twenty-first century.

---

8 Article 72 of the Cuban Penal Code.

In the audience the night *Minority Report* was shown was a student by the name of Frank, just arrived in Havana to study at the Universidad de las Ciencias Informáticas ("University of Computer Science") or UCI. A native of Santiago de Cuba, Frank belonged to the first cohort of two thousand students at the institution, which had opened its doors just over a month earlier. The island's first educational institution dedicated to the new technologies was late in arriving when compared to the rest of the planet, but in those difficult days for the Revolution, it was one of the rare achievements about which the regime could boast. That is why its students had been invited to meet with Spielberg.

After a short question period with the director, several excited students swarmed the stage. "Some girls were crying," Frank remembers. The object of their admiration was not the celebrated American visitor, but the ever-present Fidel, the paternal figure who had been there for them all through their childhood and adolescence. Much more than Spielberg, it was to him that they wanted to express their gratitude. Frank was also very impressed to be seeing the *Comandante* in person for the first time. In those days, he still firmly believed that the system Castro had imposed on the island was just and equitable. In the weeks and months that followed that encounter, his opinions, however, would undergo a radical change.

At university, Frank began to make frequent use of the available internet connection to inform himself via sources from off the island. Until then, his web access had been limited, and he'd had to content himself with information transmitted by the Cuban media. He spent hours and hours online. "I learned what freedom was on the internet, what people in free countries could do that we couldn't. And I also realized that *he* was not as brilliant as what television tried to make us believe," Frank says fourteen years later.

Frank is the son of a revolutionary. As an adolescent, his father took part in the resistance against the dictator Batista. While Castro and his comrades fought in the Sierra Maestra, he participated in acts of sabotage in his hometown of Holguín. A son worthy of his father, Frank, at the age of fifteen, joined the Young Communist League, the first step toward becoming a member of the Party.

A few months after the screening of *Minority Report*, Fidel Castro went back to meet the UCI students on their campus. That day, the Frank who stood in line to shake the president's hand was not quite the same man as in November at the Karl Marx Theatre. His online reading had opened his eyes. He now had his own opinions, which differed more and more from those that the regime would have preferred. He still belonged to the League, but that was just because leaving it would have caused him problems, perhaps even an expulsion from the university. That was the state of mind in which he found himself when, for the first time in his life, the uncontested leader of the Revolution, who he had blindly defended up until recently, held out his hand to him. Frank remembers the moment in detail: "I kept his hand in mine just a little bit longer than I was supposed to, and I immediately saw his bodyguards reacting, so I let go." Frank would never become a dissident. But from then on he knew that he had nothing good to expect either from Fidel or from the system he'd put in place. Frank would have to design his future on his own. And that future, he now knew, would not be found in Cuba. If he wanted to develop his full potential, to be free, he'd have to find a way to leave the island and settle in "a first-world country," it didn't matter which – the United States, Canada, or somewhere in the European Union. To reach this goal, he'd try anything.

About three years after having shaken Castro's hand, while he was still a student at UCI, Frank decided to try his luck as a *jinetero*. With a friend, he began to spend his evenings at the bar of the Hotel Florida on Obispo Street, consorting at random with foreign women having a drink there. The two comrades were seeking their rare pearl: someone who would fall madly in love with them and who, persuaded that her passion was being reciprocated, would agree to be their passport to another country. In the end, it was on a dating site that Frank was able to lure the only prey worth mentioning. She was Mexican. She wanted desperately to meet a man during her next visit to Cuba. When she arrived in Havana, she and Frank spent an evening together. They drank, talked, and she invited him up to her room. Even though he was not attracted to her, he accepted. Once in the room, they got undressed and began the preliminaries. But Frank didn't get an erection.

If he'd had an erection that night, he might have been living in foreign climes for some time. He would have married the Mexican woman and joined her in her country. They would have lived together more or less happily until one fine morning Frank packed his bags, left a little note on the kitchen table with his thank yous and excuses, and took off for the American border without looking back. He would have asked the immigration officers for asylum, which he would have been granted automatically thanks to the Cuban Adjustment Act. Then he'd only have had to make his way to Miami, where a cousin living there would have taken him in. Florida would have been the starting point for his brand-new future.

Except that Frank had too many scruples.

"I really wanted to leave Cuba, but I'd have preferred to find love along with my papers," he says. The friend with whom he'd hung out in the Hotel Florida had no such scruples. He managed to seduce an aging English woman whom he soon persuaded to marry him. Now he's living in London, working part-time as a cook. "But basically, he's living off her," Frank says. Rather than dropping her once he achieved his goal, his friend opted to continue profiting from his sugar mama, lying all the way. "One day he showed her a photo, presumably of his father, intubated and gravely ill. He said he had to leave for Cuba urgently in order to take care of him. Once here, he rented an Audi and partied for days." The friend also conducts many extramarital affairs. "He even sometimes wangles money from his mistresses," Frank marvels, admiring his ingenuity even while he's appalled by his former classmate's total lack of empathy and morals. And Frank knows many like him. Another friend, for example, was able to obtain a European passport by marrying a citizen of the Dutch island of Curaçao, about one thousand kilometres from Cuba. "He comes back on a regular basis, because since his marriage he's had a son with another woman from here," Frank tells me, showing me an amateur video of this friend who dreams of being the star of a martial arts film.

After finishing his studies in Havana in 2007, Frank went back to live with his parents in Santiago de Cuba, looking for a way to leave the island. Since then he's been working for a state company, developing internal computer programs. His office is on a low-ceilinged mezzanine, poorly ventilated and full of old computers, in a crumbling city-centre building. He shares the cramped space with four co-workers. To get to his workstation he has to avoid being flayed alive by the naked fan blades spinning full speed between the wall and his neighbour's chair. As in many Cuban state companies, the tasks demanded of the employees are as minimal as their salaries. And that's fine for Frank. If he keeps his job, it's not so much for the one thousand Cuban pesos he receives at the end of the month, as for the internet connection, slow but unlimited and guaranteed, to which he has access at his workstation. Once he's fulfilled his daily duties, he has plenty of time to concentrate on the better-paying freelance contracts fed him by his cousin in Miami or other foreign intermediaries. And so he spends most of his time at work creating websites for Spaniards, Canadians, or Americans. His last contract paid him seven dollars an hour over a period of six months. "In the United States that's nothing, but here it's enormous."

Meanwhile, Frank is trying to launch his own business, a web platform that would enable foreign tourists to use a credit card to rent a car, a room, and a tourist guide, before they even arrive in Cuba. For the moment, all those services have to be paid for in cash once the tourists are on the island. Since this kind of business is still illegal, it's his cousin who manages the payments, which end up in an American bank account.

To finance his precious Soviet motorcycle, Frank roams the city on certain nights, offering taxi services. "Once I've paid for the gas, I'm left with six or seven dollars in my pocket."

Beyond all his projects and schemes for earning money, Frank never loses sight of his true objective: to leave. In fact, the only time over the last decade when he was not plotting to flee the island was four years ago, when his mother was seriously ill. He wanted to be with her to the end. Not long after her death, he began again to think about his departure. On the pretext of going to visit his cousin, he asked for a tourist visa for the United States. He was refused. "If I'd have received it, of course I would have stayed there." These days, he's working on several exit strategies at the same time, in order to enhance his chances of success. One of them would be to negotiate a sham contract for a working trip to Mexico, where he could easily access the United States. The problem is that such a contract would cost him up to seven thousand dollars. "And nothing guarantees that it would work." Before embarking on such an expense, he wants first to try to convince the Mexican authorities to furnish him with a tourist visa. Next month he has to go to Havana for an interview at the embassy.

Another option on the table is immigrating to Canada. As a computer engineer, Frank thinks that he could take advantage of the Express Entry program for qualified workers. "I checked. My profession is first in line among those most often requested." So as to raise his status, he's studying French at the Santiago Alliance française, and English with a tutor. Besides his immigration efforts, he is also planning to apply to a Canadian university.

To succeed in one or another of these projects, Frank needs money. For three years he's been trying to divest himself of his large family home and to find a smaller and less grandiose one for his father and aunt. Since the sale of property was only authorized in November 2011 (before that, only exchanges were permitted), it's hard to determine the value of a house and even harder to find a buyer with tens of thousands of dollars. Up to now he's received few visits and no serious offers.

One evening, between two rain showers, Frank takes me to his home on his motorcycle. It's located in what was the former bourgeois district of Santiago before the Revolution. When we arrive, his father is in his rocking chair in front of the TV. "He has a hearing problem," Frank tells me, to explain the sound's being turned up so high. Without taking his eyes off the screen, Frank's father dutifully recycles, for my benefit, the same arguments his television set has been transmitting all day long. If the Revolution has not brought Cubans a better life, he says, it's because it doesn't have enough money, and money rules the world. And if Cuba has no money, it's purely and simply because of the United States' unjust embargo against the island. Frank rolls his eyes. He tries as much as possible not to discuss politics with his father, who fought for the Revolution, studied in socialist Bulgaria, and during his active life headed many of the Revolution's institutions. He's not going to have a change of heart at the age of seventy-four.

On the news it's announced that during a session of the United Nations Human Rights Council, an American representative has made the usual accusations against Cuba. "On the eve of the American president's visit to our country, Mister [Antony] Blinken has indicated that Obama wants to underline the importance of freedom to the Cuban people, of being able to choose their leaders and to express their ideas, so that a civil society may come into being," the announcer states. "But he forgot to say that the Cuban people freely chose their destiny already on January 1, 1959." Unlike his son and me, Frank's father does not see the point in asking Cubans if they still endorse this decision fifty-seven years later.

The more time passes, the fewer friends Frank has in Cuba. In recent months, five of them have left for Ecuador. From there they've travelled up the continent toward the north, country by country, spending a fortune for each smuggler at each border. Some were stuck in Costa Rica for weeks when Nicaragua closed its land border with its southern neighbour. One of his friends only arrived in the United States the week before, after several months on the road. Frank's girlfriend will be leaving soon. Her parents have been able to emigrate to Arizona, where they've applied for family reunification so she can join them. "Cuba is a great country for people who don't want to work. But I'm thirty-three years old, and I have plans. I don't want to just sit with my arms crossed, hoping for change. Everything happens too slowly here," he sighs.

The only option Frank has not considered up to now is escaping by boat. He knows several people who have done it. Some arrived in Florida safe and sound. Others have had to turn back. These days, more and more smugglers offer to make the crossing by motorboat, much faster and safer than the improvised craft usually used. From what Frank has heard, a place on board costs between five and ten thousand dollars. He wouldn't hesitate to pay … were it not for the sharks roaming the strait. "A mile from the coast, if the coast guard finds you, the smugglers sometimes make you jump into the water so as not to get caught and go to prison. According to the law, the coast guard can't force you to climb into their boat if you don't want to be rescued. But then you have to swim to shore on your own." It's the only risk he's not prepared to take to reach his goal.

Frank is not much preoccupied with Cuba's future. He thinks above all about his own, which he'd like to disconnect from that of his country. What concerns him most about the unlikely scenario whereby a sudden regime change would lead to chaos on the island, is not so much the chaos itself. It's the possibility that if ever that happened, he might not yet have managed to leave.

FROM ONE EDITION TO ANOTHER

Beneath the arcades of Havana's Bolívar Avenue, near the Capitol, a street hawker is spreading out books on a piece of cardboard lying on the ground. Between a dictionary of the four thousand most common words in the English language and a collection of articles by a Cuban historian, I spot a copy of the new edition of *1984*. It was launched a few days ago at the book fair, but it's not yet available in the capital's bookstores.

The literary bootlegger has posted the price of his merchandise using pieces of old torn paper he's slipped into the books. A Chinese horoscope is selling for twenty-five pesos, an old biography of a comrade of Che Guevara is going for forty, a novel by Paulo Coelho for sixty, and a guide to personal growth for eighty. Among the selections, you can also find *Diálogo con mi sombra*, Pedro Juan Gutiérrez's last book. It's one of the only works by the author of *Dirty Havana Trilogy* to have been published in Cuba. As with *1984*, you can find a copy at the fair these days at the subsidized price of fifteen Cuban pesos. For Gutiérrez's book, the reseller is asking sixty pesos. As for Orwell's novel, the surprise created by its release seems to have enhanced its value. At 120 pesos, it's the most expensive book on this mini black market.

*

In the early 1990s, Fabricio spent entire days at the José Martí National Library on Revolution Square. He got there early, asked at the counter for a book, waited fifteen minutes or so before receiving it, then read as much as he could without stopping, before returning it at closing time. That's how he was able to read, notably, H.P. Lovecraft's horror novels, and *Brave New World* by Aldous Huxley. At the time he didn't know that he could very likely have filled out an order slip for the librarian to hand him a copy of *1984* identical to the one he obtained secretly from a friend.

In October 2005, an English librarian by the name of John Pateman wanted to prove that anyone wishing to read George Orwell in Havana could do so with impunity. He went to the José Martí National Library, searched through the file drawers to find the references to his books, then asked to consult a few of them. He was given them without anyone inquiring as to his motivations. In his article, "Reading Orwell in Havana," Pateman recounts having also been able to leaf through the books of other authors such as Reinaldo Arenas and Guillermo Cabrera Infante, whose works, according to the regime's detractors, were banned on the island.[9] He then repeated his experiment in another of the capital's libraries, with the same result.

He attained his objective. He proved that it was possible to obtain, in an official manner, anti-communist literature or literature critical of the powers in Havana, without running any danger. Pateman thus allowed himself to conclude that, since the books by Orwell and the others were available in certain of the country's public libraries, that meant that "there are no authors banned in Cuba."

Three years before he conducted his experiment, the Cuban government had awarded John Pateman a medal for his contribution to the development of Cuban libraries. The following year, during an international cultural congress in Havana, he had shared the stage with Fidel Castro at Castro's request. And so John Pateman can hardly be considered an impartial observer of Cuban life.

On February 23, 2016, a little less than eleven years after John Pateman, I also pay a visit to the José Martí National Library to repeat his experiment. The woman responsible for signing up new members is courteous to a fault. Between two *mi amor*s, she asks me for identification, then hands me a form printed on very thin, poor-quality paper, much

---

9   John Pateman, "Reading Orwell in Havana," *Information for Social Change*, no. 26, Winter 2007–2008.

like those I've often filled out in ex-USSR public institutions that have not yet exhausted their reserves from times past. With her help, I darken the form's empty spaces, and in exchange for two Cuban pesos I receive a valid membership card that is good for three years. Before letting me leave, the woman insists on providing me with all the information she considers important: the library's opening hours, the procedure for renewing my membership in three years' time, and the way to gain access to the *nacional* internet network, a connection restricted to *.cu* domains, available to users at no cost.

Like Pateman, I easily find the catalogue cards for Orwell's books. Like him, I count fifteen. Most of the titles are in English. There are two editions of *Nineteen Eighty-Four*, dated respectively 1949 and 1958, but only one in Spanish, published in Havana in 1961 by Editorial Librerías Unidas. I fill out a borrowing slip, and a few minutes later I receive this first Cuban edition of *1984*, about whose existence I'd learned shortly before my departure for Cuba in one of the online articles announcing the imminent appearance of the second. Its cover is not much more appealing than Arte y Literatura's: a tricolour background in grey, black, and red, on which there appears the name of the author and that of the publishing house, the place of publication, and the four figures of the title in huge white letters. Inside, there is very little information as to the edition's origins. The title page includes the publisher's logo, a matchstick man holding out a poster on which you can read "Editorial Edilusa," probably a shortened form for **Editorial Librerías Unidas S.A.** On the other side of the page, this simple, laconic message:

All rights reserved to the author, in Cuba, to the publishers.

Nowhere in the book do the names of the publishers appear, nor that of the translator. Only the colophon at the end of the book provides a few useful details:

The printing was completed in
January 1961 – studio and office
of Luz-Hilo. Printery
Económica Integral, S.A. –
Havana, Republic of Cuba.
PLAZOLETA DE BELÉN

I leaf through the book looking for more information and, unable to find any, I close it and return it to the librarian in exchange for my membership card. My experience confirms that of John Pateman. In 2016, as in 2005, it's possible for foreign users to borrow a book by George Orwell from the National Library without having to answer any questions concerning their choice of reading material. On the other hand, I have learned very little about the origins of this Cuban edition of *1984*. As best as I can tell, around the middle of 1960, just as the revolutionary government was alienating Washington a bit more each day, someone or some group of people had the idea of embarking on the publication of this science-fiction novel. Was it a way to warn the Cubans of the dangers posed by their Revolution's totalitarian drift while they were still in the process of defining the institutions and the ideology that would guide it in the future?

A few hours later, I'm telling my partner Zeenat, over the phone, of the disappointing results of my research up to now. A coincidence: during a course on the Cold War at the Art Institute of Chicago's school, she has just read an article concerning a translation program for books and articles that was created during the 1950s by the United States Information Agency (USIA).[10] The program targeted Latin America in particular, and its main goal was to "make influential foreigners more receptive to the assumptions of U.S. foreign policy, and to do so in ways that will not be recognized as originating with the U.S. government." In the books translated by the USIA, the agency's contribution is never mentioned.

10   Warren Dean, "The USIA Book Program: Latin America," *Point of Contact*, vol. 1, no. 3, September–October 1976.

According to the article, during the first twenty-five years of its activity, the USIA sponsored twenty-two thousand editions of books in fifty-seven languages, for a total of 175 million volumes printed. Its program was not secret, but was virtually unknown to the general public. During this time, much more secretively, the CIA also financed the publication of books in foreign countries. Before a Senate committee in the middle of the 1970s, one of its former agents characterized this activity as "the most important weapon for strategic propaganda" utilized by the American Secret Service to counter Soviet influence.

This discovery puts me on a new track. Was the mysterious publishing house Librerías Unidas S.A. a front for the USIA, the CIA, or another creature of the American government? Would the Eisenhower administration have resorted to Orwell's prose in a last desperate attempt to prevent the island's alignment with the Eastern bloc? I would have to await my return to a more internet-friendly environment before testing this hypothesis.

*

In the copy of 1984 that I consulted at the José Martí National Library, a hand-written signature showed that it had once belonged to a certain María Antonieta Henríquez. A sticker on another page indicated that it had been offered to the library on March 25, 2009. Inquiring further online, I discovered that Henríquez was a musicologist of considerable reputation in Cuba, a founder in 1970 of the National Museum of Music. She died on November 28, 2007, at the age of eighty.

The most likely hypothesis is that her inheritors donated her book collection to the National Library after her death. It would appear that the library had already owned one or several more copies of this edition of 1984 for a number of decades. The poor condition of its file card in the library's drawers betrays its age, and John Pateman, who had consulted one of the two English-language editions and not the Cuban one, confirmed to me that he saw this card in 2005, that is, four years before the donation was made.

It is therefore most probable that the Librerías Unidas edition was available for consultation during the 1990s, when Fabricio was spending his days in the library. Even if he had then known it, he would probably not have taken the risk of ordering a copy, he tells me when I share my discoveries with him. "You can't compare the political climate of 2005 to now. In those days, if you wanted to work in the tourist industry in particular, *they* checked out your background with the Committee for the Defence of the Revolution [CDR] in your neighbourhood to see if you were a good revolutionary." Who knows if the records of borrowings were not sent to the CDR? Probably not, but who can say for sure? In that context, who would want to risk tarnishing their revolutionary reputation and compromising their social advancement just for having borrowed the wrong book at the library? A few Cubans must have done it. And probably they were not interrogated and did not suffer any consequences. But for Fabricio, the repressive climate that reigned when Fidel Castro was still in command was enough of a deterrent for him to abstain. His sense of danger was perhaps exaggerated. But the fear that prevented him from reading Orwell's novel with the full knowledge of the regime was very real.

NEIGHBOURHOOD LIFE

It only takes a few nights at Sonia's for the president of the neighbourhood's Committee for the Defence of the Revolution, who lives three houses down, to inquire about my presence.

"I think you have a foreigner living in your house ..."

"Yes, he's a friend of Armando. A Canadian visiting Cuba."

Sonia obviously says nothing about the "photo equipment for lodging" arrangement I'd made with her son. She just confirms that I'm not paying anything to stay there. According to this version the illegality of my visit is only partial, and the CDR president is willing to tolerate my presence. The fact that Sonia is very involved in the organization certainly weighs in the balance. She's a member of the CDR subcommittee for the environment, attends all the meetings, and when there's an election, she sits on the electoral committee. She has also registered her son as a volunteer during blood drives.

The CDRs were created in September 1960, when the Revolution was still fragile. The new government wanted to be able to count on the core of loyalists in each block of houses. These militants were given the responsibility of ensuring revolutionary decisions were respected, and denouncing neighbours suspected of counter-revolutionary activities. Officially, three quarters of Cubans over the age of fourteen still belong to the 133,000 or so CDRs across the country. The president of each committee still keeps detailed files on each of the citizens in the neighbourhood. They must gather as much information as possible regarding their activities, their tastes, the company they keep, their pastimes, their opinions, and even the condition of their health. If they determine that someone represents a danger, they report their words and behaviour to their superiors, who perform an inquiry and decide if there are grounds to take action.

So much for the theory.

In practice, in 2016, if the president of a CDR were to report every instance where someone in the neighbourhood departs from the revolutionary script, he wouldn't have time to sleep. Sonia tells me how one of the neighbours, who works in a state store, steals bottles of chlorine from her workplace and resells them to her friends at a lower price. Another does the same thing with eggs, and a third with powdered milk. Sonia is no holier than the others. Rather than denouncing them, she takes advantage of the bargains. Like almost everyone else, she also has illicit sources of revenue. A red Lada that doesn't belong to her is parked in her garage. It belongs to a criminal lawyer who rents her parking space for thirty CUC per month. She asked for less, but he insisted on giving her that amount, because he knew that with Sonia, his car would always be safe. "He makes a lot of money, because his clients pay him under the table," Sonia explains.

Even if she has as many things to reproach herself for as her neighbours, Sonia believes that the Defence Committees contribute to the cohesion of Cuban society. "It's thanks to them that we're at peace. Here there's no violence, no theft, no guns." It's unlikely that the CDR president is not aware of Sonia's arrangement with the owner of the Lada, just as it did not take him long to learn of my presence. He asks questions, gathers information, compiles files. But in the end, he knows that it's often better to avert his eyes. To safeguard the Revolution today is to allow it to live in denial by sparing it the details of the gangrene eating away at it on the inside.

*

The municipal delegate who represents the district where Sonia lives is not overly responsive to his electors. When the citizens complain about the appearance of a pothole in their street or the sudden rise in the price of a foodstuff, he's slow to react. "Some people are already saying that they won't vote for him the next time round," Sonia tells me. She herself is hesitating. It's true that he doesn't take initiatives, but on the other hand, since the beginning of the fumigation campaign against the *Aedes aegypti* mosquito, which transmits the Zika virus, he's been very effective.

Every two and a half years, Cubans go to the polls to elect their municipal delegate. The candidates are screened by the authorities and are not allowed to campaign. The day of the election, voters must base their choices on candidates' biographical notes, posted at the entrance to the electoral office. According to law, there must always be more than one name on the ballot for each municipal delegate post being contested. For the provincial and national deputies' seats, it's the opposite. Only one candidate is authorized per riding, and the electors can only vote for whoever is chosen by the Party. At each election, at whatever level of government, the turnout is in the neighbourhood of 90 percent.

Once, Fabricio tried to avoid voting. The day of the election, knowing that someone would come knocking at his door at some point, he left the house very early. "The building where I was living was positioned in such a way that no one could see the outside door without coming very close. Returning late that evening, when I turned the corner, they were there waiting for me in front of the entrance."

"Good evening, Mr. González. It's election day today, have you forgotten? I'm sure you want to vote."

"But of course."

Daniel, for his part, has already openly refused to play the game. When members of the Committee for the Defence of the Revolution appeared at his door, strongly suggesting that he participate in the vote, he replied that voting was a right and not a duty. They left, and he never heard from them again. But Daniel is part of a minority that dares to defy the implicit obligation to vote. For most, taking part in the masquerade still seems a better option than confrontation.

*

When Armando has a problem with his teeth, he does not go to see his neighbourhood's official dentist. He finds her slow and incompetent. Instead of receiving free care, he prefers to consult, illegally, another dentist, to whom he gives a *regalito* at the end of the visit to thank her for her "flexibility." His neighbourhood's family doctor, on the other hand, offers very good care. For a minor health problem, Armando and Sonia go straight to her. Recently, the government raised doctors' salaries from nine hundred to twelve hundred Cuban pesos (fifty-eight Canadian dollars) per month. It's a very low salary compared to that of health professionals in the United States, Sonia agrees, but being a family doctor in Cuba has other advantages: she didn't have to spend a penny for her education, she has the right to free lodging, and all her fixed costs are paid by the State. Still, her official salary is not enough for her to benefit from the new opportunities that economic change has brought to the island. She cannot easily buy a smartphone, or a family meal in one of the new restaurants frequented by foreign tourists, or go regularly to surf the internet at one of the Wi-Fi hotspots recently installed in certain parks. To indulge in these luxuries, she must seek out additional sources of revenue, by, for example, urging her patients to offer her "little gifts" for care that is supposed to be free.

*

Ten years ago, just before leaving for Spain, Armando brought people together in his neighbourhood to revitalize a little triangular park. He wanted to turn it into a modest public artwork. All the residents put time, money, and resources at his disposal to renovate and repaint the community space. Armando and his painter friends took care of the murals.

When he returned from Europe almost a decade later, the park was just a shadow of itself. In his absence, no one had looked after its upkeep.

Since getting back, Armando has been trying to urge his neighbours to return the park to its former glory. He has already succeeded in getting authorization for the project from his municipal delegate. But his first contacts with his fellow citizens have not been conclusive. Still, Armando is not discouraged. "They have to understand that it will be good for all of us," he says. I'm surprised by his idealism. After all those years of obligatory collectivism, his fellow citizens seem more interested in bettering their own lives than in investing in yet another collective enterprise. Despite everything, I wish him luck. If he succeeds in bringing his park back to life, he will have proved on a small scale that there is still hope that Cubans will one day recapture their will to work together for the good of all, on their own terms.

A few weeks later, Armando declares that the project has been stalled. His friend Félix, who is helping him to convince the neighbours to participate in the revitalization, has made a gaffe. He told the people nearby that if he and Armando could not get the money they needed from the neighbourhood populace and the authorities, they could eventually ask for a grant from the American embassy. "It was just an idea he threw off like that, naively. But the discussion became heated, and other people heard about it. It reached as far as the municipal delegate and the security services opened an investigation."

The Committee for the Defence of the Revolution confirmed its efficacy. In the months to come, Armando and Félix will keep a low profile. They will no longer try to make life better in their neighbourhood.

ACCESSING THE WORLD

From a technological point of view, travelling to Cuba at the beginning of 2016 represents a great leap backwards. While almost everywhere in the world you can at all times carry the internet around with you in your pocket, it's impossible to access on a Cuban cellphone. The letter E that appears at the top of smart phone screens for those subscribed to the state telecommunications monopoly ETECSA indicates that they are connected to a second-generation transmission network for cellular data. This connection only enables them to send and receive email via the address provided by the company. All other functions are blocked. To justify this limitation, ETECSA claims a technical incapacity to reply to an ever-increasing demand, as well as the high price of the investments needed to respond to it. Only one undersea fibre-optic cable, online since 2012, links the island to the worldwide network, via Venezuela. It's Hugo Chavez who installed it, out of solidarity with his friend Fidel's regime. For the rest of the traffic, ETECSA says it must resort to very expensive satellite links.

Only a handful of Cubans possess an internet connection in their homes. To enjoy that right, you need to have an official function. There are very few who, like Jean-Guy, are privileged with unlimited service. The ex-scientist Sonia is restricted to seventy hours a month. Fabricio uses the connection – also limited – available to his father, who is a foreign correspondent. At Sonia and Fabricio's, the connection is dial-up, the technology used in North American households in the early days of residential internet over twenty years ago. It is so slow that to open a single page can take dozens of minutes. The privilege this connection ought to represent is compromised by many frustrations.

As of 2009, the Obama administration authorized American telecommunications companies to work with ETECSA to improve the country's connectivity. It would only have required 150 kilometres of cables under the Florida Strait to provide the entire island with a high-speed connection within a few months. But the Castro regime saw the gift as a Trojan horse. Rightly so, in all probability. The Americans' goal was clear. By helping the Cubans to access more information they would be providing them with a clearer perspective on their lives, enabling them to better communicate with each other, and inducing them to demand political change. The Cuban government preferred to block all the projected partnerships.

And so the inability of ETECSA to connect Cubans with the internet is not a simple matter of cables and inadequate funds. The slow process of betterment is a distinctly political choice. On the one hand, officials continually insist in *Granma* that it is essential to draw on new technologies to further the exchange of knowledge and to stimulate the country's development. On the other hand, the government is always finding excuses for slowing this same progress that is deemed so indispensable.

Given the grumblings from the population and the need to adapt the Cuban economy so it does not continue to decline, the authorities had no choice but to improve their offer one way or the other. In the summer of 2015, the first Wi-Fi terminals were installed in big city parks. In Havana, there are half a dozen. At two convertible pesos per hour, three or four times cheaper than the connections offered up to now in luxury hotels, the service cost of Nauta (the internet branch of ETECSA), is still exorbitant. Especially since the connection is often unstable and the download speed irregular. Nevertheless, the appearance of these invisible terminals has made the internet available to thousands of Cubans who had rarely – or never – accessed it. In the parks there is no sign indicating the availability of a wireless network. But at any hour of the day or night, you only have to spot a few people strolling along with their eyes riveted to their telephones, tablets, or computer screens, to know that you're in a Wi-Fi zone.

Most users take advantage of their precious minutes online to update their profiles on social networks, check their email, and empty their outgoing mail of the messages they've written offline. But the greatest boon in this little revolution is the video conference call. Thanks to the terminals, families torn apart by exile have been able to re-establish more regular contact. For years, they could only communicate by telephone, and less than five minutes of conversation cost them as much as an hour's connection on Nauta. Since the private conversations take place in public spaces, it is still uncomfortable to address certain intimate or sensitive subjects. As if the regime wanted it thus. Still, these calls allow grandparents to see for the first time ever their granddaughter born in Tampa Bay, or enable a *balsero* to reassure his family after a perilous sea-crossing.

Even if all the information passes through the regime's servers when you're navigating in a Nauta zone, the authorities do not seem to be using, on a grand scale, the Orwellian surveillance power that would permit them. Unlike China, Cuba has not set up an army of web censors. All the most popular sites of the opposition remain accessible, except for one: 14ymedio, the portal of the blogger Yoani Sánchez.

In Cuba, it's the slowness and the expense that act as de facto censors.

The relative democratization of the virtual world on the island has, in other terms, had a significant impact on the real world: that of facilitating the emergence of new money-making ventures in the parallel economy. Around each Nauta zone there roam a handful of people reselling access cards, trying discreetly to attract the attention of potential clients while hoping not to draw the eyes of patrolling police. There are also clever operators who connect to the internet through a Nauta terminal with their laptops, then redistribute the connection to other users, whom they bill at a fraction of the price. In the end, they pocket a profit, while their clients save money.

There is much scarcity in Cuba, but no lack of ingenuity.

*

The most avid connectivity geeks did not wait for the government to act before finding a way to communicate among themselves. Lacking access to the internet, they created their own network. They call it the SNET, for "Street Network," *La red de la calle*. No one can claim its authorship or ownership. It's a collective project. Its proper functioning and its durability depend on the active contribution of each of its members.

A friend puts me in contact with José, one of the user-contributors. José is studying at the University of Computer Science, the same institution where Frank, and most of SNET's pioneers, also studied. There are probably about five or six thousand SNET users in Havana. Maybe many more. No one knows for sure. The network is so compartmentalized that it's hard to determine where it begins and where it ends. Other variants of SNET exist in parallel in other cities.

José greets me at his parents' home in Vedado, and takes me to his bedroom and his old PC, connected to an Ethernet cable. He bought the cable on the black market for four or five Cuban pesos per metre. He doesn't remember exactly. On the other hand, he knows its exact length: eighty-three metres. The cable leaves his computer, crosses the apartment, then exits through the window to make its way to the roof of the neighbouring twelve-floor building. That's where the wireless router that he shares with a friend is located. It enables them to exchange data with nearby servers that act as relays to others set up at the capital's four corners. SNET is a network of antennas. The more users are able to lay hands on additional material to develop it, the more the network expands.

When it was created ten or so years ago, SNET was essentially an entertainment network, José tells me. Its founders were gamers who wanted to be able to compete at a distance via the internet, as is done elsewhere in the world. "In time, it also became a way of exchanging information." You can download software and applications, consult other users' pages, or browse Revolico, a classified ads site. The intranet also has its own social networks. There exists, for example, a copy of Facebook, almost identical to the original.

Like everything informal in Cuba, SNET is illegal. And since it's illegal, its survival depends entirely on the will of the regime. If the authorities decided one day that SNET was harmful to the Revolution, it would vanish in a few days. José opens a page that sets out the guidelines for the network. Under the title "What Not to Do or What Not to Publish," it's stated in black and white that users must avoid in their postings references to politics or personalities in power as well as images showing drugs or pornography. It is also forbidden to initiate debates on religion. The moderators in charge ensure the disappearance of comments or pages that might provoke the anger of the regime. José is not overly troubled by the restrictions. "Everywhere in the world there are problems when you talk about politics. For us, these rules are necessary to preserve the network's integrity." After all the work and all the money each one has invested to build it, self-censorship is in his opinion a small price to pay.

When he and his friend decided to connect to SNET two years ago, they didn't have too much trouble acquiring the Ethernet cable. On the other hand, the router was more problematic. They first had to find the money to pay for it. In the United States, you can get them for fifty dollars, but once they arrive here they're resold for 150 dollars. No store on the island sells this kind of equipment. They have to be brought in from abroad in personal baggage. But computer material that comes through Cuban customs is subject to import fees equivalent to 100 percent of the product's value. Once the routers are put up for resale on Revolico, the Miami purchase price has tripled. "When you succeed in finding a router, you take good care of it," says José, who has already lost one, struck by lightning. Since that incident, as soon as there's a storm on the horizon, his friend rushes to turn off their precious equipment.

Every month, José pays one CUC to an administrator for the funds needed to maintain the neighbourhood network. Sometimes servers are stolen or broken, cutting off entire sectors of the network. But since it's in the interest of all the SNET users that things be up and running as soon as possible, each contributes to solving the problems. In short, SNET is a kind of incarnation of the socialist dream, born atop the ruins of a system that has failed to realize that same dream.

At university, José has access to the internet, but his monthly consumption is limited to forty megabytes. "And besides, the connection is very slow." As for the Nauta terminals, he's tried them once and has never gone back. If you have to pay that much to use a shaky connection while standing at the corner of a busy street, you might as well stick with SNET. "What you don't know, you don't miss," José philosophizes. One day, all Cubans will probably have access to high-speed, stable internet at home. That day there will be no more need for SNET. If he will want to thank it warmly for all those years of help, José will still not mourn its demise.

*

There is no way to get together with Fabricio on a Tuesday morning. He is never available. Because Monday is the day of the *Paquete*. At about 10 or 11 o'clock, a delivery man knocks at the door. In exchange for a convertible peso, he hands Fabricio a one-terabyte external hard drive. Over the next few hours Fabricio scans through its contents and copies what interests him onto his hard drive: the latest episode of a foreign television series he's following, some late-night American shows, British comic broadcasts. He also transfers some films or documentaries that have just been released to theatres or are on DVD in the United States. When he's lucky, he finds the latest issue of *The New Yorker* in PDF.

The *Paquete* isn't perfect. Fabricio would also like it to include digital books, foreign magazines, obscure documentaries, and classic films. But it's better than nothing.

Every week, *El Paquete Semanal* ("the weekly package") gives millions of island residents access to Cuban and foreign cultural content and a variety of other useful files. Practically everyone who owns a computer is signed up for it. Obviously, the service is as illegal as the SNET. It's tolerated, but under close surveillance. Forget political and pornographic content, which can only be shared on a smaller scale, through USB drives.

Like the SNET, the *Paquete* relies on people working together. Gathering the content needed to make up each edition requires the participation of an army of informal collaborators. Some record broadcasts from American networks that they access with illegal satellite antennas. Others download files or applications from the Nauta terminals. This content is then transferred to a small number of individuals responsible for assembling the folders of "Films," "Apps," "Magazines," and so on. Once the edition is complete, the original hard drive is copied, then recopied and recopied again and again. From Havana, couriers transport the copies to provincial cities, where they are once more recopied to be distributed ever more widely.

If the *Paquete* were a business, its founder, receiving a dividend for every copy produced, would certainly be the richest person on the island aside from the regime's apparatchiks. But this would also mean becoming a target for the authorities. And so it's better for everybody that the *Paquete*'s structure remain nebulous and flexible. Every contributor only receives a few pesos for work done. Since almost all the content shared by the *Paquete* is the result of pirating, it would in any case be frowned upon for the compilers to claim copyright for its distribution.

As for the regime, not only does it tolerate the trafficking of these hard drives, but it profits from it. "*They* are really hypocritical," says Fabricio. "On the one hand, *they* denounce the pseudoculture behind the *Paquete*, but on the other, *they* have no problem rebroadcasting on State television pirated American films that *they* have obviously taken from the *Paquete*."

To counter the influence of these hard drives, the government has decided to launch its own offering of cultural products, baptized *La Mochila* ("the backpack"). "But their problem is that there's not enough content produced in Cuba to compete with the *Paquete*." On occasion, there are rumours that the authorities intend to do away with the *Paquete*. "*They* would be crazy to do so," says Fabricio. "Thanks to it, we are entertained. And during that time we can say to ourselves: life here is a drag, but I'm going to watch the latest episode of whatever-series-I'm-following-at-the-moment, and I'll forget everything about my condition. To kill the *Paquete* would be a very bad political decision."

MAGIC, OR THE HABITUATION OF BELLIES

At the Cienfuegos bus station, I see my first name on a sheet of paper. The man holding it in his hands is short, thin, greying, moustachioed, and wearing a smile so welcoming that you'd trust him with your life without a thought. I have come to Cienfuegos just for him, though I know nothing about him, except that he speaks a little French. He doesn't know much more about me, other than I'm the friend of the son of the friend of a friend. Or something like that. That's all he's needed to greet me. And I, no more than that to make this trip to see him.

Emilio has prepared for my arrival. To find me a place to stay, he made the round of the *casas particulares* without my asking. "Almost all of them were already taken," he tells me. But he was able to find me a room on the Prado, the city's main street.

Emilio knows Cienfuegos and its history like the palm of his hand. Along with his friend Oscar, he gives me a guided tour of the centre of town. When the opportunity presents itself, he points out the traces of French architecture in the buildings, tells me the stories of the people who were important to the town, and the events that marked its history. He sometimes slips into the language of Molière for a date or an expression, then returns to Spanish.

After the tour, I suggest to Emilio and Oscar that we go to eat at a restaurant. They are suddenly ill at ease.

"It's just that, you see, we haven't brought any money with us," Emilio tells me.

"You don't understand. I'm inviting you. It's the least I can do."

Three burgers, three cold lemonades. A bill of three convertible pesos. I leave fifty centavos as a tip.

Emilio is sixty-two years old, the father of two adult children, and works at the National Office of Statistics. Oscar is nearing forty and is an accountant in an outpatient clinic. I'm thirty-two and a half and have no stable income. I invite these two older men who have kept the same jobs for years to a restaurant in their own hometown, where I am taken aback at the absurdly low price for each item, while they are indulging in a luxury their budgets would never allow them.

The next night, Emilio reciprocates by inviting me to dinner at his home, which he shares with Oscar. They've prepared fish and rice with beans. I've brought pastries for dessert. Emilio has already bought some. The small house is on two floors. The ground floor includes the living room and kitchen, as well as a tiny bathroom. The bedroom is upstairs. Emilio has a television set, a sound system, a pressure cooker, a rice cooker, and several other items that his official salary would never have allowed him to afford. "We Cubans, we do magic," he explains. "Look, I wear good clothes, always clean. I have several conveniences. If you see children coming out of school, they're wearing impeccable uniforms. They all have nice shoes, bought with convertible pesos. We live quite comfortably. How do we do that? Even we sometimes don't know." Almost every product and appliance has a story that connects it to one person or another. The T-shirt he's wearing was brought from Chile by a friend. A Miami friend offered the coffee machine. Oscar's cousin, who's a cook in Varadero, gave them the bottles of ketchup and mustard that are on the table.

Unlike many of their fellow citizens, Emilio has no family abroad to send him money on a regular basis. Once deducted from his salary, the twenty-five Cuban pesos he has to pay each month for his mortgage and the fifty for his refrigerator, bought on credit, leave him with exactly 253 pesos to take care of his monthly needs. Ten dollars and twelve cents. He earns little, but also works little. He arrives at work at 8:15 a.m. If he has no door-to-door calls to make to gather data, he is sometimes gone by 11 a.m. He and the State are even.

At the end of the meal, Emilio offers me a coffee. To boil the water in which he will mix the powdered milk that will go with it, he uses an alcohol burner whose flame he then extinguishes with wet rags made from pieces of old pants. "Life is not easy," he sighs. I become suspicious.

Is he trying to arouse my pity in the hope that I'll slip him money or buy him a domestic appliance? Is this burgeoning friendship really fake? Or is it my own stinginess that's making me paranoid? Perhaps, knowing that I'm a writer, he just wants to tell me about his daily struggles in order to flesh out my account of Cuban life?

Emilio takes out his ration card. He shows me the series of columns and lines that list from month to month the products he has obtained for ridiculously low prices at the state store. Bread, cooking oil, eggs, rice, coffee, flour, sugar, meat. It's impossible, however, to get through a whole month on the small amounts of each foodstuff that the *Libreta* guarantees to all Cuban citizens, Emilio explains. This aid only allows you to feed yourself for ten or so days, fifteen at the most. The rest you have to purchase at full price on the markets, official or black depending on availability. "But we're never hungry," Emilio assures me. "Our bellies are used to it."

Emilio informs me that his propane tank has been empty for several days. He'll only be eligible for another at a subsidized price in July. "At the State store, ten litres cost seven pesos. In the street, it's ten CUC." Almost thirty-six times more expensive. In the meantime, he'll try to make do by exchanging tanks with his children. He also has to replace a faulty stove burner. In the street, he'll pay five CUC. In theory, he could buy one in the State stores for half the price, but they never have any in stock. As soon as new supplies come in, they turn up on the street without appearing on the shelves. Cuban magicians also have dirty tricks.

In a month, Barack Obama will be arriving in Havana on an official visit. Emilio observes that after all these years of demonization, this sudden cozying up to the United States is disconcerting to Cubans. What are they now supposed to be *thinking publicly* about their imperialist neighbour? The government has not yet made itself clear on the subject. "Before the parades, we shouted: ¡*Cuba, sí!* ¡*Yanqui, no!* Now, it will be: ¡*Cuba, sí! Yanqui … ¿que?*" says Emilio, not without irony.

There's a knock at the door. It's Claudio, Emilio's brother. In one hand he's holding a wad of bills. He's just won seventy-five convertible pesos on the *Bolita*. He gives Emilio a five-CUC bill as a present, then leaves. In the month following the Revolution, Fidel Castro's government did away with all games of chance. Up to then, the casinos and racetracks were almost all controlled by the American mafia, which benefitted from the dictator Batista's complicity. The ban did not, however, lead to the total disappearance of gambling. Every day, at around 2 p.m. and 8 p.m., Cuban bet takers connect to Miami radio and television networks to find out the winning numbers in the Florida Lottery. It's based on these that they dole out their prizes. The *Bolita* is illegal, but the bettors are at least certain that no one on the island can manipulate the results.

Emilio is concerned about his brother, who is hooked on gambling and alcohol. His problems have already cost him two marriages. He also doesn't like to see him walking around with so much money for all to see in the streets of Cienfuegos. Even if crime is rare, you never know what might happen. Unlike his brother, Emilio is in excellent health, both physical and mental. If he continues to age this well, he shouldn't have any problem matching and exceeding the age of 76.9, the life expectancy of a Cuban male. If ever his health begins to deteriorate, he'll be taken in hand by the public health system. Conditions won't be ideal, but he'll be able to count on the doctors and nurses treating him to the best of their knowledge and abilities. All care will likely be delivered free of charge, even if the medical personnel might let him know that a little *regalito* wouldn't hurt. That is how Emilio's old age should unfold, assuming that in 2031, when he's 76.9, Cuba still has its universal healthcare system.

*

The host Emilio found me in Cienfuegos is a doctor who specializes in prenatal screening. María is in her fifties and has two children from two different marriages. Her current husband works in a retirement home. The blended family lives in a spacious apartment in a colonial building on the Prado. María began renting their vacant room four years ago. She earns almost as much by giving me a place to stay for four days as she does over a whole month detecting cases of Down's Syndrome in fetuses. Still, the government has been forced to raise her salary in recent years. It's trying desperately to staunch the bleeding caused by the Cuban Medical Professional Parole Program, put in place by George W. Bush in 2006, whose overt goal was to incite the island's doctors and nurses to defect. Once they arrive in the United States, candidates receive support to quickly and easily integrate into the American medical system. The Cuban government denounces loudly and clearly what it sees as an attempt on the part of the United States to undermine its universal healthcare system. María has seen several of her colleagues leave without warning to take advantage of this policy. She herself has no plans to emigrate. Since she has been renting a room to foreign tourists passing through, her family's situation is much improved. In the beginning, however, it was hard to make ends meet. The cost of a licence to operate a *casa particular* was very expensive. "We had to put together as much money as possible during the tourist season to be able to pay for the licence during the months when we were less busy. We were just barely holding on," she remembers. The government later lowered, bit by bit, the operating tax. It also became possible to suspend the licence in low season, or when they wanted to do renovations.

One afternoon after lunch, I go with María to the pediatric hospital. On the way, she drops off her daughter at the Guerrillero Heróico Elementary School, named after the most famous picture of Dr. Ernesto Guevara, taken by the photographer Alberto Korda in March 1960, and reproduced on innumerable T-shirts. In her uniform's buttonhole, the child is wearing that same portrait of the late revolutionary, and on her head, a beret similar to Che's. Emilio was right. María's daughter's outfit, like that of the other children, is impeccable.

At the hospital, María shows me her department. The laboratories are well taken care of, but the machines are old and the American embargo makes it hard to replace them. I expected worse.

A local TV crew is there. These days, all everybody talks about is Zika. The aim of the report is to explain to citizens the dangers and consequences of the virus. María replies to the usual questions. *What is Zika? Is it really responsible for microcephaly? How can you prevent the transmission from mother to fetus?* In some Latin American countries, they're advising women not to get pregnant for the next two years. In Cuba, a vast fumigation campaign is underway. The army has been mobilized. Once a week, every citizen has to open their house to soldiers armed with a fumigator. The campaign is universal. It seems to be working. The authorities have detected only a few isolated cases of infection on the island. This is one of the rare kinds of mobilization that are still working and giving results. Doubtless because the Revolution has been able to convince everyone of the importance of public health. And perhaps also because insecticide does not sell well on the black market.

*

In Cienfuegos, you only have to venture beyond the limits of the charming historic centre, barely a few dozen metres to the north, to feel that you've been duped. Two streets from Plaza de Armas, where the cruise passengers who have stopped at the port for a few hours pass through like the wind, the city becomes much less photogenic. The buildings are rundown, at best patched up with whatever is at hand. Some streets are in such bad shape that they're unnavigable by car or horse-drawn carts, a common means of public transport in provincial Cuba. Black water, malodorous and stagnant, gathers in the depressions, perfect breeding grounds for the Zika-carrying mosquitos that are elsewhere being fumigated so zealously. Children scurry along, accompanied by cats, chickens, and stray dogs. There is a sense of chronic negligence. The only traces of the Revolution's greatness are the slogans painted on the walls. Like everywhere, they proclaim the inevitability of a future victory, the invincibility of a movement toward the future, toward eternity. Coincidence or not, the neighbourhood is populated primarily by Afro-Cubans, who historically have been left behind. The Revolution officially did away with any discrimination where they are concerned. But clearly, inequality is more tenacious than ideals.

Southwest of Plaza de Armas, the scene is less depressing, but is still in marked contrast to the lovely façades of the centre of town. I pass in front of a house where two plump women in their thirties in tank tops and shorts, and one who is older, are leaning against the outside wall. For a fraction of a second I imagine an instance of prostitution in the light of day. As I try to dismiss this facile conclusion from my mind, one of the young women calls out an unambiguous "¡Niño! ¿Quieres chica?" I decline the offer with a slight shake of the head that probably goes unnoticed, and continue on my way.

*

One of Emilio's prized possessions doesn't belong to him. It's an electric bicycle "assembled in Cuba" and supplied by his employer to facilitate his movements around town when he has to collect census data. "It's worth five hundred CUC!" Emilio still marvels, as that represents more than three years of his salary. If he ever left his job, he'd have to return the bicycle to the National Office of Statistics. That's one of the reasons he keeps working. I remark that with all his free time and his encyclopedic knowledge of the city's history and geography, he could easily make extra money as a tourist guide. "The problem is that the law doesn't permit me to have a second job," he replies. If he decided to offer his services illegally and his employer found out, it would be a reason to fire him, and he'd lose his electric bicycle at the same time. But the question doesn't even come up, because while the economy around him is in flux, Emilio's biggest flaw is that he's honest. Yet he's perfectly aware that by confining himself to the established rules, he's increasingly putting himself at a disadvantage. With every new docking of a cruise ship, he sees his fellow citizens crowding the port to badger the tourists. With three or four English or French words tacked onto a smile, they're able to tease three or four dollars out of the pockets of these lost souls just landed on solid ground. *Looking for cigars? Rum? Vous cherchez un bon resto? Follow me!* No need for any special talent. You just have to leave your scruples at home, get to the right place at the right time, and wait for the fish to bite. "Even a beggar in a tourist spot earns more than me," Emilio observes. Someone holding out his hand just has to come up with a single convertible peso or even fifty centavos in a day to end up richer than the statistician.

If economic liberalization continues over the coming years, the beggars and other fishers of tourists will continue gaining ground on Emilio. While he's gathering up statistics for a moribund institution, the more resourceful will be busy, through licit and illicit means, piling up money that will make them the small or even big entrepreneurs of tomorrow's Cuba. And the day when the quasi-inevitable great wave of "rationalization" of resources will be decreed, Emilio risks paying for his honesty. If he doesn't lose his job, he'll be stuck with the same, virtually symbolic, salary. If he looks for another job, there's little chance that he'll find one in his area of expertise. Who will want an old-school statistician after the great change has taken place?

In the years preceding the dismantlement of the USSR and those that followed soon after, millions of employees of Soviet state businesses and institutions were let go. Full employment, one of the central policies of the communist regime, was abandoned. Fifteen or so years later, when I was travelling through post-Soviet territory, almost all the watchmen and watchwomen for buildings, stores, or museums were former engineers, technicians, and other specialists who had been forced to accept any small job they could find in the wake of privatization or the shutting down of the state enterprise that had employed them. They were all highly qualified, but overnight their skills had lost their usefulness.

If Cuba's new economy does come in for a landing, I hope that Emilio and the other good soldiers of the state apparatus will have a smoother descent than their equivalents in the former Soviet Union.

*

It's Saturday night on San Fernando Street, in the centre of Cienfuegos. Couples, families, and animated young people share the sidewalk and its festive air. In front of a theatre, a ventriloquist's show attracts a few bystanders. Strains of music from loudspeakers along the street go head to head. Emilio is strolling along with some of his friends. We pass from time to time, and then lose sight of each other. It's still early when I decide to return to the *casa*. I have to take a bus the next morning. Before leaving, I wait to run into Emilio one last time, to say goodbye. When I announce my imminent departure, he seems disappointed and taken unawares. In the end, he really did seem to expect a gift from me. He would never have dared ask, especially here in the middle of the throng and surrounded by his friends, but if I'd offered, he certainly would not have refused. Money, a T-shirt, a bag of coffee, a stove burner. Anything to help him out. I'd ignored the signs. I'd wanted to ignore them. Partly because I'm stingy, it's true, but also because I don't know how to handle charity given to an honest worker twice my age, while respecting his dignity and the idea that our relationship was one of friendship before being mercantile.

Followed by Emilio's bittersweet gaze, I melt into the crowd.

THE INTERNAL EMBARGO

When the waiter sets the bowl of fries down on the table, Mayrelis, the owner of the Esto no es un Café, comes out with an astonished "oh!" She hasn't eaten potatoes for months: not fried, not mashed, nor any other way. "We bought them from a seller *por la calle*, on the black market," she says, to explain their sudden appearance before us. For about two years, the tuber that ensures the survival of a large part of humanity has been almost unfindable in Cuba. A few farmers produce them, but the harvests are almost entirely reserved for the tourist industry. When Mayrelis opened her restaurant in Old Havana in April 2014, she preferred not to take any chances: there would be no potatoes on her menu. "I tried to include the ingredients that I knew I could obtain at any time, never mind the season. But I'm still terrified of waking up one morning and finding that I can't offer certain dishes on my menu. In other restaurants, they're always telling their customers we haven't this, or that, or that. Here, if it's on the menu, we have it."

Before going into business, Mayrelis was the curator for exhibitions at the Wifredo Lam Contemporary Art Centre for ten years. Her restaurant, which she sees essentially as a "cultural project," is an outgrowth of her former career, right down to its name. "This is not a café" is an allusion to "*Ceci n'est pas une pipe*" ("this is not a pipe"), from the canvas *The Treachery of Images* by the surrealist Belgian painter René Magritte. Each main course is inspired by the work of a major twentieth-century artist: Klein's Blue is a lamb stew served in a deep-blue dish, echoing the unique colour patented by Yves Klein with France's National Institute of Industrial Property in 1960; the Pollock Chicken requires the dripping of different coloured sauces according to the technique popularized by Jackson Pollock; as for the roast pork, called Duchamp's Fountain, it's served on a urinal-shaped plate, reminiscent of Marcel Duchamp's controversial readymade. "Coming in here, I want the customer to have an artistic experience, to become a spectator," says Mayrelis.

Among the ingredients used in the preparation of meals at the Esto no es un Café, only the vegetables and cheese come from farms near Havana, with which Mayrelis deals directly. The meat, seafood, and spices are almost all imported. Mayrelis is perennially anxious about being able to find them. Even if her restaurant has only ten or so tables, she's had to hire a buyer whose entire job is, every day, to come up with the ingredients on both the official and black markets. "Sometimes the chicken we find is from Canada, sometimes from Brazil." Despite all her efforts, shortages sometimes win out. In January 2015, Mayrelis's nightmare came true. The Pollock Chicken and all the other dishes made with fowl had to temporarily be removed from the menu. "For a month, it was impossible to find any kind of chicken. The government had not yet made its import order, and production within the country was not up to meeting the demand. Can you believe it? Chicken! The easiest thing of all to raise!" she sighs.

For Mayrelis, this kind of situation shows that not all of Cuba's problems can be attributed to the American embargo. "The embargo is internal first of all. The country is not meeting its demands. We have hardly any local production. Cubans are not used to getting up early, having responsibilities, producing. They prefer to say that such and such a thing is impossible. Our material condition is dependent on the udder of whatever foreign cow is prepared to help us out. The Soviet Union, China, Venezuela …"

Esto no es un Café is situated near the cathedral in Old Havana, on the Callejón del Chorro, "jet alley," where in the sixteenth century the city's first aqueduct was situated. Even before the reforms in the mid 1990s allowed for the opening of privately owned restaurants – known as *paladares* – the alley was known for its clandestine establishments. "Tourists and Cubans came knocking at the doors, as if they were going to eat at a friend's. They were let in and were offered food. It was as secret as if they were being sold marijuana," Mayrelis says. Today, the alley has eight *paladares*, whose clientele is "about 80 percent" foreigners.

To open her restaurant, Mayrelis had in any case to look abroad. She already had the location – her house, which she was prepared to turn into a business – but no liquidity. A Cuban friend and her European husband agreed to come in on the project in exchange for a percentage of future profits. Since foreigners are not permitted to invest in private ventures in Cuba, the European husband was taking a big risk, Mayrelis confesses. No document attests to his involvement in the business. What is more, since the restaurant opened, he separated from his wife. At any time, the two Cuban women could stop paying him his share of the profits, and he would have no recourse against them. Several foreigners who have made investments, trusting a friend, a partner, or a simple Cuban straw man, have lost everything. "In their place, I would never invest under such conditions," Mayrelis admits, swearing that she has no intention of doing such a thing to her investor.

Once she found the necessary money, the paperwork required to register the business was surprisingly straightforward. On the other hand, equipping the space demanded a great deal of ingenuity. Mayrelis gives me a tour of the restaurant, telling me the story behind every piece of furniture and equipment. The bar's marble counter was made to measure in Italy. She was able to import it non-commercially, passing it off as a residential countertop. In principle, she ought to have bought the kitchen's stainless steel workspace from a state enterprise, the only one in the country authorized to sell it. Except that, paradoxically, this same company is not permitted to sell it to *cuentapropistas*, small private business people, like Mayrelis. To get around this absurdity, Mayrelis had to scramble to find one on the black market. "It's surreal, I tell you!" I point my finger at the drink cooler. "It comes from Panama. It probably costs six or seven hundred dollars there. I bought it from a private importer for twelve hundred dollars." To get good quality plates, glasses, and utensils, Mayrelis orders them from the Metro retailer in Italy, then has them delivered by air cargo. "We only have the right to five kilos of personal imports, so I register each package in the name of a different restaurant employee. The government doesn't want us to import anything, because it wants to preserve its monopoly. But I'm not interested in buying poor quality dishes from the State that are going to break the first time you use them." Even her business cards, shaped like a Magritte pipe, come from abroad. "Printed in Mexico," she says.

Mayrelis doesn't hesitate for a second when I ask her what sort of change would make her life as a restaurant owner easier. "A wholesale market." She dreams of a place where she could go to buy certain products such as cooking oil, napkins, and condiments in large quantities, at a lower price than she pays retail. "At the moment, running my cafe costs me double what State hotels and restaurants pay, because they can buy wholesale."

Since the Cuban government tentatively opened the country up to private enterprise, it has continually played at carrot and stick with those who have gone into business. The regime's fear is that the *cuentapropistas* will become rich. Rich and thus independent, powerful, and perhaps a political threat. But the State can't get along without the energy they are injecting into an otherwise stagnant economy. The regime's businesses are inefficient and produce little. *Cuentapropistas* like Mayrelis, motivated by personal profit, do miracles with nothing. In addition to the constant shortages they must manage, they have to systematically resort to the black market to run their businesses. When the regime needs them to stimulate the economy, it eases its rules. And when it feels that they're starting to get too comfortable, it comes down hard on the one foot they need to have in illegality.

Despite the obstacles, Mayrelis is happy with her first two years as an entrepreneur. She has good employees, and wants to keep them. She redistributes 10 percent of her total revenue to them. With their salaries and tips, each one earns thirty to fifty CUC per day, depending on the number of customers. In addition to guaranteeing the loyalty of her employees, she believes that this model discourages them from stealing the stock, as they did when they were working for the State. She doesn't yet make enough of a profit to think of buying a car or taking vacations abroad, but her situation is gradually improving. Among her other ambitions, there is that of opening a private agency specializing in art tours. But for now, tourism is monopolized by the State, or more specifically, by the all-powerful Revolutionary Armed Forces. It is very unlikely that this sector will open itself up to competition in the near future.

Mayrelis also has another dream, much more personal, and in fact very simple: she'd like to keep the same hair colour all year round. Because for now, she has to be satisfied with the reddish tint she's able to find on the State store's shelves, which, from month to month, is never exactly the same.

DOUBT

Sunday, the day of the Lord, I'm walking through the Miramar neighbourhood, looking for the Santa Rita de Casia church. Fabricio had told me the day before at which intersection I would find it. I should have noted it down. It seemed to me that he had talked about the corner of 30th Street and 5th Avenue. That's where I am. No church. Just embassies. I continue along 5th to the corner of 28th. Still nothing. I find some shade on 28th, take out my phone, find Fabricio's number on my list, and call. On the opposite side of the street, a diplomatic bodyguard in front of the Algerian embassy comes out of his sentry box. A few seconds earlier, I'd thought of asking him for directions. While the phone is ringing in my ear, I hear him whistling to attract someone's attention farther down the road. I have a bad feeling. After two or three rings with no reply, I hang up, put the phone back in my pocket, and as if nothing were up, I go back to 5th Avenue. I've just taken a few steps toward 26th Street when a man hails me. He crosses the road, walking fast. As he gets closer, I feel him studying me. He's trying to figure out who he's dealing with. I already know who he is. I've seen this man dozens of times in the past. In Belarus, in Russia, in Iran, I've seen him roaming around opposition demonstrations. He's burly, his face is stern, his hair is cut short. He's dressed in black and carries a little bag over his shoulder. He so much doesn't want to seem the person he is, that it's obvious that he's exactly that. My defence mechanisms kick in at once. I start playing a role. I deaden my gaze and downgrade my ability to communicate. Crossing the sidewalk, the man places himself in my path, blocking my advance. He looks me up and down from head to toe, decides what tone to adopt, then asks me what I'm doing there. In exaggeratedly bad, hesitant Spanish, I inform him that I don't speak his language. Isolating each syllable, I add: "I am walking," miming the action with two fingers. In his next sentence, spoken too quickly for me to be able to get it all as I continue to evaluate the situation, I catch the word *"iglesia."* He suspects me of wanting to go to Santa Rita de Casia. I shake my head to show that I don't understand. He inspects me for a moment more. Is this foreigner in front of him a lost tourist or a phony innocent who knows exactly what's going on? Irritated, he curtly orders me to turn around and continue my morning walk along 28th Street, in the direction of the sea. Nothing on the horizon warrants my way being barred. No crowd, no cataclysm. The avenue is deserted. Nothing in his dress, either, gives him the authority to tell me where to go. No uniform, no badge. But I don't protest. I stay in my role. I'm just a tourist wandering through Miramar on a Sunday morning. I start down 28th Street and don't turn back. On the left, on the right, I admire the elegant houses from pre-revolutionary times. Five hundred metres farther on, I arrive at the beach. I stop for a moment to take in the Florida Strait, still without looking behind me, then I stroll through the neighbourhood's streets and avenues. After a few minutes, I begin to check out my surroundings to be sure I'm not being followed. I'd be surprised if that were the case. But given the slight possibility that someone has decided to keep me under observation, it's best not to take chances. It's just when you start lowering your guard that questions arise. If the agent in civilian clothes had asked to see my identification papers and had wanted to know where I was staying, what would I have said? Armando had warned me not to reveal that he's putting me up, because that could cause problems. To have the president of the Revolutionary Defence Committee close his eyes to my illegal presence in his house is one thing; to be questioned by the security services is much more delicate. I also wonder if I've gotten Fabricio in trouble. Do *they* have the technical capacity to identify the person I was trying to reach by phone before I was stopped? If so, would *they* try to do so? Did *they* take my photograph while I was talking to the agent? Am I now part of a file? All that is very unlikely. But I have no way of knowing for certain. Like Winston before his telescreen.

> How often, or on what system, the Thought Police plugged
> in on any individual wire was guesswork. It was even con-
> ceivable that they watched everybody all the time. But
> at any rate they could plug in your wire whenever they

wanted to. You had to live – did live, from habit that became instinct – in the assumption that every sound you made was overheard, and, except in darkness, every movement scrutinized.

My plan had failed. I had not been able to reach the Santa Rita de Casia church. I hadn't been able to attend Mass in the company of the Ladies in White and the other dissidents who meet there every week. I'd not been able to follow them during the demonstration they have persistently organized every Sunday after the service ever since the Black Spring of 2003, during which seventy-five dissidents were arrested and condemned to prison sentences lasting between six and twenty-seven years. And I did not see, either, the members of the Rapid Response Brigades harassing or even brutalizing these dissidents, as they sometimes do. If I'd known beforehand the exact location of the church and had approached it with confidence, perhaps the agent in civilian clothes might not have intercepted me in time. Perhaps I would have been able to attend the Mass. But would I have then gotten into real trouble? Unless that's already happened, and *they* are just waiting for the right moment to move in? Until the end of my stay, until I've gone through passport control at the airport, this doubt, however minimal, will continue to haunt me.

EXIT THE WALL

"Every joke is a tiny revolution ... a temporary rebellion against virtue, and its aim is not to degrade the human being but to remind him that he is already degraded," wrote George Orwell in "Funny, but Not Vulgar," an essay published in the London magazine *Leader* in July 1945. For Orwell, humour must necessarily disturb the established order. "The truth is that you cannot be memorably funny without at some point raising topics which the rich, the powerful, and the complacent would prefer to see left alone." Orwell sees humour as "dignity sitting on a tin-tack. Whatever destroys dignity, and brings down the mighty from their seats, preferably with a bump, is funny. And the bigger they fall, the bigger the joke."

Under an authoritarian regime, the force of a joke is ten times amplified by the danger it represents for the person telling it. To laugh at the powerful is to tempt the devil. And to tempt the devil is damned funny. As long as you escape unscathed.

In Guantánamo, at the extreme east of Cuba, I talked with Alexis Ayala, a member of the satirical group Komotú, about the challenges of being a professional comic on the island. His group's last show, called *El Muro* (*The Wall*), deals overtly with the limits imposed on a society, limits that at times, incrementally or abruptly, advance, retreat, or disappear.

In the same city, I met Yosmel López Ortiz, a puppeteer and vice-president of the local section of the Hermanos Saíz Association, a State group of young artists. By mounting plays for children and adults, he also feels that he is contributing to an enhancement of the Revolution's cultural tolerance, even if he's doing it subtly and prudently. In his opinion, the Cuban social system offers artists a different kind of freedom than that enjoyed by their fellows in countries ruled by the law of the marketplace.

In Havana, I spent some hours with the stage and film director Juan Carlos Cremata Malberti. His artistic approach is much bolder, and he has paid the price. In July 2015, his adaptation of *Exit the King* by Eugène Ionesco, judged a bit too close for comfort to Cuban reality, was shut down by a theatre after only two performances. During our meeting, he quoted the comments made by the bureaucrat responsible for censoring the play.

Since I'm talking about transgressions, allow me to commit one in turn and to briefly interrupt my story to present a one-act play inspired by my interviews with these three artists.

EXIT THE WALL

CHARACTERS

The DIRECTOR

The PUPPETEER, who is imbedded in a wall of bricks

The PUPPET, who is manipulated by the Puppeteer but has an
independent cast of mind

The COMIC

MADAME CENSOR

The KING

*A wall on rollers that is about two metres high, made of
Styrofoam bricks, divides the stage in two. Stage left, about
halfway between the wall and the wings, a few steps lead to
a throne on which the KING is sitting, thin and old. He's
wearing a military uniform, a false grey beard, and a crown
bearing a red star. Aloft, near the wings, there is suspended
a medallion bearing the portrait of José Martí. Stage right,
a large suitcase is lying on the floor.*

*The curtain rises as the last notes of the song "Puro Teatro,"
interpreted by La Lupe, are still echoing. The stage is
cloaked in darkness. Only the portrait of José Martí is
gleaming, like a moon in the sky. Stage left, the public can
make out the silhouettes of the KING on the throne and of
MADAME CENSOR near the wall. The latter unscrolls a
royal-looking communiqué and begins to read.*

MADAME CENSOR

"In the theatre, as in all things, in Cuba we are capable of creation,"
said José Martí, visionary and defender of our native land. Today,
as we struggle to fashion a country appropriate to our needs, in
the midst of crises, conquests, and the ideals inherited from a past
and a present in constant flux, the stage has become a space wide
open to reformation and change. When we can appreciate in the
creators and in the followers of a cultural institution their role
as "agents," we may equally acknowledge their ability to generate
modes of behaviour, and thus their capacity to transmute, to
reconstruct, to reappraise, and to further explore new possibilities
for the stage. Given the developmental strategies for Cuban
theatre, given the ongoing dialogue between our institutions,
and the day-to-day artistic activity whose goal is to forge ever
more constructive affiliations between the poetic passions of our
creators and the nation's cultural policies, the National Council
of the Performing Arts and the Havana Theatre Centre have
decided to suspend the presentation of the work *Exit the King*,
a production of the El Ingenio Theatre. In its place, the Tito

Junco Hall in the Bertolt Brecht Cultural Centre will offer other programming options.[11]

The lights come up little by little as MADAME CENSOR, dressed in a suit and a beige blouse, pushes the wall a few metres. Stage left, the DIRECTOR, dark glasses on his nose and straw hat on his head, comes out of the wings gesticulating.

THE DIRECTOR

I've been censored! I've been censored! I've been censored! Two performances and then, ¡*Basta!* How could she do that to me? She's just a little bureaucrat who only has a job thanks to her Party card. She knows nothing about theatre!

In his excitement, the DIRECTOR bumps up against the wall, barely budging it. He stares at it, then gives it a kick before stomping away, exasperated.

MADAME CENSOR

I have followed your career from the very start. You've accomplished much over the years, and we've always left you alone. But now, enough is enough. I put my faith in this play and you betrayed me.

THE DIRECTOR

(*astonished*) Betrayed?!

MADAME CENSOR

You could at least have used metaphors, for heaven's sake! How dare you laugh like that at an old sick man? It's unacceptable! You know perfectly well that I couldn't let you get away with that. I'm a *fidelista*!

---

11 "Cambios en la programación, sala Tito Junco, Teatro Bertolt Brecht," a communiqué of the National Council of the Performing Arts, *Cubarte*, July 7, 2015.

THE DIRECTOR

For Fidel? (*aside*) What I wanted to say was, you're a *fidelista*??
Have you seen a doctor for this problem, madame? Because it's a
problem today to still be for Fidel. Times have changed, you know.

PUPPETEER

It seems he burned a Cuban flag onstage …

THE DIRECTOR

What?! Who said that?

PUPPET

(*coming out of the wall*) Over here! In the wall, the Puppeteer!

THE DIRECTOR

But it's false! Super-false! I adapted the play, I profaned the
national anthem, I distorted José Martí's words, but I did not burn
the flag! (*pause*) That said … I could very well have done so if I'd
wanted to. Here's what really happened. (*coming around the wall,
going to the KING, and looking him up and down*) Ah no, my King
did not have this beard! (*ripping off the false beard and tossing it
toward MADAME CENSOR*) Rise, I beg you.

> The KING rises.

THE DIRECTOR

In Ionesco's play, there is this scene where the King falls for the
first time …

> The DIRECTOR gently pushes the KING and makes him
> tumble down the stairs. The KING falls face down onto
> the ground.

THE DIRECTOR

And the people are dancing because they think the King is dead …

> The DIRECTOR dances and waves his arms in the air.
> MADAME CENSOR brings her hand to her mouth.
> Painfully, the KING gets back on his feet.

THE DIRECTOR

... Except that the King gets up again.

MADAME CENSOR

That's exactly how Fidel fell! You did it on purpose!

THE DIRECTOR

I invented nothing, it's all in Ionesco's text!

> *Suddenly the lights go out. The wall pivots ninety degrees. A video[12] is projected onto it. There we see Fidel Castro completing a speech, then striding away from the podium. He doesn't see the steps dividing him from the hall, and he takes a brutal tumble. A dozen panicked people run to help him up. End of video. The wall returns to its former position.*

MADAME CENSOR

(*indignant*) You see! It's identical!

THE DIRECTOR

(*to MADAME CENSOR as she leaves the stage*) That's the way you see it, Madame! (*aside, after a pause*) Of course I knew I was going to remind everyone of Fidel's fall.

PUPPET

(*coming out of the wall*) But why provoke her like that?

THE DIRECTOR

Why not? Why not say what I want to say directly? I've had enough of metaphors! I don't want to keep repeating that something is rotten in the state of Denmark! I want to talk about this King.

> *The KING, looking confused, picks up his false beard and sticks it back on his chin. He struggles back up the stairs*

---

12 The video, titled "Caida Castro/Castro falls," is available on YouTube at youtu.be/FixSd3DVcjY.

and sits down on his throne. At the same time, we hear
the COMIC scaling the wall.

THE COMIC

If I may … (*reaching the top of the wall and straddling it*) I respect
what you're doing, sir, and there ought to be room in this country
for your way of practising the performing arts. But … I also think
that you ought to negotiate a bit more subtly with the mental
barriers of …

THE DIRECTOR

(*interrupting*) I'm done with negotiating! If you never raise the bar
for negotiation, you'll never achieve anything!

THE COMIC

At least let me finish! You have to know how to negotiate, I was
saying, with the mental barriers of the spectators. It's not just
bureaucrats who are sensitive, you know. The public can be
sensitive, too. If the spectators grind their teeth during your show,
if they feel uncomfortable at the idea of sitting in a theatre where
you dare to say this sort of thing, are you really any further ahead?

THE DIRECTOR

Pffft! If they don't like what I'm saying, they're free to leave!

THE COMIC

Wouldn't that be too bad? Like you, I'm trying to twist the knife
in the wounds of the problems besetting our society. (*whispering*)
I'm laughing at the King too, you know …

The KING, drowsing on his throne, shudders, looks around,
suspicious, then relapses into his stupor.

THE COMIC

Except that I prefer to say things more subtly, using double
meanings, irony. Besides, that's just where you find your creative
challenges in our … in our … (*clearing his throat*) in our
situation. When you can find a way of saying what you want to

say without doing so directly, while being certain that everyone in the audience knows very well what you want to say, then you've got the beginning of a joke. And when the spectators laugh and applaud, that means they've understood and are supporting you. From that point on, we're not all alone to say what we are saying, we are hundreds! A thousand! A whole theatre full!

The COMIC takes a brick from the wall and lets it drop.

PUPPET

(*coming out of the wall*) There's a crack in the wall!

The KING wakes with a start.

THE COMIC

In our show *The Wall*, there's a sketch that takes place at a fictional monument honouring the fourteen Chinese people fallen in combat. A spy has been sent to deal with an embarrassing situation. (*taking from his pocket a PUPPET clothed in black and wearing dark glasses*) A potential suicide is standing at the top of the monument and is threatening to throw himself into the void. (*doing a brief imitation of the desperate man*) Except that on that very day, a Chinese delegation is arriving in the country. And you don't want to make the guests feel uncomfortable. The spy's mission is not to save the man's life, but … to persuade him to kill himself somewhere else or on a different day!

The KING bursts out laughing.

THE COMIC

The spy climbs up and talks to the desperate man, who reveals the reasons for his unhappiness. (*entering into the role of the potential suicide, who addresses the PUPPET representing the spy*) The problem is my salary. It's much too high! And my boss doesn't want to lower it. He says that would be an illegal act!

Laughing uncontrollably, the KING slaps his thighs.
MADAME CENSOR re-enters stage left and mimes the
KING's laughter.

THE COMIC

At the end of the sketch, the spy persuades the man to abandon his plan. He even gives him back his zest for life, to the point where the man flings out his arms to embrace that life and ... (*pushing the spy PUPPET into the void*) Oops ...

The KING gets up from his throne, applauds loudly, loses his footing, and again falls down the stairs. At the same time, the COMIC takes another brick out of the wall and lets it drop.

PUPPET

The crack is getting wider! My God, everything's going to come down!

MADAME CENSOR, appalled, looks in turn at the KING and the wall, hesitates, and decides to go first to pick up the brick that has just fallen and to put it back in place. Then she runs to help the KING get back on his throne.

THE COMIC

Twenty years ago, it would have been unthinkable to put on a show here like *The Wall*.

THE DIRECTOR

Twenty years ago, I would have been put in prison for my play!

PUPPET

When the King was still himself, it would have been prison for sure, yes!

THE COMIC

You see, the walls are perhaps invisible, but they can move. And we can help to make them move.

The wall begins to edge toward stage left.

THE COMIC

We just have to be careful to keep our balance in the process.

THE DIRECTOR

(*pushing the wall so it will advance more rapidly*) And I, I think stirring up controversy is the only way to make anything change. If we stop our polemics, nothing will go forward!

> *MADAME CENSOR runs up and brings the wall to a halt. The COMIC on top teeters and almost falls off. For a moment, MADAME CENSOR and the DIRECTOR push in opposite directions. Nothing budges. They give up.*

PUPPETEER

(*in the wall*) Me, I like it here.

THE DIRECTOR

(*looking around*) Excuse me?! Who said that?

PUPPET

Over here! In the wall, the puppeteer!

PUPPETEER

I've spent time abroad. I've seen how artists live. The first month, I quite liked it. But then I stopped enjoying my work. All I could think of was how to find a way to please the public in order to make money and survive. There was no room left in my head for creation. Here, my salary is not very high …

THE DIRECTOR

(*interrupting*) That's an understatement!

PUPPETEER

… but at least I know that I'll get a cheque every month, whether I produce or not. I can take my time and concentrate on my creative process.

THE COMIC

Even here, with the economic changes, there are more and more temptations. There are cabarets in the capital that are offering us big bucks to present *The Wall*. But we prefer the quietness of the provinces. We aren't ready to trade our creative freedom for more money.

THE DIRECTOR

(*astonished*) Your freedom?! I'd love someone to tell me how much freedom I'm entitled to in this country. Is there a ration card for that too? If so, then give me my monthly ration now!

PUPPETEER

Me, if I have a criticism to make, I address it to the authorities directly.

The PUPPET beckons MADAME CENSOR to come closer, and murmurs something in her ear. MADAME CENSOR nods her head and moves off.

PUPPETEER

Before, our puppet theatre was very didactic. We wanted to teach children love of country, respect for the rules. Today, we deal with themes more tied to the children's concerns, like the death of those dear to them, illness, and even homosexuality!

PUPPET

You have to admit that the King is much more deaf than before. He's getting soft...

THE DIRECTOR

I've still been censored! They censored me!

PUPPET

Oh! But you've been asking for it a little, all the same ...

THE DIRECTOR

My job is to open minds. I only want to be free. The truth is, they don't even know how to defend their censorship. Have you seen their impenetrable communiqué? They're insinuating that I'm an agent. An agent of whom, of what?

MADAME CENSOR

(*stuttering*) I – uhh… umm … ah!

THE DIRECTOR

You see?

PUPPETEER

There's that phrase they've repeated to us ever since we were children. "Revolution …"

The KING, suddenly full of energy, rises and shakes his fist in the air.

ALL TOGETHER

"… IS TO CHANGE EVERYTHING THAT MUST BE CHANGED!"

THE DIRECTOR

For me, to be a revolutionary is to force things to evolve. For them, it means clinging to what's already there. I know the next generation will reject me, as I rejected the work of those who came before me. And so much the better. That's Revolution. Perpetual motion!

PUPPETEER

I'm a revolutionary too, you should know! I'm mounting a play that will feature the four great ladies of Cuban song, including La Lupe and Celia Cruz, who were banned for a long time and who died in exile!

PUPPET

Brilliant! It quietly corrects the errors of the Revolution, rather than attacking it head on! That's being a revolutionary!

MADAME CENSOR

To be revolutionary, is … to be revolutionary!

THE COMIC

There you are! In the end, we all agree. We want revolutionary change in the real sense of the word. So society will progress.

The DIRECTOR starts moving back and forth between the wings. He brings out clothes and other personal effects that he puts into the suitcase on the ground.

THE COMIC

But ... but what are you doing?

THE DIRECTOR

I'm leaving.

MADAME CENSOR

Good riddance!

THE COMIC

For good?

THE DIRECTOR

I ... no ... yes ... no. I've just been invited to a festival.

THE COMIC

Where?

THE DIRECTOR

Over there, obviously. (*stopping and turning toward the audience*) I've hesitated for a long time, but I can no longer bear this wall. There, or rather elsewhere, I'll be nobody, it's true. Maybe I'll have to work in a supermarket to survive. But maybe also I'll be able to shoot films and put on plays.

PUPPET

Wait a bit! The wall won't be there for long. The King is dying, you know that! He's bound to be taking his metaphors with him into the grave!

THE DIRECTOR

(*pause*) That remains to be seen. See you soon, perhaps.

The DIRECTOR closes the suitcase and disappears into the wings while we hear "Cuando Salí de Cuba," sung by Celia Cruz. The other actors stay where they are.

Fade to black.

The End.

BEFORE LEAVING

After our interview at his house in the Nuevo Vedado neighbourhood, the director Juan Carlos Cremata Malberti gave me the phone number of the dissident Eliécer Ávila. "He lives right nearby. You should go and see him. You'll see, he's very intelligent," he tells me.

In 2008, when he was studying at the University of Computer Science, Eliécer Ávila became notorious for having embarrassed Ricardo Alarcón, then President of the National Assembly. Rising to speak during a meeting in an auditorium, the young Ávila first swore that he was a communist and a revolutionary. He confessed that his most cherished dream was to one day undertake a pilgrimage in Bolivia to where Che was killed in 1967. And he could not understand why Cubans had to obtain the permission of the government to leave the island (a stipulation that was removed five years later), nor why, after decades of Revolution, an airplane ticket still represented years of salary for a State employee. More than Ávila's questions, it was Alarcón's response that went down in history: "If everyone could travel where they wanted, air traffic all over the world would be enormous, don't you think?" Alarcón's reply soon became an object of ridicule, and the exchange propelled the good communist Ávila, more or less despite himself, into dissidence. Today Ávila heads a political movement called Somos+.

On his way to Ávila's house for the first time, Cremata says, he was afraid of being followed. "But in the end there was no surveillance. I spent the evening talking with him. We even talked politics."

I noted Ávila's number, but I hesitated to call. I asked the advice of someone I trusted in Miami. "He's a dissident, and these days they're arresting dissidents," came the response. "If you meet him, you'll have the security services on your back. They could arrest you and confiscate your equipment and your notes. In any case, many people question Ávila's convictions. His movement is really only a webpage. And he owns a house in Havana. Where does the money come from for him to have all that, do you think?" According to my contact, Ávila is merely a sly fox who has found that dissidence can pay. Lots of people in Florida are eager to finance any dissidence on the island, even if it bears no fruit.

I had already talked about Eliécer Ávila with Frank in Santiago. He'd known him slightly at university. Frank thought that his ex-classmate was not a fake dissident, but in fact a true agent of the Cuban State. "You can't support the system and suddenly change your mind completely," Frank said, although he had undergone the same mental transformation as Ávila, without, however, proclaiming his dissidence from the rooftops.

For all these reasons, and with all the mystery surrounding the inner workings of Eliécer Ávila's soul, I very much wanted to meet him. But after the incident near the Santa Rita de Casia, and because one false step could compromise my notes and my project's future, fear trumped my curiosity. The dissident's number in my notebook remained unused.

*

It was a few years ago, at the funeral of a dissident who had died of natural causes. Family and friends were gathered together around the coffin when, suddenly, State security agents entered the funeral home. They weren't disrupting this solemn assembly to arrest someone, but to deliver flowers and a card supposedly signed by Fidel and Raúl. In their message, the leaders saluted the contribution to the Revolution of this "patriot," who had always worked for the good of his native land. Reading the note, those close to him were shaken. Their friend, their brother, was he a mole of the regime? Had he been passing on information about them for all those years? Was he a traitor to their cause? Or was this message a deliberate attempt to cast doubt on the integrity of a man who could no longer defend his honour? "*They* have a highly developed sense of black humour," says Fabricio, who is telling me this story that came to him, no doubt embroidered along the way, by word of mouth.

Was the publication of *1984* another of the regime's cynical jokes, designed to confuse observers as to its true intentions?

*

During the week preceding my departure, I badger the secretary of the Cuban Book Institute's president, trying to get an appointment with her at last. If there's one person on the island who must be in on the circumstances surrounding the publication of *1984*, it is certainly Zuleica Romay. The Cuban Book Institute ("Instituto Cubano del Libro," or ICL) links virtually all the publishing houses, including Arte y Literatura, with the Ministry of Culture. When the publishers come up with a list of books they intend to publish during the year, it's her task to approve them. Unfortunately, her secretary explains, this is a bad time. The Havana International Book Fair is touring the provinces. The president, who also heads the event, is for the most part outside of the capital, and in any case is very busy.

Without an appointment, I go directly to the ICL's imposing headquarters on Obispo Street with a friend who is an employee of one of the publishing houses that has its offices there. Since his face is familiar, we get in with no questions asked. In a corridor we by chance run into someone who in fact worked on the new edition of *1984*. My friend knows her, introduces me briefly, then pulls her aside to talk to her. I wander off, as if the subject of their conversation is of no interest to me. Their dialogue is hushed. It seems that she knows more than your average Cuban about how this book came to be, but not very much, really. Only what she had to know to do her job. But she does substantiate one thing: the idea of publishing Orwell did not originate with Victor Malagón, the director of the publishing house. Malagón would not in a hundred years have dared to initiate such a project. The two of them laugh at the very idea of such a thing happening. He's very nice, wouldn't harm a fly, but polemics are not his cup of tea. Malagón is more the timid type who cares too much about his position to risk upsetting the Revolution's literary establishment. The directive came from "higher up" than the publishing house's editorial committee, says our informant, confirming what Fabricio already thought. How much higher? She shrugs her shoulders and smiles. She doesn't know or doesn't want to say. She does add that the book's publication would "absolutely" not have been authorized without the inclusion of a preface to the original text. It was "absolutely" essential to tell Cuban readers how to read Orwell, so they would make the connection between 1984's Oceania and its political police, and today's United States with its national security agencies and their Big Brother inclinations. A research chair on the United States had been approached to write the introduction, but none of the researchers involved wanted to perform the task. And so the publishing house turned to the historian Pedro Pablo Rodríguez. Not because he was an adept reader of Orwell, but because he was a loyal member of the Communist Party and a respected scholar. What is more, he had overseen a critical edition of José Martí's work. A "Martían" like him would be able to find the words to guide readers toward a "revolutionary" understanding of the novel.

Our informant leaves to go back to work. To learn more, I would have to gain access to someone higher up in the pecking order. Another time, on another trip, I hope it will happen.

*

The night before I leave, less than a week before Obama's arrival, conciliatory signs are everywhere: after an interruption of almost five decades, the papers report that direct postal service between Cuba and the United States will be reinstated as of the following day. An airplane will assure the delivery of letters and parcels between the two countries. It's only a pilot project for now, it's made clear, but the service will become permanent if the test runs yield positive results.

The two main official dailies on the island also publish a communiqué from ETECSA, announcing it has signed a cooperative agreement with the American telecommunications company Verizon. According to the agreement, calls between the United States and Cuba will be put through directly, in other words they will no longer have to pass through a third country. That will drastically reduce the costs and will improve the quality of the connection.

The same day, the White House unveils a series of new measures whose aim is once more to work around the embargo that Congress refuses to lift. From now on, Cubans will be able to perform international bank transactions via the United States, and even open an account in that country. It's Daniel who informs me of this latest news when I drop in to say goodbye. "That means I can get paid directly by my publisher in Miami without having to wait for him to come to Cuba and give me my fee in cash," he rejoices. Like many of Obama's decisions concerning Cuba, the goal of these decrees is to reduce as much as possible the effect of the embargo on the lives of ordinary Cubans.

If the reconciliation continues at this pace, I tell myself, no matter who succeeds Obama as president in November, a return to the past seems more and more improbable.

MARCH 17 TO SEPTEMBER 5, 2016

BETWEEN TWO TRIPS

AN ABSENCE OF PROOF

On April 11, 1946, Ihor Szewczenko, a young academic of Ukrainian origin who learned English by listening to the BBC, wrote a letter to George Orwell. He had just finished reading *Animal Farm* and wanted to translate it into his mother tongue for the two hundred thousands Ukrainians stuck in displaced persons camps in Germany and Austria a year after the fighting stopped in Europe. Orwell was delighted with the proposal. He agreed to write a preface intended specifically for this edition, and insisted that he wanted no royalties. In his preface, he explained how he came by this animal allegory of the Russian Revolution, and deplored the blindness of so many English intellectuals and workers, who, despite Stalin's totalitarianism, continued to believe that the Soviet Union was working its way toward socialism. "And so for the past ten years I have been convinced that the destruction of the Soviet myth was essential if we wanted a revival of the Socialist movement."

Колгосп тварин ("the animals' collective farm") was published around the middle of 1947 in Munich. However, only two thousand copies made their way to the displaced persons. About fifteen hundred others were confiscated by the American military and handed over to the Soviet authorities who were in charge of repatriation, and they lost no time destroying them. The Cold War was only beginning, and the Americans didn't want to upset the Soviets with whom they had to collaborate, especially in determining the fate of the uprooted population. In a letter to the writer Arthur Koestler dated September 20, 1947, Orwell deplored the attitude of American authorities and invited his friend to respond positively to Szewczenko, who hoped to translate one of Koestler's books. He also advised Koestler to remain discrete where this project was concerned, given its "more or less illicit" character. "I have been saying ever since 1945 that the DPs were a godsent opportunity for breaking down the wall between Russia and the West. If our government won't see this, one must do what one can privately," Orwell confided to Koestler.

Fairly rapidly, as the Cold War set in, the American and British governments also became aware of how books, Orwell's in particular, could serve as anti-communist propaganda. As early as 1947, the British writer was contacted by the American State Department, which wanted to produce a radio version of *Animal Farm* aimed at countries vulnerable to communist influence. Orwell accepted. The next year, the State Department financed a Korean edition of the same book. During that time, the brand new Information Research Department (IRD), created by the British Foreign Office, and which would become one of the most important sources of literary propaganda all through the Cold War, orchestrated the appearance of an edition of *Animal Farm* in the Telugu language. In newly independent India, a peasant rebellion supported by the Communist Party was inflaming a Telugu-speaking region. In distributing this book, the IRD wanted to warn Indians off an illusory dictatorship of the proletariat.

In 1949, anti-Stalinist Russian émigrés made contact with Orwell; they were trying to finance the translation of *Animal Farm* for a Russian-language magazine aimed at German regions under Soviet control. The author saw in this proposition a new way to have his book travel as far as the USSR in the suitcases of Red Army soldiers who would one day return home. He went so far as to suggest financing the project out of his own pocket. When his agent told him that he was on the verge of closing an agreement for selling the rights to the book in Persian, Orwell insisted that he not demand too steep an advance, "as it is important that this translation should go through."

Before he died on January 21, 1950, Orwell encouraged all initiatives, private or governmental, whose aim was to distribute *Animal Farm* in countries under the yoke of a totalitarian regime, or that were at risk of having one installed. When *1984* was published in June 1949, he followed the same course with his new book.

Orwell's death did not slow the growing popularity of his books within British and American propaganda organizations. That same year, the IRD had comic strips inspired by *Animal Farm* published in newspapers in numerous countries, including the *Times of India*. In 1951, in an internal memo, the American Secretary of State Dean Acheson described *1984* and *Animal Farm* as works "of great value to the [State] Department in its psychological offensive against Communism." He even ordered the London embassy to aid foreign publishers in producing new translations of these books.

From its creation in 1953 to the fall of the Berlin Wall, the United States Information Agency alone ordered the translation and distribution of Orwell's books in more than thirty languages. An undetermined number of other editions saw light via front organizations of the CIA and the IRD. Ironically, if George Orwell became one of the most-read English-language authors during the twentieth century, it's in large part thanks to American and British propaganda organizations.

Although very critical of Western capitalist countries' imperialism, Orwell supported these initiatives, estimating that the battle against communist totalitarianism was more urgent. Were he still alive a few years later, he would probably have been less impressed by the fact that these same imperialists took it upon themselves to alter his works in order to further their cause.

In December 1954, an animated version of *Animal Farm* was released in British movie theatres, and then in the United States a month later. It was subsequently translated and distributed in several other countries. Those familiar with the original text were surprised to discover that, on the big screen, Orwell's tale did not end in the same way as it did on paper. In the book's final pages, as the pigs are celebrating their new alliance with the neighbouring farmers in their ex-owner's house, the other animals are secretly observing the scene through the window. They see that it is almost impossible to differentiate the pigs, who are now walking on two feet, from the humans. With this ending, Orwell wanted to expose the striking resemblance between the old capitalist systems of oppression and the new communist tyrannies. But in the film, the humans are missing from the last scene. And rather than resigning themselves to their exploitation by the new ruling class, the animals revolt.

The animated film ends with their storming the house and preparing to overturn their porcine dictatorship.

Two years later a modified film adaptation of *1984* appeared. In the final scene, rather than declaring that he loves the Party leader, as in the book, Winston cries out "Down with Big Brother" from the midst of a crowd. The torture to which he has been subjected has not succeeded in breaking him completely. Human nature is stronger than dictatorship. In case the message was not clear enough, the film ends with a warning: "This, then, is a story of the future. It could be the story of our children, if we fail to preserve their heritage of freedom."

Years later, it was revealed that both productions were financed by the CIA, and that it was the American agency that insisted that Orwell's defeatism in the face of the all-powerful totalitarian regimes be replaced by calls for resistance. If ever the people on the other side of the Iron Curtain were able to see these films, they might perhaps think of rising up against their oppressor.

There is a wealth of material chronicling the use of *1984* and *Animal Farm* as propaganda tools during the Cold War. Among the articles and books I was able to consult, none mentions Cuba as a target of these programs.

In an email exchange, the research librarian of the American State Department responsible for the documents of the USIA – disbanded in 1999 – confirmed that nothing in the archives suggests that the agency was involved in the publication of *1984* in Cuba in January 1961. The same with the National Security Archive, a non-governmental organization that collects declassified documents from American agencies – including the CIA – in order to ensure more transparency from these agencies. There is no trace anywhere of Librerías Unidas S.A., nor of any connivance between Cuban publishing houses and American authorities at that juncture. However, on either side I am reminded that an absence of proof is not a proof of absence.

As I previously noted, there is no mention of the translator in the first Cuban edition of *1984*. Comparing the text with other Spanish editions, I can see that the translation used was that of Rafael Vázquez Zamora, produced for the Ediciones Destino in Spain. This is the publishing house that at the time held world rights for the book in Spanish. Although the book denounces all forms of totalitarianism, Franco's regime authorized its publication in 1952, like the Americans and the British seeing it primarily as a powerful anti-communist propaganda tool.

At the A.M. Heath Literary Agency, responsible for George Orwell's literary legacy, I'm told that they've never heard of the first Cuban edition of 1984, nor of that of *Animal Farm*, which appeared at the same time with Librerías Unidas, but of which I've not yet been able to find a copy. It seems that there was never a contract for a rights transfer in either case. The literary agent Bill Hamilton is not really surprised. Given the political context, he writes me in an email, it is very unlikely that the publishers behind Librerías Unidas would have tried to obtain permission from Ediciones Destino in Franco's Spain. "During the Cold War period, when publishing was controlled in many places by the state, the only available editions of such books were underground, samizdat, and the Orwell estate had no control over these and of course expected no royalties. They took a view that the books had a right to distribution by unorthodox means in places where the state had censored them, and where copyright itself was compromised."

Given Orwell's active support, during his lifetime, of all the clandestine publications of his books, it is easy to imagine that he would have encouraged the appearance of his Cuban editions, whether behind Librerías Unidas there were anti-communist Cubans or British or American propaganda services.

*

During the months separating my first two visits to the island, I carry out online searches enabling me to draw up a list of other titles published by Librerías Unidas. As far as I can see, the house only existed from 1959 to early 1961. Aside from Orwell's novels, other books in the catalogue clearly reveal the anti-communist, anti-totalitarian orientation of the publishers. They are almost all editions of works already published abroad: in *La Gran Estafa* (*The Great Swindle*), the Peruvian ex-communist and former Moscow agent Eudocio Ravines reveals and denounces the tactics used by the Soviets during the 1930s to extend their influence in China and Latin America; in *La Nueva Clase* (*The New Class: An Analysis of the Communist System*), the Yugoslavian Milovan Djilas, a former comrade of Tito who defected, exposes the way in which the communist elite in the USSR and Yugoslavia were able to put in place totalitarian regimes from which they were the first to profit; the novel *El cero y el infinito* (*Darkness at Noon*), by Arthur Koestler, another formerly ardent communist, recounts the misadventures of an early Bolshevik arrested, imprisoned, and condemned for treason by the government he had helped put in power. Like *1984* and *Animal Farm*, the translations of these three books were also published in various languages around the world with the help of the CIA, the USIA, or the IRD. Arthur Koestler was in fact an IRD consultant and a CIA informer during those years.

Two other books published by Librerías Unidas do, however, cast doubt on the political convictions of the publishers, and at the same time on their potential links with the American and British agencies. Among the first titles published by the house at the beginning of 1960, we find, in fact, *Fábula del tiburón y las sardinas: América Latina estrangulada* (*The Shark and the Sardines*), by Juan José Arévalo. In this brass-knuckles essay, the first elected president of Guatemala fiercely condemns the United States' imperialist policies toward the Americas. The book initially appeared in 1956, two years after the coup d'état in Guatemala that overthrew Jacobo Árbenz, Arévalo's successor, he too democratically elected. The United States defended its operation, citing their suspicions that Árbenz was preparing to embrace communism and ally himself with the Soviets. A few months after the release of *Fábula* by Librerías Unidas, Fidel Castro ordered another edition from a State publisher, of which fifty thousand copies were printed and distributed across the island at a low price.

In February 1961, one month after having brought out translations of *1984* and *Animal Farm*, Librerías Unidas published *La tragedia de la diplomacia norteamericana* (*The Tragedy of American Diplomacy*) by the American historian William Appleman Williams. An important figure of the New Left, Williams presented himself as a critic of his government's official historiography. He argued that since its creation, the United States had not just propagated freedom around the world but had also acted as an imperialist force. Two months after the release of the Cuban edition of his book, the intellectual condemned the Bay of Pigs invasion, as he had condemned that of Hungary by the Soviet Union in 1956.

During the Cold War, the British and the Americans tried in different ways to win over leftist intellectuals around the world in order to head off Soviet influence. The CIA, for example, founded the Congress for Cultural Freedom in 1950, an organization with many outposts, including one in Cuba that was dissolved at the end of 1960. The Congress published magazines in different languages and organized international conferences and seminars. Its mandate was to promote leftist ideas, socialist but anti-communist and anti-Soviet, targeting the intelligentsia of various countries. From time to time, however, conflicts arose within the organization when its directors blocked the publication of texts criticizing America's interventions around the world.[13] During its two decades of existence, most of the members of the Congress ignored or wanted to ignore the fact that the money that paid for their activities, their salaries, and their publications, came from Uncle Sam's secret pocket.

If the Americans and the British did invest in such leftist projects, it seems to me unlikely that they founded or even financed a Cuban publishing house like Librerías Unidas, which denounced their imperialism

---

13 See Frances Stonor Saunders, *Who Paid the Piper? The CIA and the Cultural Cold War* (U.S. title: *The Cultural Cold War: The CIA and the World of Arts and Letters*) (London: Granta Books, 2000; New York: New Press, 2013).

just as fiercely as it did that of the Soviets. But again, the absence of proof is not the proof of absence.

During my next visit to the island I would continue my research at the National Library, and enter into conversation with people I met, seeking additional clues to the identity and purpose of *1984*'s first Cuban publishers.

MEANWHILE

FRIDAY, MARCH 18, 2016

The U.S. Coast Guard rescues a boat with eighteen Cubans on board, dehydrated and short of supplies. They had embarked twenty-two days earlier. During the journey, nine lifeless bodies had to be thrown overboard. It was a cruise ship, the *Brilliance of the Seas*, that spotted the drifting craft two hundred kilometres off the Florida coast.

SUNDAY, MARCH 20

The Obama family lands at the Havana airport. *"¿Que bolá Cuba?"* (What's up, Cuba?), the president tweets, on exiting the plane. A few hours earlier the Ladies in White had held their weekly demonstration at the door to the Santa Rita de Casia church, singing "Obama, we have a dream: a Cuba without Castros." A group of regime supporters showed up and began to taunt them. They came to blows, and fifty or so protesters, including the well-known graffiti artist El Sexto, were arrested.

MONDAY, MARCH 21

Barack Obama deposits a wreath of flowers at the foot of the José Martí monument in Revolution Square. The poet and politician, dead over a century earlier, is venerated both by the anti-Castro exiles in Miami and Fidel's supporters in Cuba. Obama then holds a press conference along with his counterpart, Raúl Castro. Jim Acosta, a CNN journalist of Cuban descent, asks the Cuban head of state if he is still holding political prisoners, and if so, why they are not being freed. Unaccustomed to this sort of democratic exercise, Raúl is enraged. "What political prisoners? Give me a name or names. After this meeting is over, you can give me a list of political prisoners. And if we have those political prisoners, they will be released before tonight ends." After the press conference, the Obama administration declares that it long ago submitted a list of fifty-three names to the Cuban authorities. But the regime does not consider any of these people political prisoners. The incident does not lead to anyone being freed.

TUESDAY, MARCH 22

At Havana's Gran Teatro, Barack Obama delivers a speech in which he dissects one by one the regime's criticisms of the United States and liberal democracy, while at the same time appealing to Cuban pride. He also evokes the need for reconciliation between Cuban Americans and those living on the island. The speech is broadcast live on national television. Some excerpts:

> [The embargo] is an outdated burden on the Cuban people. It's a burden on the Americans who want to work and do business or invest here in Cuba. It's time to lift the embargo
>
> ...
>
> I've made it clear that the United States has neither the capacity, nor the intention to impose change on Cuba. What changes come will depend upon the Cuban people. We will not impose our political or economic system on you ...
>
> As Martí said, "Liberty is the right of every man to be honest, to think and to speak without hypocrisy" ...
>
> I've had frank conversations with President Castro. For many years, he has pointed out the flaws in the American system – economic inequality; the death penalty; racial discrimination; wars abroad ... But the fact that we have open debates within America's own democracy is what allows us to get better ...
>
> So here's my message to the Cuban government and the Cuban people: the ideals that are the starting point for every revolution – America's revolution, Cuba's revolution, the liberation movements around the world – those ideals

find their truest expression, I believe, in democracy. Not because American democracy is perfect, but precisely because we're not ...

El futuro de Cuba tiene que estar en las manos del pueblo cubano ...

Cuba doesn't have to be defined by being against the United States any more than the United States should be defined by being against Cuba ...

The tides of history can leave people in conflict, and exile and poverty ...

It is time now for us to leave the past behind. It is time for us to look forward to the future together – *un futuro de esperanza*. And it won't be easy, and there will be setbacks. It will take time. But my time here in Cuba renews my hope and confidence in what the Cuban people will do. We can make this journey as friends and as neighbours and as family, together. *Sí se puede. Muchas gracias.*

(*Applause.*)

After his speech, Obama meets a dozen dissidents, then, with Raúl Castro, attends a friendly baseball game between the Tampa Bay Rays and the Cuban national team. The obedient crowd chants "*¡Raúl! ¡Raúl!*" The Rays win, four to one, and Obama gets back onto Air Force One to fly off to Argentina.

FRIDAY, MARCH 25

On an outdoor stage in front of Havana's Ciudad Deportiva, the Rolling Stones perform for 500,000 people. Armando and his friends are in the crowd, as is the stand-up comic Alexis Ayala, who has flown in from Guantánamo. Also in the crowd, against his will (he likes his rock progressive), is Fabricio, there to serve as the eyes and ears of his father, whose night vision is weakening, but who still must write an account of the show for *El Mundo*.

TUESDAY, APRIL 19

The Seventh Congress of the Cuban Communist Party ends after four days of deliberations. Fidel Castro speaks. Before the one thousand invited delegates, he broaches the subject of his imminent demise. "I will soon be ninety years old … The end comes for us all, but the ideas of the Cuban communists will remain," he manages to say in a voice that is only the shadow of what it once was. His brother Raúl is re-elected First Secretary of the Party, and declares: "This Congress will be the last led by the historic generation, which will be placing the Revolution's banners in the hands of new growth." He also repeats his mantra, where reforms are concerned. "We have continued to steadily advance in this process, without haste, but without pause." *Sin prisa pero sin pausa.* No important new reforms are announced, except for one: as of the next Congress in 2021, the leading roles in its organization will no longer be filled by anyone over seventy years old. The vice-president, Miguel Díaz-Canel Bermúdez, also stays in place. He remains the designated successor to Raúl, who has already announced that he will leave the presidency at the end of his second term, on February 14, 2018.

MONDAY, MAY 2

Just one day after Cuba's Labour Day parade, the cruise ship *Adonia*, from Miami, docks in Havana with seven hundred tourists on board. Ten days earlier, the Cuban government had authorized the arrival of boats full of Americans to the island, after a ban of five decades.

SATURDAY, AUGUST 13

Fidel Castro celebrates his ninetieth birthday, and appears in public for the first time since the Congress. He attends a gala in his honour at the Karl Marx Theatre in Havana. In a column titled "El Cumpleaños" ("the birthday"), and published the same day by the daily paper *Granma*, he recalls the attempts on his life over the years. He also salutes the "great courage and intelligence" of the Chinese and Russian peoples, and criticizes Barack Obama for not having formally apologized to the Japanese people during his visit to Hiroshima in May. José Castelar, a cigar roller in the capital, fashions a ninety-metre cigar to mark the event, even though he knows that the *Comandante* has not smoked for thirty years.

TUESDAY, AUGUST 16

Jean-Guy Allard dies in Havana at the age of sixty-eight, from the effects of the rheumatoid arthritis that afflicted him for years. His ashes are scattered in the waters of Havana Bay, facing the statue of the explorer Pierre Le Moyne d'Iberville, who was born in Montréal and died in Havana in 1706 from mysterious causes. It was Jean-Guy who had urged the Québec government to erect this monument. *Granma, Juventud Rebelde*, and the *Journal de Québec* all devote articles to his death.

WEDNESDAY, AUGUST 31

Twenty minutes late, JetBlue's Flight 387 leaves Fort Lauderdale and lands an hour and fifteen minutes later in Santa Clara. It's the first commercial flight between the United States and Cuba since the October 1962 missile crisis. Several other flights between American and Cuban cities are inaugurated the same day.

THURSDAY, SEPTEMBER 1

The International Olympic Committee announces that the Cuban discus thrower Yarelys Barrios has tested positive for acetazolamide, an anabolic steroid. The organization orders her to return the silver medal she won at the 2008 Summer Olympic Games in Beijing. The thirty-three-year-old athlete denies any doping and declares that she is not in a position to give back the medal: in June, she sold it on eBay for the sum of 11,655.55 American dollars.

SEPTEMBER 6 TO 22, 2016

SECOND TRIP

¿QUÉ BOLÁ, CUBA?

The *casa particular* in Havana where I'm staying for the length of this visit is the same where I spent the final nights of my first trip. Its owner sends a driver to pick me up at the José Martí Airport. I see that he's not the same one, Maykel, who drove me out when I left six months earlier, and on the way unburdened himself of all his grievances against the regime. Maykel was a soldier in the Cuban army during the Angolan Civil War. After he returned, he worked as a factory manager, for a long time "participating in the lie" by collaborating with security services. He excused his years of indoctrination by evoking the powers of persuasion of the smooth-talker-in-chief, *El Tipo*, "The Man," as he called him. The day of his disillusionment, eighteen years earlier – he didn't tell me what caused this rupture – he'd tried to convince his family of the "great national lie" in which everyone was implicated. All those close to him thought he was crazy. Now that he was a private, illegal driver, he was earning much more than before, and no longer had to be a yes-man. Although he was no longer part of the system, Maykel still had some friends in the security organizations. They'd told him that all the tickets for the baseball game Raúl and Obama attended had been handed out to loyal communists. "You'll see, they'll chant ¡*Viva Raúl!* ¡*Viva Fidel!* ¡*Viva la Revolución!* And there'll be no one there to make waves." His prediction proved accurate. At the end of our conversation, Maykel asked me if I was really a journalist, as the keeper of the *casa* had probably told him. Just a few years earlier, he would never have dared to openly criticize the regime, even less in front of a foreigner, he told me. "I would have been locked up for four or five years. But now I'm no longer afraid." I deduced that his long digression was not just a form of therapy, but that it implied a real desire to have his words leave the country and be reported somewhere or other. Now it's done.

Juan, the new driver for the *casa*, is much less chatty. During the ride, he replies factually to my questions without offering his own opinions.

When we arrive at the *casa*, the manager explains to me why Maykel was replaced. "He talked politics too much. It frightened the tourists."

The fear, it seems, has changed sides.

*

Havana's walls still show signs of the mid-August celebration. On many, the same stencilled graffiti shows the bearded one who was fêted, instantly recognizable in profile, with the legendary military cap on his head. The silhouette is not that of the hunched and emaciated leader who showed himself a month ago at the time of his birthday, but that of his great years, a half-century ago, when he was at the height of his powers, just like his Revolution. "90+" is inscribed beneath the drawing. Ninety more years are being demanded of the one who has already lived as many. As everyone knows that the legend is about to give up the ghost, I suspect that this wish is more a mark of respect than a real wish to see *El Tipo* hovering over daily life on the island for nine more decades.

This graffiti sparks an idea in my mind for another piece of absurdist theatre in the style of Virgilio Piñera or Eugène Ionesco: on the day after his ninetieth birthday celebrations, a retired dictator announces that "by popular demand" he is calling a halt to the end of his life, and resuming his duties for a new mandate of ninety years. Unsettled by this unforeseen change in plan, his courtiers, who were already preparing for his funeral and pondering the best way to legitimize their power through the posthumous manipulation of his image while at the same time undoing his legacy bit by bit, try to flatter him into maintaining his march toward death.

*

The springtime euphoria is long gone. After having consented to Major Lazer and Rolling Stones mega-concerts in March, to the shooting of the eighth film in the series *Fast and Furious* in the streets of the capital in April, and to the Chanel fashion show on the Paseo del Prado in May, the Cuban authorities have had enough of *yanqui* artists making their country the flavour of the month. In August, the California pop group Maroon 5 learned this the hard way. After having already shipped to Cuba all the equipment it needed to shoot its next videoclip, it was refused a permit.

During the same period, internet access on the island continued to improve. New wireless terminals materialized across the country, and it was announced that soon the entire Malecón would be covered by the Nauta network.

*

Upon reflection, Sonia has decided not to turn in her Communist Party card. She would have badly missed the Party cell meetings at the Academy of Sciences, those of the neighbourhood Committee for the Defence of the Revolution, and the official demonstrations like the May 1st parade. Now that she's retired, each of these gatherings is a rare opportunity for her to reconnect with her former colleagues. Besides, she likes to offer her opinions during the meetings. She is still a member of the Party, but her assessment of the Cuban system's woeful state has not changed. "Only vital industries like oil and electricity should be under the State's control," she declares. "All the rest should be privatized. Centralization doesn't work." But I doubt that she dares to express her opinions so candidly in the presence of Party officials.

Her son, Armando, has not tried to revive his plan for renewing the neighbourhood. After the incident that led to an inquiry by the security services, he no longer wants to involve those living nearby. In any case, he's busy with a new project. For a few weeks, he's been renting a stand at the Almacenes de San José craft fair, near the train station. He and his artist friends are planning to "infiltrate commercial territory" with their creations so as to initiate the public into contemporary art. In the fair's hangar, his canvases, long thought out, are hanging side by side with all the Havana clichés popular with the tourists: an old American car parked in front of the Bodeguita del Medio where Hemingway hung out; elderly street musicians in straw hats performing in front of a mural of the glorious Che; or reproductions of old ads for Havana Club rum. "If the gallery owners knew I was showing here, they'd never include me in their exhibitions," Armando admits. "But what can I do? I've participated in several gallery shows and never sold a painting. There aren't enough foreign collectors who come to Cuba, and there's no Cuban who can pay hundreds of dollars for a work of art." At the fair, his paintings of multicoloured and multiform human and animal skulls sell rather well. So much so that he's had to hire a cousin to whom he's taught his technique, so that he can reproduce the works that sell best. He also asked me to bring him, from Canada, five cans of acrylic paint in different colours, because they're always hard to find in the State stores. Trying to cultivate a clientele at the craft fair, Armando knows he's taking the risk of having commercial gain compromise his creative freedom. He also recognizes that he's now trying to "sense what's in the air" in order to please the public. But he's trying not to lose sight of his goal: "To answer to a demand without seeming to prostitute myself."

*

The Mexican consular authorities did not believe Frank when he said he wanted to visit for a work trip. They refused him a tourist visa. And so he will prepare his immigration dossier for Canada, while at the same time working on other plans for escape.

Mayrelis's wish has come true. But only on paper. The government has opened a first wholesale outlet for hotels. But the concept of "wholesale" seems to have eluded those running the business. It's easier to find some products, but everything is more expensive than in other state enterprises. "*They* know that for businesses to work, we need these products, so *they* profit from it in order to squeeze more money out of us." Beyond this, supplies are still hard to come by. These days, Coca-Cola, even its Cuban version, tuKola, is almost impossible to find. Mayrelis has had to ask a friend passing through Varadero to get her some through a contact in a hotel. As for her espresso machine, it has to resign itself to poor quality beans rather than the imported variety it's accustomed to. Potatoes are not always available on the black market.

Obama's March visit played havoc with Esto no es un Café's normal routine. For four days the restaurant was open only in theory. "Our only clients were the American Secret Service agents." The presidential family made a scheduled visit to the cathedral, just a few steps away. Michelle Obama even passed in front of Esto no es un Café on her way to buy art at the Experimental Graphics Workshop at the end of the alley.

What disturbs Mayrelis the most these days – aside from the restaurant's main refrigerator being up to its usual tricks, and the incompetent repairman who for two weeks has been unable to solve the problem – is the Old City's being brought under the control of the military. It seems that, recently, the Revolutionary Armed Forces have succeeded in laying their hands on the Habaguanex Tourist Company, up to then under the direction of the chief historian's office in Havana. Over thirty-five years ago, the historian Eusebio Leal Spengler made a deal with Fidel: his office would receive a portion of the profits from Old Havana's tourist income, and with that money it would finance the restoration of the old buildings. Both in Cuba and abroad, his work was universally praised. But now the old man is supposedly sick with cancer and will soon die. Obviously, the newspapers do not talk about the historian's illness, or the takeover of

Habaguanex by the armed forces. Mayrelis can only go by the rumours and articles that turn up on diaspora sites if she wants to get some idea of what's happening around the corner from her business. "The city's cultural values are certainly going to change. The military know nothing about conservation, and are going to undo Eusebio's legacy, his real vision. That says a lot about the way things are going now in the country," Mayrelis asserts.

*

I didn't know that Daniel was a numismatist. I found out when I asked him what I could bring him from North America. I had to do the rounds of Montréal's antique currency shops to lay my hands on the Canadian bills of different series that were lacking in his collection, while respecting his budget. When I give him the bills, he reimburses me, cash on the barrelhead. I confess my surprise that an intellectual of his stature, otherwise not drawn to material goods, could have a passion for bank notes and spend so much money on them. He explains: for him, numismatics is not just a hobby, but an investment. If ever the economy and the two Cuban currencies were to collapse, he could sell his collection, which would without doubt have increased in value in the meantime.

Daniel hands me the January–February 2016 issue of *La Letra del Escriba,* in which he was able to publish a translation of the essay "Why I Write" by Orwell. He's just received it. At the beginning of the year, the country's printers were swamped with orders and they had to give priority to the new books scheduled to be released at the book fair in February. The printing of *La Letra* was repeatedly put off, and the journal finally came out five months late.

*

Fabricio has found a way to make much more money than he does translating novels or foreign websites. Recently he organized the visit of a group of Americans on a cultural junket. He had to be able to reply to all sorts of questions, so he was forced to do some research before their arrival. For the three days that he spent with them, he earned 350 CUC, tips included. "If I could have a group like that every two or three months, it would be perfect," he says. After a hiatus of some years, he has also resumed teaching literature at the college level.

Over the last months, his translation of *1984* has landed in the capital's bookstores. Passing each day in front of Alma Mater, at the corner of San Lazaro and Infanta, I see that the copies are rapidly flying off the shelves. So as not to be out of luck, I end up going in.

Placing two copies on the counter, I interrupt the conversation the clerk is having with a man who has come to put up a poster in the window. I know I've seen the man somewhere, but I can't remember where or when. The clerk takes one of the books, and addressing the man, says: "You see, this is a good example. You have to act quickly when things are happening, because you never know how long it might last." I ask her what they're talking about, but she ignores my question. She does confirm that *1984* is at present one of the bookstore's bestsellers.

THE MUTABILITY
OF THE PAST

In Orwell's Oceania, past events have no objective existence in and of themselves. Their survival as *facts* depends entirely on documents and witnesses asserting they have happened. And since the Party has absolute control over the documents and the minds of its members, it can alter the past as it wishes to make it consistent with the discourse of the moment. To acknowledge that it has committed an error in its predictions, or worse, that is has knowingly altered its doctrine or political line, would constitute an admission of weakness. The past is, must be, what the Party wants it to have been. This principle, called "the mutability of the past," is the very foundation of Ingsoc, which is Oceania's official ideology. It is the constant manipulation of memories, allied with a strict ban on any contact with foreigners, which guarantees that Party members cannot compare their reality with any other.

When Winston Smith tries to find out what life was like before the Revolution, he knows that the archives have been falsified, and that the memories of Party members, including his own, have been altered by propaganda. And so he concludes that his only hope of unearthing the past's true nature resides in the memories from this period still alive among the oldest members of the proletariat, that despised caste that the Party has not even bothered to indoctrinate.

One night after work, at the risk of attracting the attention of the Thought Police, Winston visits a bar frequented by the workers. He enters into conversation with an old man who he thinks must already have been an adult at the time of the Revolution. But his questions only elicit piecemeal answers, incoherent or irrelevant. The old man's memory is no more than "a rubbish-heap of details."

> Within twenty years at most, he reflected, the huge and
> simple question, "Was life better before the Revolution

than it is now?" would have ceased once and for all to be answerable. But in effect it was unanswerable even now, since the few scattered survivors from the ancient world were incapable of comparing one age with another. They remembered a million useless things, a quarrel with a workmate, a hunt for a lost bicycle pump, the expression on a long-dead sister's face, the swirls of dust on a windy morning seventy years ago; but all the relevant facts were outside their range of vision. They were like the ant, which can see small objects but not large ones.

Unable to compare the present with the distant past, Winston must resign himself, like his comrades, to accepting the Party's claim that it has continually bettered their living conditions since the Revolution. In Oceania, in the year 1984, the past is inaccessible.

In Cuba, in 2016, those who can remember life in the years preceding the Revolution and during those following its triumph are also less and less numerous every day. With the passing of years, their memories must struggle both with the wear and tear of time and the Party's revisionist propaganda, which tries to have them forget its unfulfilled promises and its ideological reversals. Nevertheless, part of this past remains accessible. The regime has not taken the trouble to destroy or rewrite it. To bring it to light, you only have to visit the National Library, fill out a few forms, and immerse yourself in the documentary proofs of its existence.

*

The librarian presents me with the thick, bound volumes of newspapers and magazines, over a half-century old. A few of them are in such a lamentable state that despite all my precautions, some of the pages crumble in my hands. Touching them, I feel as if I'm contributing both to this past's revival and its disappearance.

Here I am in January 1961. Three days after the New Year, President Eisenhower breaks off diplomatic relations with Cuba. While the Luz-Hilo workshop's presses are printing *1984*'s first Cuban edition, Havana's periodicals are on a war footing.

> The invasion is coming!
>
> Mercenary pilots are being offered $25,000 to attack Cuba's refineries.
>
> Cubans, donate your blood. We are in a state of emergency and high alert before the threat of invasion by an enemy as vile as it is powerful.
>
> Imperialism has finally stripped away its hypocritical clothing to reveal to all its evil intentions.
>
> Eisenhower confirms his aid to Cuban counter-revolutionaries; he has repeated his attacks against the Cuban Revolution in his last message sent to Congress.

On January 20, 1961, John F. Kennedy is sworn in as the thirty-fifth president of the United States. On the island, there is hope that the Democrat will be less warlike than his Republican predecessor.

> We must have a face-to-face discussion with the United States and share with them our grievances, says Commander [Ernesto] Guevara.

But as soon as the new president declares that he has no intention of normalizing relations with Cuba, the guard goes back up.

> What does President Kennedy hope to do with those bands of mercenaries and criminals?

Revolutionary fever is at its height. The Year of Education has just succeeded that of Agrarian Reform. Intellectuals and other literate individuals are sent into the countryside to teach the rural population how to read and write. In the factories, working hours are ramped up. With an invasion threatening, no mercy is shown to counter-revolutionaries, who are seen as agents of imperialism.

> "The scaffold for the terrorists," demands the working class in front of the presidential palace.

> The Revolution is entering its third year with more dynamism than ever.

> Fidel says: "THEY WILL SEE, we're going to teach people to read TO THE VERY LAST illiterate, as we are going to annihilate TO THE VERY LAST criminal."

> Three counter-revolutionaries are shot in la Cabaña.

> Cuba is producing more and more every year: in two years, Cubans have not only put in place a stable economy, but have increased production. The Revolution is succeeding in its goals.

In an ad, Coca-Cola claims to be "the hallmark of hospitality," and suggests that the teachers of reading and writing treat themselves and their students to a "joyous interlude" by drinking a tasty Coke during the lessons. A men's tailor and a furniture store both call their promotions "revolutionary bargains." A California school offers correspondence English courses, and it's Uncle Sam himself who urges prospective students to learn the language by following his "FAMOUS Rational System." Beneath the logo in their ads, most large businesses, such as the U.S.-founded Sears or the Havana-based Fin de Siglo, bear the label "Nationalized." The marketing strategies are still capitalist, but the economy is more and more controlled by the state. What is more, several articles, newspaper items, and ads strongly suggest that new alliances are being forged, and that the dawning of a new era is more and more certain.

Soviet actors and directors are in Havana for Soviet Film Week. A first.

China will welcome Cuban technicians to teach them advanced techniques in the field of agriculture.

Today one of the greatest shows in the world is coming to Cuba: the Yugoslav Ballet.

A shipment of butter from the USSR has arrived in Cuba.

Bulgaria has signed a long-term treaty with Cuba, and is granting it a credit of five million dollars.

Saturday morning, a group of professors from the University of Moscow, currently in Havana as tourists, visited the University of Havana.

The Cuban Revolution is not yet socialist, but in all the publications the achievements of communist countries are celebrated, and readers are assured that the United States is a power in decline.

In Czechoslovakia, infantile mortality is diminishing.

More than 70 million Soviets were vaccinated against polio in 1960.

Unemployment continues to increase among the American population.

China, like Cuba, is living a moment of revolutionary history where everyone is committed, where everyone is working extra hours, where everyone has production at heart along with a rise in productivity, and betterment in every field.

Eisenhower is leaving *yanqui* prestige at its lowest ebb in history.

In Soviet Uzbekistan, the irradiation of cotton seeds has reduced the growing period by two weeks, and increased the yield by two percent.

On the cover of its January 22, 1961, edition, the magazine *Bohemia* shows a twenty-year-old woman wearing a pale blue shirt tucked into her jeans. On her belt, she carries a long knife in a leather case. On her head, a black beret. At her neck there hangs a white crucifix. The Revolution is not yet atheistic. The year's fourth edition is titled "In Defence of the Revolution." The young girl is one of the hundreds of thousands of members of the new Committees for the Defence of the Revolution created four months earlier. She has responded to the patriotic call in order to defend the Revolution against its internal and external enemies.

> In calling for vigilance and the deterrence of all sorts of counter-revolutionary operations, the objective is in no way to promote unfounded denunciations and ham-fisted spying within the population, but rather to cleanse the rearguard of the nation in these times of dynamic patriotic preparations, while the terrorist vermin lurk in the shadows, plotting to sabotage all the noble desires and plans for furthering human advancement on the island.

The editors of *Bohemia* saw the risks of excessive zeal on the part of such surveillance committees. But they preferred to believe that revolutionary fervour would enable the "New Man" to transcend his reptilian instincts in the name of a cause greater than himself.

Three issues later, the same revue announces the creation of a state apparatus for press distribution.

The seller of newspapers, he who puts into the hands of the
reader printed news and points of view, belonged without
a doubt to one of the old society's most underprivileged
and neglected groups. That society's epitaph was written
on January 1, 1959, with the triumph of the Revolution.

I shut *Bohemia* and ask the librarian for the volume containing the issues
of the daily *Prensa Libre* from April 1961.

April 1961 is the month when everything changed for the Revolution.

On the sixth, we learn that "The *Yanquis* are training troops to
intervene in Cuba."

On the ninth, Fidel Castro claims that his country is the "fortress
of dignity in America and the invincible bastion of justice and revolution
in America."

On the thirteenth, *Prensa Libre* warns that "Cuba could be the
tomb of the O.A.S. [Organization of American States] were the mercenaries to attempt an attack." Kennedy affirms that he has no intention of
intervening in Cuba "under any circumstances."

On the fourteenth, it is reported that the Soviet cosmonaut Yuri
Gagarin has been "greeted as a hero in Moscow." The Soviets have just
won the first battle in the space race by sending a man into orbit around
the earth. The USSR's prestige is at its height.

"AERIAL ATTACKS ON HAVANA, Santiago de Cuba, and San
Antonio de Los Baños," headlines the April 15, 1961, edition of the paper.
Still, it claims that the attack has "not in the least affected the defensive
capacity of our rebel army." In fact, as will later be revealed, Cuban avi-
ation has been almost entirely wiped out by the bombardments.

That same day, as the Soviet Cinerama is being unveiled in Havana,
Fidel Castro delivers a speech before the Colón cemetery, where the
funerals for the victims of the air attacks are taking place. Toward the
middle of his speech, the *Comandante* appends to the word "revolution,"

for the very first time, an adjective that puts an end to all the ambiguities and hesitations of the previous months.

> This is what they cannot forgive: that we are here, right under their very noses, and that we have made a socialist revolution right under the nose of the United States! This socialist revolution, we are defending it with our guns. This socialist revolution, we are defending it with the valour that our anti-aircraft artillerymen displayed yesterday, riddling the attacking planes with our shells.

The Cuban Revolution is socialist. Castro has chosen the Cubans' camp. Twenty-eight months earlier, anti-communists fought at his side to overthrow Batista. Some even played a role in his government. But now the Revolution is socialist and aligned with the Eastern Bloc. Therefore it was always destined to follow this path. Those who do not accept this are traitors.

At 1:15 a.m. on April 17, as the rotary presses are printing the next day's papers containing Fidel's entire speech, in the Bay of Pigs, two hundred kilometres southwest of Havana, a group of fourteen hundred exiled Cubans recruited and trained by the CIA lands on the beaches of Girón and Larga with the intention of overturning the revolutionary government.

Prensa Libre, April 18: "We must defend ourselves with iron and fire against the barbarians: Cubans, onward!"

In the inside pages, the new adjective is already part and parcel of the old slogans: "Death to the invader! Long live the socialist revolution! We will be victorious!"

April 19: "The USSR is ready to support Cuba with all the military assistance necessary."

April 21: "TOTAL VICTORY: The invasion launched against Cuba by the United States has been crushed."

The defeat is indeed a bitter one for the exiles and humiliating for their powerful sponsor. Kennedy's hesitations doomed the operation. The new president did not want this to be yet another example of his country's direct interference in Latin America's affairs. But in reducing to the minimum the logistic and material support foreseen by his predecessor Eisenhower for the Cuban exiles' Brigade 2506, he guaranteed the landing's failure. And despite his precautions, the invasion was in any case seen to have been orchestrated by the United States.

The antagonism between Washington and Havana is now set in stone. Castro is still in power, stronger than ever. After two years of ideological and strategical indecision, the period of uncertainty is over.

Two weeks later, during a visit to the members of Brigade 2506 who have been made prisoners, Fidel is still qualifying, somewhat, the Revolution's orientation.

> We have decided that our regime is socialist. Entirely socialist? No, because it is a regime that has adopted a series of socialist laws, but which, in reality, has many other institutions that are not of the socialist type: and we have many small- and medium-sized industries, many medium-sized landowners, medium-sized businesses, and finally, there are many French fry stands. The revolutionary government has not nationalized French fry stands.

During the May 1, 1961, parade, in a three-and-a-half-hour speech that is reproduced in its entirety in the next day's papers, Fidel elaborates on the direction his country will take.

> Here, there is only one party: that of the humiliated ... The Revolution has no time for elections. There is no government in Latin America more democratic than the revolutionary government.

Gone are the promises, many times repeated before and after the Revolution, of a multi-party system and free elections. Cuba will be ruled by a single party whose legitimacy will reside in the popular will expressed on January 1, 1959. As of now, it must be believed that this was always the initial plan.

Before the end of 1961, Fidel will declare himself Marxist-Leninist. He will thus have always been so. Just like the Revolution.

In May 1961, the regime, communist and therefore atheist, starts to confiscate the possessions of the Catholic Church. In September, 131 priests are expelled from the country for counter-revolutionary activities. Hundreds of others flee. There is no more place for religious practice within the context of the Revolution. And so there never was. When the young defender of the Revolution with the white crucifix posed for the cover of *Bohemia* in January, her faith in God was still compatible with the faith she had in the Revolution. A few months later, she saw herself forced to choose between Jesus and Fidel.

In 1968, during the "revolutionary offensive" designed to free the country from the last traces of the old world, French fry stands would be nationalized, then closed down by the regime. The Revolution will always have intended to include only socialist institutions.

As for news sellers, in 2016 they are again among society's most underprivileged. Early in the morning, old men and women line up in front of the state kiosks to buy copies of the few periodicals still in existence – including *Bohemia* – which they resell as they wander through the streets. From their informal business they earn a handful of pesos to add to their meagre retirement allowance. Among them, very few must remember the promise the Revolution made to the news sellers fifty-five years earlier – the promise of a radiant future.

There are two sorts of classification for the books in the National Library. Some are ordered according to the author's name, while for others you must seek out the book's title. Orwell's books may be found under the letter *O*, while the essay *La tragedia de la diplomacia norteamericana* by William Appleman Williams has been catalogued under "T." Still, I manage to locate most of the books my online searches have identified as having been published by Librerías Unidas. I also discover others I hadn't known to have appeared with the same publisher.

In exchange for an order slip, I'm provided with most of these works, no questions asked. Some are not to be found, probably lost in the bowels of the library, or long vanished. In only one case do I hit a roadblock. To consult Arthur Koestler's *El cero y el infinito*, I must obtain the status of "researcher," a librarian tells me. But my library card says I'm only a "professional." Why is this book restricted? Has it been banned? In any case, how to explain that I am given, with no problem, *Anatomía de un mito*, a collection of Koestler's essays that is just as anti-communist as his novel, and also published by Librerías Unidas? Unless the available copy of his fiction is simply in such bad condition that it cannot be handled by just anyone?

I receive no answer. I will know no more.

None of the Librerías Unidas books I'm allowed to consult give me any more information regarding the publishers. All I can determine is that between March 1960 and February 1961 the publishing house brought out a dozen books. Most are essays or novels, either anti-communist or anti-imperialist, in the original Spanish or translated from English.

I turn to the reference books. In a monograph titled *La imprenta en Cuba* ("printing in Cuba"), published in 1989 by Letras Cubanas, the historian José G. Ricardo traces the history of the printing of books, magazines, and newspapers on the island. The chapter devoted to the Revolution's first years is totally mute when it comes to the existence during this period of independent publishers. The author only deals with the history of the Revolution's State publishers. Not a trace of Librerías Unidas.

In 1968, the José Martí National Library brought out *Bibliografía cubana 1959–1962* ("Cuban bibliography 1959–1962"), an inventory of the books published in Cuba – or about Cuba in other countries – during the four years following the triumph of the Revolution. In its introduction, it is specified that if the review is not exhaustive, it nevertheless contains "what is most fundamental and representative from those years." Neither *1984* nor *Animal Farm* are included among the 2,776 books listed. In fact, none of the anti-communist books published by Librerías Unidas have been catalogued. One finds only *La tragedia de la diplomacia norteamericana* by Appleman Williams and *Fábula del tiburó y las sardinas* by Arévalo, in the section "Imperialism and Anti-Imperialist Struggle." In the case of the latter book, it is noted that it was published a first time by Librerías Unidas in 1960, before appearing a few months later with Imprenta Nacional de Cuba.

Returning to the old newspapers, I come across a review of Arévalo's book in the *Diario de la Marina*'s April 3, 1960 edition. In its Sunday literary section, the conservative paper, pro-American and staunchly anti-communist, names *Fábula* as its "book of the week." Not for the merits of its argument, but because, according to the daily, Arévalo unknowingly exposes the dangers of communism. In this unsigned article, *Diario de la Marina* recognizes that the United States has not always acted in the best interests of the Americas and has often given priority to its own national interests. But it would be an illusion to think that Russian imperialism, "which Arévalo serves," would act differently in countries under its sphere of influence. "Librerías Unidas S.A. has done a great service to its readers by circulating this book, for it makes clear that if there are exploiters in business there are even more in politics, and their methods are not very different: the former take advantage of foreign workers, and the latter betray the public's faith," the paper concludes.

Adjacent to the review, a Librerías Unidas advertisement describes the book in more positive terms. It is presented as a "superb work" in which the author, in his "deft and vigorous style," has been able to tell the story of "the tragedy of the continent's peoples from Rio Bravo in Mexico to as far away as the Antarctic." The books, it says beneath the description, are on sale in bookstores for 1.50 pesos – a price six times as expensive as the edition that will be published by Imprenta Nacional de Cuba. Below the ad, a final mention of Librerías Unidas S.A. is accompanied by the logos of three of the capital's bookstores.

A month later, in May 1960, the revolutionary authorities bring an abrupt close to the 128-year existence of *Diario de la Marina* in Cuba. This termination marks the beginning of the end of critical media outlets on the island. Within a year and a half, they will all have disappeared.

Aside from the copies of Librerías Unidas books I've been able to consult, this critique is one of the only traces of the publishing house that I've found in the archives. This absence of information, although very frustrating, is not so astonishing when you think about it. The aftermath of a revolution leads inevitably to the explosion of a thousand and one competing initiatives seeking to exercise an influence on the process of redefining the nation. For a certain time all futures are still imaginable, except those that recall too explicitly the past, and each one can propose what appears to be the best, while warning against those believed to be dangerous. Then the paths to the future shrink in number, and most of the options, little by little or all of a sudden, disappear. Once the surviving future has been mapped out, the new powers that be have no interest in preserving the memory of the competing visions that, for a time, co-existed with their own, or contributed to its shaping. If the masters of the present sometimes go so far as to alter the nature of these alternatives in the archives, or to wipe the slate clean of them, it's sufficient, most often, to let time efface their memory and erode the last signs of their existence.

So it was, very likely, with Librerías Unidas and its founders.

SHE AND BAY AND THE YEARS

She
was born
to fervour for the Revolution
when the Years
still looked to the future
nineteen sixty-six
The Year of Solidarity
with other socialist peoples

She
was two years old
in January nineteen sixty-nine
when He
cancelled Christmas
It's not
that we're proposing to change traditions
it's not
that we're renouncing forever
the classic times
we will return
to normal year ends
we will return
to normal Christmases but
the machines
must do their job
the machines
must shore up
our traditions

It was the Year of Decisive Effort
when Men
still New
and Women
capitalized too
went to the fields
proud-chinned
primed for the ten million
for the Year of the Ten Million
Tons of sugar

He
however
who had for so long cursed
the cane
vowing
to free the island from the restraints
of its exportation
suddenly now
in power
He
in the name of victory
of the new day's triumph
over the old
bent back down upon the cane

You would have thought it was Napoleon
sworn enemy of the windmill
who after driving off Snowball
from *Animal Farm*
had *never in reality*
been opposed to the windmill
and *on the contrary*

had advocated it in the beginning
but now
the erection of the windmill
had led to *unforeseen shortages*
and the harvest of ten million
had reaped only seven and a half tons
and it was Snowball's fault
and it was the *Yanquis'* fault

She
was too young
to know the choreographed pain
in the thousands of spines
that put too much faith
in the theatrics and hyperbole
of long-winded words
from a man too persuasive
to be a liar
She
was too young
to see the mounting doubts
in the sweat poured out in vain
to see the years
go grey and the poets
locked up for speaking out

As early on
as seventy-three
the Years
had consumed their hopes
for new tomorrows
with nothing to applaud
but myths and anniversaries
and rows of chairs

Nineteen eighty
the Year of the Second Congress
of her fifteenth year
and of her disillusionment
She
remembers too well
At school
there was this boy
Jesus was his name
I remember
because he was called
Jesus
one day he left with his family
the Exodus
over a hundred and fifty kilometres of sea
of a hundred and twenty-five thousand unschooled
sailors
From school
we were led
to his home
to shout insults
at his empty house
children shouting insults
at an empty house

Eighty-eight
Year Thirty of the Revolution
the year when Bay
came into the world
came out of Her belly
into the belly of Her world
it was a year
of sweet stagnation and Russian money

of victory in Angola and an Olympic affront
one of the good years
it would soon be said

Because soon came January ·
nineteen ninety
year thirty-two
of a receding dream
Bay
was not yet two
when He proclaimed
the beginning of the end
of what could be borne
a time of uncertainty
and of grave threats
a special period
in time of peace
so special *that there are things*
that escape our will
that slip through our hands
but be reassured
the Revolution will not give an inch
to anything
nor to anyone
the Revolution will not declare
capitalist reforms
bourgeois reforms
because
if the Revolution is the greatest and most extraordinary
reform in history
then why
in the absolute
should it change?

In nineteen ninety-four
the fourth year of the great involution
when despite the inches surrendered
and the bourgeois reforms
anger and hunger
again launched boats
onto the bay facing Her and Bay
She
remembers
watching the exiles for hours
dots adrift on the waters
destinies trading
one peril for another
She
remembers
having gone back home
having taken a pot of paint
having taken a brush
having painted
a single wall
for hours
with one and the same colour
and until this day
She
knows why they left
but does not know
why she painted that wall

It was also during those years
of Oceania and soup from peelings
when *it was almost normal for people over*
thirty to be frightened of their own children
that for Christmas

which no longer existed
She found
a tiny tree
and made little Bay promise
to keep their little secret
The same day at school
before parents and children
a teacher
began to curse Christmas and the infidels
of the Revolution
and Bay
turned to me
a finger on her lips to swear
that she would not talk

Since then
twenty more years have vanished
from their lives
today tomorrow
She
could leave
a bed is there for her in the north of the world
but She wants to stay
where She is herself
but Bay
she
wants to leave
just a few years
the island's shadow behind her
then return
perhaps return
she would see
but to leave only

if for all her pains
she would not find herself
cleaning toilets
in a New York McDonald's
which is what could very well happen

Hoping for a lucky star
and to no longer have to depend on her mama
at the age of twenty-seven
like Cuba relying on her lovers
at fifty-seven
Bay
lays down
her highbrow books
compromises
her pride
works as a hawker
of knick-knacks in a craft fair

One afternoon Bay and I
sipping coffee at the *paladar*
a call from a friend an offer
not to be refused
Three hundred say-oo-say
per month
entertainer in an old town hotel
shake a leg
make doe eyes
for oldsters
who have come there out of the cold
energized by the sun
and their buying power's
power

an offer
she will refuse
she can't go
that low

With Jota
her gay friend
there's a last chance plan
they call Z
The first to arrive on other shores
comes back to the island to wed the other
and to leave again
hoping not to have to mouth the alphabet
all the way down to the last letter

Bay
like She
doesn't like it
when I
in the midst of our sharing
name the hurts
evoke the contours
probe the Years
ask
for textures to be described
the exact taste of bitterness
the impact of barbs
on the heart's depths
and that *even if the potatoes*
and their absence
are political
even if *the sweat*
on the baker's brow

on his hand on the bread in the belly
of Bay's disdain
is political
even if each one or almost all Her poems
bear the signs of the ambient air
between the lines of daily life

Two thousand and sixteen
Year fifty-eight of what remains
of fifty-nine
the insidious fear the failed dreams
the distorting mirrors the inner hyena
the precariousness of hope
the erosion of meaning in words
Victory
Eternal
Invincible
Just
Popular
Loyal
Solidarity
Social-ism
Social-ist
De-mo-cra-tic
DEMO-CRACY
Free
FREE-DOM
LIB-ER-TY
re-vo-lu-tion-ary
REVOLU-TION

While She
while Bay
plug their ears
to breathe
while they
free invincible loyal revolutionary
in their fashion
care for words
In the shade cast by pedestals
the blank pages of what is to come
are wondering
how high revolutions
are able to count

THE WALLS IN WORDS

An old literary critic receives me at his home. "You'll see, Fernando knows the Cuban literary world inside out," a mutual foreign friend has told me. "And you can bring him a bag of ground coffee. That will make him happy." Fernando's apartment is tiny, poorly lit and poorly ventilated. The piles of books crowding the room speak eloquently of its denizen's priorities. A fan does its best to compensate for the cruel absence of circulating air. On this hot and humid September day, my sweat falls in large drops onto my notebook.

The friend is right. Fernando knows Cuban literature like the back of his hand. When he mentions an author, he invariably adds to his name the list of prizes they've won and the honours they've received, to attest to the worth of the work of the author in question. When I talk to him about the first years of the Revolution, he tells me the story of the birth of Imprenta Nacional de Cuba, which published and sold classics of world literature such as Cervantes's *Don Quixote* and political polemics such as *Fábula del tiburón y las sardinas* at absurdly low prices so as to make them accessible to the people. On the other hand, Fernando has never heard of the short-lived Librerías Unidas.

A light dims, the fan slows, then stops. A power failure. My drops of sweat grow larger.

During the 1960s, Cuban authors wrote little about "present realities," Fernando notes. They preferred to situate the action of their novels at the core of the heroic struggle the Cuban people had led some years earlier against the dictator Batista. It's only recently that a new generation of writers has begun to address the present day. "They're talking about it in a very raw way," Fernando says. "They're even dealing with problems such as the black market and prostitution." What Fernando omits is that there have always been Cuban authors talking about "present realities." It's just that their books were not published on the island, and they were often forced into exile because of the very nature of their writings. When I bring up the role of the censor to explain the absence of current affairs in Cuban literature over the decades, Fernando protests. The word "censor" irks him. He prefers "content revision."

"It is possible that before, there existed a process of content revision."

"It is possible or did it exist?"

"It's possible that it existed. But no longer."

These days, according to him, what is posing problems is not so much "content revision," as shortages. The "special period" was by far the hardest for literary and journalistic production. But today the lack of resources is being felt once more.

"Last month, the radio was rebroadcasting programs in order to economize on technicians and hosts."

"Does that mean that Cuba finds itself in a sort of mini special period?"

"No, no! Because the President of the Council of State Raúl Castro has said that we are not in a special period, but that we must cut costs."

Between his own assessment of what is real and the president's denial, Fernando chooses – in my company, at any rate – the second option.

I suggest to him that in this time of reforms and apparent openness, the powers that be ought sooner or later to authorize the creation of independent publishing houses. "That could happen. But there will still have to be controls. Because it must be clear to the outside world: this State is ruled by a Party." He utters his last sentence in a vexed tone of voice, as if carried away by an earnest patriotic élan. "Nowhere in the world is there freedom of the press. Everywhere, owners decide what will be published or not."

Fernando admits that the Revolution has in the past adopted certain "bad policies." He cites the removal from the shelves of the novel *Paradiso* by José Lezama Lima just after its appearance in 1966, because of certain homoerotic passages. "The error" has since been corrected. In 1991, the publisher Letras Cubanas republished *Paradiso*, which had in the meantime appeared in many languages abroad and been recognized as one of the greatest Cuban novels of the century. The recent release of *1984* is also "proof of the current openness," says Fernando. On the other hand, he provides no example of what remains to be "rectified" in the Cuban literary ecosystem. He restricts himself to pointing out what has been corrected.

Fernando, like the writers of previous decades, prefers not to launch into an analysis of the current situation, and even less to project himself into the future. He confines himself to the past, a much more certain time, because it has already been authoritatively written down, and in some instances rewritten. When I try to get to the bottom of what he is thinking, I feel his words running up against inner walls. Just when his opinions are on the verge of streaming forth, they are brought back into line. Fernando knows many things and has just as many thoughts about them, but he dares not tell me all. On sensitive questions, he dulls the impact of his facts by surrounding them with *I think* and *It's possible that* in order not to commit himself. I doubt that he still believes in the regime's infallibility or frayed ideology. But the residue of an ancestral fear born of repressive times seems to hinder him from expressing himself freely.

*

The Revolution liberated Julio Travieso Serrano. Literally. On January 1, 1959, when the rebels entered Havana a few hours after the flight of the dictator Batista, they opened the door to his cell. He had just spent an entire year there, during which time he had been beaten and tortured with electroshocks.

Before his arrest – his third and last – Julio had participated in acts of sabotage and attacks against the Havana security forces. He was part of the urban branch of Fidel Castro's 26th of July Movement. He had joined it in 1955, at the age of fifteen, even before the return from exile of its founder on board the *Granma*. Julio had just read *History Will Absolve Me*, a manifesto based on the powerful four-hour testimony Fidel gave at the time of his trial after the attack on the Moncada Barracks, the Revolution's first false start. The leader's words had convinced Julio to risk his life trying to overturn Batista. After putting the book down he told himself that Cuba deserved better than the injustices and inequalities it had known up to that point. Julio could have easily remained indifferent to the fate of his fellow citizens. Until joining the rebellion, he had not suffered from hunger or repression. His father was a sales agent. His family was middle-class. At home, there was always bread on the table. But young Julio had a thirst for social justice and freedom. After the triumph of the Revolution, he put his shoulder to the wheel and his hand on the machete like millions of Cubans who wanted to build a new world.

"We thought the future would be glorious, that we would win all it was possible to win, and that we would have a life unlike anywhere else. Those were years of enthusiasm …"

"And the years now…?"

"Are years of less enthusiasm!"

A man of letters, the author of several novels, and the translator of some great literary classics, Julio seems unable to share the words he must have long since applied to his current feelings in this post-enthusiastic time. All through our conversation in the yard of the National Union of Writers and Artists, he hides behind euphemisms, metaphors, and the unsaid, what appears to have been a great disappointment, if not a feeling of betrayal. He vividly describes what he felt when he was still in step with the Revolution, but leaves me to guess at the rest of his personal path.

"At the time, a minority was against the Revolution and a majority supported almost all the measures it adopted. Imagine if, in Canada, a leader promised you many things and, for a time, he fulfilled his promises. How would you feel?"

"The difference between Canada and here is that …"

"It's that you do not believe in great leaders!"

"No, that's not what I'm saying. The difference is that every four years we can let the leader know that we are no longer enthusiastic."

Julio emits a brief burst of laughter, approving and embittered at the same time.

"Of course, I understand. It's hard to grasp today our feelings back then. We hated the Americans and all the measures taken against them seemed to us to be good for the Revolution. But I was not the owner of a factory or a company. I didn't even own a house. No one took anything away from me. Those who had their properties confiscated were against these measures. Now, I understand the problems this posed for free enterprise and freedom of religion. At the time, I didn't."

Around 1961, Julio found himself a copy of *Animal Farm*, published by Librerías Unidas. The book is still on his shelves.

"Did you see the connection between *Animal Farm* and Cuba when you read it for the first time?

"Then, no."

"And later, yes?"

Julio pauses.

"It's a criticism ..."

He stops himself. He will go no further.

To evade my embarrassing questions, Julio resorts to a variety of strategies. Sometimes he tells me that my question "requires an answer that would take days," before offering me one that is short and evasive. At other times he brings forth contradictory arguments, nebulous and illogical, which leave me perplexed, and force me to abandon the struggle for coherence. When I underline the anti-communist nature of *1984* and suggest that its publication by Librerías Unidas seems to have been intended to warn Cubans against the danger of a totalitarian drift if there were an alignment with the USSR, he assures me that it is not an anti-communist book as such.

"Orwell was, perhaps. But Orwell and *1984* are not synonyms. The novel talks of a utopia. It criticizes utopias."

"But that's just it, in Cuba people wanted to build a uto–"

"Here, there was never any question of a utopia."

"Then it was a question of what?"

"Of reality. Not a utopia."

My aim was not to corner Julio or to at all costs face him with his contradictions. I resigned myself to respecting his walls, without believing for all that that they represented the true limits to his reflections.

It's Fernando the critic who led me to Julio the translator. He'd told me that recently, during the launching of a new edition of his translation of Bulgakov's *The Master and Margarita*, Julio had praised Arte y Literatura for at long last republishing *1984*. He had gone so far as to express the wish that *Animal Farm* would also know a second life in Cuba. Julio confirms this. That is what he said on that day. Still, he does not expand on the reasons why he was moved to praise Orwell's books in public. I can only guess by looking at his history as a translator. From the Russian, Julio has translated a few politically inoffensive classics by Gogol and Turgenev, for a Mexican publishing house. He also produced for them a translation of *We* by Yevgeny Zamyatin, which first appeared in 1920, and is considered the precursor to Huxley's *Brave New World* and Orwell's *1984*. Like *The Master and Margarita*, Zamyatin's novel was banned in the USSR during Stalin's time. It would appear that Julio has a penchant for translating books banned by communist regimes.

"Fifty years ago it would have been impossible to publish such a book," Julio says of *1984*. "But today, we are in different times."

"And they please you, these different times?"

"Of course."

In his introduction to *The Master and Margarita* – which appeared first with the Mexican publisher before having been picked up by Arte y Literatura – Julio cites an introduction by the German author and playwright Goethe to his play *Faust*:

> Whether the book *Faust* does or does not possess a goal,
> does or does not tend towards a sublime or epic state …
> there is no need to say. I firmly believe that even with a

crystal-clear intelligence and good judgment, many [readers] will have to work diligently if they are to become masters of all the secrets contained in my fable.[14]

Julio continues his prologue, saying "the secrets in *The Master and Margarita* are so numerous that the intelligent reader will have to discover them for himself."

Talking to him, I feel as if I'm being invited to play the same game that Goethe and Bulgakov urged on their readers.

*

Before the Revolution, the Kohly neighbourhood was populated by Havana's upper crust and some foreign families. Some of the residents owned pleasure boats docked on the Almendares River, the natural border on the neighbourhood's east side. The dictator Fulgencio Batista himself owned a house in Kohly. After the Revolution, the sumptuous dwellings abandoned by the aristocrats were handed over to generals and senior officials in the new regime. In the neighbourhood streets, today, the olive-green uniform is widely seen, and the Batista house has been transformed into a medical clinic for the employees of MinInt, the Ministry of the Interior.

Unlike most of the residents of Kohly, the former Senate president Lucilo de la Peña did not flee the island after the triumph of the Revolution. He remained there until his death in 1971. The revolutionary authorities allowed him to keep his large colonial mansion, which he had bought from Batista's mother-in-law. For a while he was also allowed to run his printing works and his publishing house, both called Luz-Hilo (Light–Wire), situated on Luz Street in Old Havana. It is on the presses

---

14 Translated from Julio Travieso Serrano's Spanish translation. It was not possible to locate the German original Travieso attributed to Goethe.

of Luz-Hilo that all the Librerías Unidas' books I was able to consult saw the light of day, including the first Cuban edition of *1984*.

I first heard Lucilo de la Peña's name from Julio Travieso, when I asked him if he knew what lay behind the appearance of Orwell's novels in Cuba in January 1961. According to him, de la Peña had not only printed those books but had also published them. But he advanced no tangible proof. Still, the theory was worth exploring. For the first time I had the name of someone who was perhaps closely, or at the very least distantly associated with Librerías Unidas.

Researching online, I discovered that in addition to his commercial activities and his political past, de la Peña was for a time the arbiter of duels. On the other hand, I found no proof of his presumed links with Librerías Unidas.

A column published in the Society section of a San Diego newspaper also revealed that in February 2016, during a trip to Havana, his granddaughter Mary Drake, a philanthropist living in California, found her grandfather's house while driving through Kohly in a taxi. María Elena – Mary's given name – was only eight years old when she left the island for the United States. Her father, Lucilo's son, was an officer in Batista's army. Going to knock at the door of her ancestral home, she was delighted to discover that her aunt Conchita, with whom she had had no contact since she left, still lived there. Conchita was then in Guatemala with her husband, visiting their daughters, but Mary promised to return very soon to at last be reunited with her aunt.

I contacted Mary, who gave me Conchita's number.

On the telephone, I took Lucilo de la Peña's daughter to be an old eccentric. "I have a question for you, but it will make you laugh," she tells me, when she learns where I'm from: "Are the Great Lakes Canadian or American?"

When she and her husband Enrique receive me in the backyard of their Kohly house, they confess that her problem is more serious. For years, Conchita has suffered from psychiatric problems for which she is receiving serious treatment. "Her psychiatrist has told her not to delve into her family's past," Enrique explains. "She is too emotionally affected when she talks about her father. She has also lost part of her memory of those times. If you want to talk about the books Lucilo published, there's no problem. But you must not talk about his political involvements."

Conchita's condition does seem serious. But I can see that beyond the memory loss and the pain that the awakening of certain memories might provoke in his wife, Enrique wants at all costs not to risk having any difficulties with the authorities. "I'm a retired doctor. I was a government civil servant, assistant director of the Oncology Institute for twenty-two years. And this period for Lucilo was very ... very upsetting," he admits.

"We don't want to live in the past," Conchita adds. "We are living in the present. My life today is with my husband, my children, in our house. And the rest ..." With a wave of her hand, she rejects anything beyond the perimeter to which she confines herself in order to maintain a certain mental equilibrium.

Enrique does not know if his father-in-law was behind the publication of *1984*. As far as he knows, Lucilo only published books under the rubric Luz-Hilo. "The books he published were chosen for their popularity and not their politics," he says. "If he felt that a book like *1984* might sell, he could have published it. But it's certain that he had nothing to do with questions of anti-communism or anti-capitalism."

Enrique remains evasive as to the position Lucilo de la Peña took regarding the new government after 1959. Once again, illness is a convenient alibi. "In the beginning he supported the Revolution, but then senility set in and he talked no more about it. When I met him for the first time in 1962, he was already not all there."

Enrique assures me that Lucilo did not have his businesses confiscated in the course of the nationalization of publishing houses toward the middle of 1961. According to him, they were sold to the State. "The revolutionary government had no reason to seize the businesses of people who had done nothing wrong."

I remain skeptical. Perhaps it's true that Lucilo de la Peña managed to reach an understanding with the regime in order not to lose everything. But this would clearly have been an exception. Compensation for the rich was not a common practice in the newly communist Cuba of 1961. "My father is one of the only two members of the Senate to have continued to receive his complete pension after the Revolution, because he was an honourable man," adds Conchita in one of her rare interventions.

Are there collaborators of Lucilo still alive and able to talk to me about his last active years as a printer and publisher? Enrique barely lets me finish my question. He excludes that possibility without even taking the time to consider it. As for Lucilo's archives, they were in the house's garage, and were destroyed when a cyclone tore off the roof a few years ago. I read Enrique and Conchita an email from their niece María Elena in which she asks me to pass on her "kisses and much love," promising to come and see them very soon. Enrique, who has never met her, remains on his guard. "After almost sixty years without any news, what does she want, exactly? Why not have written earlier? Why initiate a relationship now?" I point out that María Elena was a child when she left the island and that until recently communication was difficult between Cuba and the United States. "My mother was also there for a long time and I talked to her every month, or almost," Enrique replies. "It was difficult, but not impossible."

No point insisting. Enrique and Conchita are not interested in reliving memories. For almost six decades they have succeeded in having their aristocratic history forgotten. Enrique is known as a "good revolutionary." Why plunge back into a time when his social status cast doubt on his convictions? Better to leave the past where it is.

I have made little progress in my quest. Lucilo de la Peña was certainly the printer of 1984's first Cuban edition, but I'm pretty sure that he did not initiate its publication.

Once again I get closer, and then fall back.

WHY ORWELL

George Orwell never set foot in Cuba, or on the American continent. At the time of Orwell's death in January 1950, Fidel Castro was just a young lawyer newly graduated from the University of Havana, and an Orthodox Party militant. He had participated in some political actions outside the country but was still unknown to the international media. It is almost certain that George Orwell had never heard of him. As for Fidel Castro, a great reader, it is very likely that at one time or another in his life he read at least one of Orwell's classics. Who knows, perhaps he even got himself copies of the Librerías Unidas editions of *1984* and *Animal Farm* a few weeks before he shut down all the independent publishers on the island?

In his writings, Orwell many times warned against the dangers of authoritarian drift in the wake of a revolution. "History consists of a series of swindles, in which the masses are first lured into revolt by the promise of Utopia, and then, when they have done their job, are enslaved over again by new masters," he declared in a 1946 essay on the political scientist James Burnham. "You can achieve nothing unless you are willing to use force and cunning, but in using them you pervert your original aims," he wrote in an essay on Arthur Koestler, later that same year. In *1984*, Orwell suggested that the primary motivation of revolutionary movement leaders was without doubt more to slake their thirst for absolute power than to realize the ideals they were claiming to defend. "One does not establish a dictatorship in order to safeguard a revolution; one makes the revolution in order to establish the dictatorship."

Whether or not he read Orwell before or after he took power, Fidel Castro clearly did not seek to forestall the authoritarian drift of his revolution. In fact, if the *líder máximo* took any inspiration from Orwell's writings, it was certainly the better to reproduce the authoritarian apparatus the author was trying to warn his readers against.

Like Daniel and Fabricio, though in a sociopolitical context very different from theirs, I read Orwell's two antitotalitarian novels at about the age of eighteen. They shook me as well, and influenced my way of seeing the world. The co-occurrence of 1984's republication by Arte y Literatura with my first stay on the island impelled me to once again delve into the English writer's work and to inquire into his intellectual evolution. I reread his novels, and for the first time lingered over his essays. As I went on reading, Orwell and his writings assumed more and more importance in my reflections on Cuba and on the writer's political role.

One afternoon I sat down at a café in Old Havana to read "Why I Write," which Daniel had just published in *La Letra del Escriba*. Orwell sets out four factors that impel him to write:

1. Sheer egoism;
2. Aesthetic enthusiasm;
3. Historical impulse;
4. Political purpose.

Every writer tries to appear intelligent, hopes that people will talk about them, and hopes they will continue to be read after their death, Orwell writes, backing up his first point. It would be dishonest on the part of the writer to claim the contrary.

Aesthetic enthusiasm is the pleasure a writer may feel "in the impact of one sound on another, in the firmness of good prose or the rhythm of a good story." Even pamphleteers and the authors of school textbooks have recourse to certain words or expressions that serve no useful purpose and that are employed for aesthetic reasons only, he observes.

As a citizen and chronicler of his time, Orwell hopes to make a contribution by telling the story of his time to future generations. This historical motivation for writing is the "desire to see things as they are, to find out true facts and store them up for the use of posterity."

As for the political influence of his prose on his contemporaries, Orwell hopes that his writings will enable him "to push the world in a certain direction, to alter other people's idea of the kind of society that they should strive after." Thus he sees politics "in the widest possible sense," and not just as the simple defence of a cause or ideology.

"It can be seen," he goes on, "how these various impulses must war against one another, and how they must fluctuate from person to person and from time to time."

These four reasons to write, as enumerated by Orwell, are a bit like a horoscope: every writer who hopes to find themselves there will do so. That is probably what accounts for the popularity of the essay, without in any way detracting from its relevance.

Why am I writing a book about Cuba?

Out of *sheer egoism*? In part, obviously. I am not free from wanting people to interest themselves in my work, to find me intelligent, and of wanting my writing to survive me and to perpetuate my memory beyond my death.

Out of *aesthetic enthusiasm*? "When I sit down to write a book," Orwell says in "Why I Write," "I do not say to myself, 'I am going to produce a work of art.' I write it because there is some lie that I want to expose, some facts to which I want to draw attention, and my initial concern is to get a hearing. But I could not do the work of writing a book, or even a long magazine article, if it were not also an aesthetic experience." I could not have said it better.

By *historical impulse*? That is my primary reason for writing this book. Trying to encapsulate Cuba's present, I want to offer to those who will study this period in the future an added point of view regarding the events and people who will have made a mark upon it; an external perspective, different, inevitably, from the accounts of Cubans themselves.

As for my *political purpose*, I am under no illusion that my writing will be read by the great decision makers of today or tomorrow, in Cuba or elsewhere. So I doubt that I will be able to have the tiniest influence on the way things will play out. Despite this, like Winston when he writes in his diary while still being certain that it will never be read, I cannot stop myself from trying, at the very least, to paint a portrait of the present, and in the long run, to fashion a better future.

*

When Fabricio juggles with a lie or with an ethical dilemma, he sometimes turns to Orwell and asks himself what he would have done in his place. "A bit like the Christians with Jesus," he notes. Not that he is conferring on him a status akin to sanctity. It's just that he admires Orwell for his intellectual honesty and his clairvoyance, two qualities rare in his time, as in every other. "What is important to retain from his work and his life," says Daniel, for his part, "is his position as an intellectual in a very difficult context. He was simultaneously criticizing Stalinism, Nazism, and the imperialist designs of the British and American governments. He didn't care about making enemies. He defended his ideas and expressed his opinions as he understood them."

Since his death, some have criticized Orwell for the disdain he seemed to have for homosexuals, for his suspicion of Jews, for his opposition to abortion, and for the fact that he wrote essentially for a masculine readership. In his books, women characters rarely demonstrate much capacity for thought and independent action. While clearly on the Left, Orwell remained in certain respects a man of his time. Had he lived in our day, his views on these subjects might have been different. But perhaps not. What makes him now a moral authority is his capacity to face unpleasant facts, something he rightly recognized in himself, and which, he explained in "Why I Write," represented one of his primary reasons for taking to his typewriter.

Orwell knew how to denounce these disagreeable facts not only when he detected them in the declarations, the writings, and the causes of others, but more important still, in his own life, his own work, and the putting into practice of his own ideals. "Orwell as a writer was forever taking his own temperature," quipped the philosopher Christopher Hitchens in his book *Why Orwell Matters*.[15] "If the thermometer registered too high or too low, he took measures to correct matters."

---

15 Christopher Hitchens, *Why Orwell Matters* (New York: Basic Books, 2002).

Even if he declared himself to be a partisan of democratic socialism, there was no question of Orwell remaining silent when it came to the crimes of those who would have been his natural ideological allies. "I believe that the first duty of a writer is to preserve his integrity and not to allow himself to be persuaded to tell lies, to suppress facts, or to falsify personal feelings on the pretext that the truth would be 'inconvenient' or would 'play into the hands' of one or another evil influence," he said in 1947, in an interview for the French magazine *Paru*.

In "Politics and the English Language," he weighed into the poor use of the English language by his peers. But he did not fail to note that anyone reading his essay would surely decide that he is committing "the very faults I am professing against."

If he dreamed of an egalitarian, just society, he was aware that a callow idealism could prove almost as perverse as the various forms of outright discrimination. "Of course, everyone knows that class prejudice exists, but at the same time everyone claims that *he*, in some mysterious way, is exempt from it," he wrote in *The Road to Wigan Pier*, his 1937 sociological inquiry into the conditions of the working class in the north of England. "The fact that has got to be faced is that to abolish class distinctions means abolishing a part of yourself." He knew that the first battleground in working toward a more just society is to be found deep in one's own heart. Rather than to deny his prejudices and flaws, he had the courage to expose them and force himself to combat them in order to limit their influence on his actions.

All through his short life, in his actions and writings, Orwell demonstrated that the only true loyalty was to intellectual honesty. For Fabricio and Daniel, as for me, that is what explains why, sixty-six years after his death, George Orwell remains as relevant as when he was alive.

*

In 1943, six years before the appearance of *1984*, in his essay "Looking Back on the Spanish War," Orwell was already concerned that the first-hand account he had written in *Homage to Catalonia* would not in the future carry sufficient weight when faced with the propaganda and revisionism of the parties implicated in the conflict. When the time came for historians to establish the facts concerning different episodes in the war, the truth of the one would be just a valid as the truth of the other. "This kind of thing is frightening to me, because it often gives me the feeling that the very concept of objective truth is fading out of the world," Orwell wrote. He sensed the emergence of a society where a leader could dictate an unarguable alternative to the sum of two and two. And this perspective, he confessed, frightened him "much more than bombs."

*

Periodically, I find myself drawn into a debate with writer friends who contend that "everything is only fiction," and that it's vain, if not dishonest, to claim that you can "write the real," as I am trying to do. Even if I understand their desire not to let anything at all get in the way of their creative freedom, and I know that the debate will have no end, I can't stop myself from throwing myself into it. The stakes seem to me too high.

It's clear that our capacity to perceive or not certain aspects of reality, and our interest or lack of it in doing so, has an influence on the account one gives of an event. However, beyond these differences in perception, some facts remain. More frightening than bombs indeed is the idea that you can deny the very occurrence of a bombardment or the count of victims, on the pretext that objective truth does not exist. Without this bedrock of certainty, the convictions of all sorts of negationists have the same weight as the testimonies of eyewitnesses.

In 1984 Orwell talks of a world where this negation of objective reality is pushed to an extreme. In Oceania, the authorities try to control reality not only in the way it is consigned to the archives, but in the way Party members can privately perceive it.

> The Party told you to reject the evidence of your eyes and ears. It was their final, most essential command. His heart sank and he thought of the enormous power arrayed against him, the ease with which any Party intellectual would overthrow him in debate, the subtle arguments which he would not be able to understand, much less answer. And yet he was in the right! They were wrong and he was right. The obvious, the silly, and the true had got to be defended. Truisms are true, hold on to that! The solid world exists, its laws do not change. Stones are hard, water is wet, objects unsupported fall towards the earth's centre. With the feeling that he was ... setting forth an important axiom, he wrote: *Freedom is the freedom to say that two plus two make four. If that is granted, all else follows.*

If I write, it is to help ensure that in Cuba, as elsewhere, today like tomorrow, two and two continue to make four. And to arrive there, George Orwell has shown himself to be an excellent travelling companion.

TALES OF FAILURE

In the Museum of the Revolution, "there where all of history is to be found," according to the slogan inscribed on the building's exterior, the Revolution stops at 1990. The last rooms in the museum are devoted to the years 1975 to 1990. "During this period," we read, "there was a political and state restructuring as well as social and economic improvements throughout the country." Newspaper clippings, charts, and photographs attest to the advances made in several areas, such as culture, sport, and agriculture. It would of course be surprising to find in such a propagandistic museum any reference to the dismantling of almost all these gains during the "special period in time of peace" that followed. And because there have been no significant achievements since that time, and the country has never regained its former level of development, it's not unexpected that the history of the first decade and a half of the third millennium would not be included. Under the circumstances, this omission would seem to be the least depressing option.

For a movement or an individual that does not acknowledge any errors, or so few, the only failures that can be talked about are those that have been overcome, or those that allow one to more definitively affirm one's status as a victim.

The museum's first rooms contain a detailed presentation of the attack on the Moncada Barracks on July 26, 1953. That day, which was the day after the *carnaval* in Santiago de Cuba, thinking to capitalize on the soldiers' hangovers, Fidel and Raúl Castro had planned to make off with the Batista army's reserve of arms and ammunition. The poorly planned operation turned into a fiasco. Almost half of the 135 rebels were killed. The others, including Fidel and Raúl, were arrested. Nevertheless, this failure is still today regarded as the Revolution's opening act.

A bit farther on, in a room recounting the last months in the mountains before the triumph of the Revolution, I come across a reference to a man I met on my first trip to Cuba: "On October 25, 1958, the fourth front, 'Simón Bolívar,' was officially opened, under the leadership of the commander Delio Gómez Ochoa." On the photo above the text, I cannot, however, identify Ochoa among the fifteen other bearded men, all about the same age, armed and smiling. Is that him crouching down at the centre of the photo, casually pointing his revolver toward the horizon? Or is he not rather another, standing just behind, a machine gun in his hands, the shadow of whose cap masks part of his face? If the photo was in colour I would probably have had no trouble recognizing Commander Ochoa. Even if he were fifty-eight years younger, I would have been able to pick out his eyes, a rare azure blue, which, unlike the rest of his body, have made it through the years virtually intact. Before his eyes, it was his commander's uniform, however, that had attracted my attention when I saw him for the first time after the launch of a mediocre book at the fair in February. His uniform and his cap were olive green, both bearing a black and red diamond, a yellow star in the middle, symbols of the 26th of July Movement. Because even if he has commanded no more battalions during the last two-thirds of his life, Delio Gómez Ochoa still wears his uniform at public gatherings.

Like his brothers in arms, Commander Ochoa lived through the triumph of January 1959. But six months later he also experienced a defeat. A defeat that the Revolution prefers not to include in its museum.

On June 14, 1959, at the demand of Fidel Castro, Delio Gómez Ochoa landed on a beach in the Dominican Republic at the head of a small group of Cuban and exiled Dominican guerrilla fighters. The goal of these combatants, trained in Cuba over the previous months, was to replicate the Cuban scenario by overthrowing their own dictator, Rafael Trujillo. For the Cubans, it was their first attempt to export their Revolution to a neighbouring country. But the operation soon turned into a catastrophe. Most of the insurgents were killed soon after stepping onto Dominican soil. Ochoa was one of the rare survivors. He spent the next two years in the dictator's jails, where he was tortured. It took Trujillo's assassination at the hands of his own soldiers in May 1961, for him to receive a general amnesty and to return to Cuba.

Not being Joseph Stalin, Fidel Castro did not harshly punish his comrade for this failure, for which he himself was partly responsible. Ochoa was, in fact, named to a number of important posts. For a time, notably, he was the manager of Cuba's National Marble Company. His position as an apparatchik of the regime allowed him to live more comfortably than most Cubans. But he received no public honours. Castro never mentioned him in his speeches, and Ochoa had to wait until 2004 to receive an honorary rank in the Rebel Army.

In the Dominican Republic, on the other hand, his historical role is looked upon very differently. He has long been recognized as a national hero. Every June 14, he is invited to tell the story of his feat of arms in all the forums, and his valour is praised. The Dominican state awarded him two pensions. He was offered a car, an apartment, and even Dominican citizenship. There, the failed operation he headed is considered the starting point for the long struggle leading to the fall of the dictator. His failure was the first defeat *before* the great victory. In Cuba, his Dominican adventure represents the first reversal of the Revolution *after* its great victory. Hence the desire to forget it.

When I met Commander Ochoa at the book fair, I knew nothing about his past. Only his uniform and his clearly advanced age told me that he must have participated in the revolutionary struggle. A woman, probably one of the few people who knew his identity, whispered his name to me and confirmed his role in the Revolution. This was the day after Barack Obama's visit to Cuba had been announced. I hoped to get a reaction from one of the first anti-imperialist fighters to this attempt to bring the two countries closer together. "It's very good news," Delio Gómez Ochoa said to me in a hoarse voice as he leaned on his cane. "Obama is the first president to seek dialogue. He wants to put an end to this climate of perpetual tension. That's good for Cubans. We will no longer have to buy all our products from China and Russia. We'll at last be able to open ourselves to the world, and the world to us." Rather than demanding, like his predecessors, an abdication, Obama was offering, according to him, a new path. It had to be taken. Ochoa's analysis matched the official line of the regime he had served all his life and which, if it had not glorified him, had at least assured him the privileges due to his unfailing loyalty.

At the end of our short discussion, I took a photo of the old commander, with his permission. As I started to leave, he raised his index finger to stop me. He had something to add. "Delio Gómez Ochoa." He had assumed that I had only been drawn to him by his uniform and that of course, like most Cubans, I was not aware of his name nor his place in history. A few minutes earlier, his intuition would have been right.

*

In another room of the Museum of the Revolution, I recognize once again, in an old photograph, a person I've recently met in the flesh, in a very different museum from this one.

The photo in question, clearly cropped, shows two men. The one in the foreground is easily identifiable. It's Ernesto "Che" Guevara. His hair disheveled, his jacket soiled, his gaze grim, the guerrillero is not in a happy state. His hands are out of frame, but the position of his arms suggests that they are tied together. Che then has only a few hours left to live. He has just experienced his last defeat. His attempt to export the Cuban Revolution to Latin America has come to an abrupt end. At his right is one of the jailers, a young, strapping man, freshly shaved, his eyes cold. "During the year 1967," the photo's caption explains, "the CIA launched an aggressive operation against the guerrilleros operating in Bolivia. On October 9 of that same year Commander Ernesto Guevara de la Serna was assassinated in La Higuera. CIA agents of Cuban origin participated in his assassination, including Félix Ramos Rodríguez, who appears here with the prisoner Che."

When I interviewed Félix Rodríguez in January 2016, at the Bay of Pigs Museum in Miami's Little Havana, he had shown me this same photo of himself with Che. Guevara's capture was one of the highlights of his career even if, in reality, he had failed to fulfil the mission with which he had been entrusted. "We'd received orders from the CIA to bring him in alive at any cost, because we knew that there was tension between him and Castro. But the Bolivian government decided to kill him. I was the last person to talk to him," Rodríguez told me, with a certain boastfulness.

In this photograph, Félix Rodríguez is twenty-six years old. But his fight against the communists in general and the Castrists in particular had already been going on for almost ten years.

When the Revolution overthrew Batista's "constitutional government" – as he characterized his dictatorship – Rodríguez was studying at a military college in the United States. Six months later he joined an anti-communist legion and went to the Dominican Republic to defend Trujillo's tyranny against Delio Gómez Ochoa and his band's landing. In February 1961, a few weeks before the Bay of Pigs invasion, he secretly entered Havana to prepare for the taking of the capital, which was anticipated to take place once Brigade 2506 had routed the revolutionary armed forces. When the operation failed, Rodríguez took refuge in the Venezuelan embassy, where he remained stuck for five months before being given safe conduct off the island thanks to a diplomatic convention. Until Lyndon B. Johnson put an end, in 1965, to all the schemes to oust Fidel Castro's regime, Félix Rodríguez was involved in planning every one of them. Aside from the operation to capture Che in Bolivia, he took part, for the CIA, in many other missions designed to do away with the communist threat, notably in Vietnam, Ecuador, and Peru. But the "liberation" of his native island remained the fight of his life.

Times have changed since the end of the Cold War, but the convictions of Félix Rodríguez, now president of the Bay of Pigs Veterans Association, have not moderated in any way. Nor has his strategy to overthrow Castro's dictatorship. "Rather than opening up to the regime, we must close all doors in order to make their economic situation so untenable that they will have to open up," he contends. That this strategy has not worked for five decades when it has been applied by the United

States is not enough to convince him that it might not work in the future. And so he sees Obama's opening toward Cuba as a betrayal of his cause. According to him, its only effect will be "to prolong the suffering of the Cuban people and the life of the communist regime." That Obama has chosen this path does not surprise him, however, because he is convinced that the American president is a Muslim and a communist secretly sympathetic to the Castro brothers.

For dissidents like Félix Rodríguez, the failure of the Bay of Pigs invasion was the first defeat preceding a victory that, fifty-five years later, is still to come, a bit like the failed Moncada Barracks attack for Fidel Castro and his revolutionaries or, for the Dominicans, Delio Gómez Ochoa's catastrophic landing with his men in June 1959.

While waiting for the rest of the past to be worthy of the telling, the Bay of Pigs Museum, devoted to the Cuban counter-revolution, has only a single display room.

THOSE WHO KNOW

Everyone calls him Juanito. Even his email address at the Cuban Book Institute, the Instituto Cubano del Libro, or ICL, uses this nickname. Is it because he's so short that this affectionate appellation suits him well? Or might it be because Juan Rodríguez Cabrera, an energetic and likable young fifty-year-old, inspires more familiarity than formality despite his elevated status, attested to by the air conditioner in his office. I don't dare ask.

At first, it was not him but his boss who I wanted to meet. But the president of the Institute, Zuleica Romay, just back from a mission abroad, explained to me in an email that she was too far behind in her work to receive me. She therefore authorized the editorial vice-president to reply to my questions. In my initial request, I had avoided mentioning the main reason for my wanting to talk to a member of the ICL's upper management. I had simply explained that I wanted "to discuss the plans for developing the Cuban book industry, as well as the challenges it must face, such as, for example, the supply problems caused by the American embargo."

When I enter Juanito's office that Thursday morning, my plan of attack is clear: I will begin by asking him questions about the changes and challenges in the industry, and as soon as an opening presents itself, I'll try to learn more about the circumstances surrounding the publication of *1984* by Arte y Literatura.

I begin the discussion by referring to the reform of the publishing houses' economic model three years ago, which transformed some of them into "companies." "They still receive grants from the State, but only for the printing of books and the salaries of their employees," Juanito explains. "For the rest, they must rely on their sales revenues. But that doesn't mean that they can put any price they want on their books. It's the Institute that determines this, taking into account the readers' ability to pay." In what way this new model is profitable for the State, the publishers, or the readers, Juanito is unable to say. The "companies" that sell more copies certainly see more revenue, although the difference is modest given the absurdly low sales prices, and this increase only compensates for the lost grants. Since book production is still entirely controlled by the State, an increase in print runs adds to the burden on budgets. And it means printing more copies than before, which is almost impossible, given the constant shortage of paper and ink and the long delays at the printers. I begin to think that if I do not understand the logic behind this reform, it's simply because there isn't one. But Juanito is not one to question official decisions. He executes; he does not decide.

On the editorial side, the ICL's vice-president assures me that the new model has not changed the way things are done. Every publishing house, business or not, is "free to publish what it wants." Each has an editorial committee whose task is to decide on the titles that will be included in its yearly plan. This plan is submitted to the Institute, which determines whether its proposals "are compatible with the country's editorial policies." Juanito adds that the Institute sometimes recommends titles to the publishers. "But we never order them to publish anything at all." As proof, he picks up a book on his desk, called *Guía de edición* ("publishing guide"). It's a manual published in a Latin American country, and he intends to ask the Nuevo Milenio publishing house to bring it out. "But they can easily say no if they want to."

Juanito seems to have no problem explaining to me in detail the approval process for the publication of a foreign book in Cuba. The door has opened. I make my move.

"Last February, Arte y Literatura published a new edition of *1984* by George Orwell. I have to say that that surprised me. It's an anti-communist book, after all ..."

Juanito's expression suddenly changes. His gaze, up to now amiable and direct, begins to elude mine.

"We have criteria ... but the publishers can publish what they want," he repeats. "There is no censorship. As long as the book contributes something to our society, obviously."

I see him thinking aloud, looking for the right words and an escape hatch.

"We publish books that, in our opinion, stimulate thought. Books that respect our country. Not those that directly attack our thinking, that attack Cuba. We publish books that help to build a better society. I think that many people will buy [1984] and will draw their own conclusions. A book can criticize totalitarianism and socialism, but we have our views, which we also present ..."

"In the introduction?"

"In the introduction. You know, there are some writers who are very controversial, and are published here all the same. Leonardo Padura, for example ..."

"But who makes the decisions?"

"The publishing house, in collaboration with the Institute."

"But in the *precise* case of *1984*, was it the publishing house or the Institute that initiated the project?"

He pauses, his eyes still avoiding mine, and seems to be wondering what I'm getting at.

"The publishing house. In fact, you really ought to talk to the director of Arte y Literatura. He'll be able to tell you more than I can."

"Good idea. But tell me, do you sometimes have to ask the Central Committee of the Communist Party what it thinks of a book?"

"No. It's assumed that the Institute and the Ministry of Culture know what ought to be published."

Juanito finally decides to counterattack to escape the ambush I've set for him.

"Look, at first you wanted to meet the President of the Institute. I thought you wanted to discuss the book industry and not one book in particular. I was not prepared for this sort of interview."

The window has shut. I back off.

"Of course! We can return to that if you wish. They say that independent publishing houses may soon be making an appearance on the island ..."

The tension drops. We talk for a few minutes more, then he gives me to understand that he must return to his regular duties.

Just before he lets me go, he becomes anxious again.

"Do you still want to meet the President of the Institute?"

"I would have liked to, but as you know she is very busy these days. That's why she referred me to you."

"And what use will you make of our interview?"

"As I said, I'd like to write a book based on my research in Cuba. But our conversation is just one among many others."

Juanito is not naive. He sees very clearly that my goal in meeting him was to learn more about the publication of *1984*. As we part, the vexed gaze overtopping his cosmetic smile speaks volumes. I have caught him unawares. He was *not prepared for this sort of interview*, as he said himself. He didn't know what lies to tell me. Perhaps he didn't even know what truth he was to hide from me. Only his sudden shift in expression suggests to me that the logic behind the appearance of this anti-totalitarian and anti-communist novel in the communist and authoritarian regime he serves has not been entirely assimilated by all the cultural bureaucrats.

*

As Juanito has recommended, I am climbing the few floors that lead from his office to that of Arte y Literatura. If I have not tried to talk to its director, Victor Malagón, before, it's because I first wanted to try to get answers from further up in the book industry's hierarchy. My friend's conversation with an informant in the Institute's hallways during my first trip had already convinced me that I could not expect a great show of independence from the head of Arte y Literatura, given his concern for safeguarding his own position.

A secretary tells me that Victor Malagón is on a bus, on his way to the Institute. An hour later he arrives and is quick to apologize for keeping me waiting. I point out that he could not have known that I was coming.

"We have been a 'company' since 2013. We publish classic writers from various countries. In general, we try to have the copyrights and translation rights ceded, because we don't have the means to pay for them ..."

The opening comes more quickly than with Juanito.

Unlike his hierarchical superior, Victor Malagón has no trouble explaining to me how *1984* ended up in his catalogue. And I'm not the first one to have posed the question. He says he has received many such inquiries by phone and email from all over the world. If this book has not been published before, he explains, it's in the first place a question of copyright. Orwell's work has been in the public domain only since the year 2000. And then they would have had to pay for the Spanish translation. So came the idea to commission a new translation on the island, which would be much less expensive. "We would have liked to publish the book a year earlier, but the translator's computer broke down," he adds. Even if I know that the delay was really caused by Fabricio's procrastination, and that his computer never ceased to function during this period, and that he never used this as an excuse, I do not contradict Malagón. Never mind flawed memories and little lies, what interests me are the real reasons behind the publication.

"Orwell's essays are much better, but *1984* is a classic, it's his best-known book," Malagón goes on. "They say it's a critique of socialism, but I don't think Orwell was anti-communist."

"All the same, he criticized authoritarian regimes ..."

"Which are the most authoritarian regimes in our day? Those of the great empires, the great powers! Look at England, there are cameras everywhere in the streets!"

The director of Arte y Literatura assures me that, contrary to what many people have assumed, *1984*'s publication had nothing to do with "the changes now taking place" in Cuba. To prove it, he asserts that the decision was taken even before the announcement of warmer relations between the United States and Cuba – which I knew already.

"But who exactly had the initial idea to publish the book?"

"I don't remember, because these are decisions taken together, during our editorial meetings."

"Was there no one in particular on the committee who proposed the book?"

"No, we all proposed it together."

"And the decision didn't come from higher up?"

"Of course not!"

Victor Malagón is categorical. It's the publishing house that initiated the publication of 1984, and its approval by upper echelons proceeded as smoothly as with other books. The information I've received from other sources, indicating that the order came from "higher up," incites me to be just as categorical: Victor Malagón is lying. That moment of astral coincidence when the members of the editorial committee *all proposed together* the republishing of a book that first appeared sixty-five years earlier, never occurred. Malagón probably knows, better that Juanito, the smallest detail of how 1984 turned up in the publication plans of his publishing house. Unsurprisingly, he prefers not to share that with me.

As I get ready to leave his office, Malagón hands me the latest issue of *La Letra del Escriba*, which he has just received. It's the January–February issue that includes Orwell's "Why I Write." "You should propose your book on Cuba to the publisher Nuevo Milenio, for translation into Spanish," he suggests, standing in the doorway. Hiding my astonishment as best I can, I thank him, and assure him that I intend to follow his advice.

SMALL FATES

It's 6:30 a.m. I've been awake for a good while, trying to think about what I still have to do and the people I have to meet before leaving Havana tomorrow. Through the window, I hear the wailing of sirens: fire engines. I get up, dress, and go out to see what is happening, hoping at the same time to catch the sunrise on the Malecón. A column of smoke, visible in the first light of dawn, guides me toward the site of the fire, four streets away from my *casa particular*. A yellow ribbon of the PNR, the National Revolutionary Police, is blocking access to a section of Campanario Street, between Concordia and Neptuno. Surrounded by a cloud of smoke, the firemen are battling the flames, already invisible. The fire must have been small, and there are probably no victims.

A few of the curious, early risers, late-to-beds, insomniacs, and light sleepers, are taking a look at what is happening on the other side of the yellow ribbon. In the zone that is now out of bounds to ordinary people, a police officer is filming the scene with his telephone. I pull out mine and begin taking photos. After two clicks, an officer lowers my arm. "No photographs," he tells me, without any particular emotion.

Tomorrow, in the paper, there will be no fire at 253 Campanario Street, in Centro Habana. There will be Raúl Castro Ruz, who is receiving a foreign dignitary, and vice-president Miguel Díaz-Canel, who is assessing the progress of important projects somewhere in the country. There will be the celebration of the fifty-eighth anniversary of a revolutionary action, and a reminder in the headline that the embargo is the main obstacle to development in Cuba. But there will be no mention of the fire. Because there are never fires in Cuba, as there are never murders, never suicides, never robberies, never car or workplace accidents, never instances of prostitution, never scams, and of course, never shortages. Unless you can blame the United States, a mosquito, or Mother Nature, life in Cuba, officially, knows no hazards.

It is easy to forget, at a distance of five decades, that things were once different. There was a time when the newspapers still spoke of the imperfections of the aspiring "New Man," and of the world in which he lived. It was in leafing through 1961's newspapers that I came to this realization. At that time, the Revolution had not yet taken control of all facets of life and of all accounts of the surrounding world in the media. For a few months more, it was possible for an independent publisher to print anti-totalitarian novels and for papers to feature miscellaneous news items.

In its column "The Police Roundup," in January 1960, the daily *Prensa Libre*, for example, reported the following events:

> The young Migdalia Morejón Ruiz, twenty years old, residing at 273 Nueva del Pilar Street, was found dead by the cleaning services of an establishment at the corner of Cristina and Arroyo. Near the body was a bottle containing the residue of a rapid dyeing solution.

> Luis López López, fifty-three years old, residing at 2614 37th Avenue, suffered serious injuries when the car he was driving collided with a PNR patrol car driven by the security guard Ismael Suarez, at the corner of 41st Avenue and 112th Street in Marianao.

> The PNR has arrested the brothers Luis and Pedro Sánchez Vera, respectively seventeen and sixteen years old. They are accused of being the perpetrators of a robbery of more than five hundred pesos, committed in a house belonging to René Mesa and situated at 5838 41st Avenue in Mariano.

> The worker Gilberto Torres González, thirty-four years old, living at 61 O'Farrill in La Vibora, suffered serious injuries in falling from a building under construction on 3rd Street, between I and J, in the neighbourhood of Dolores. He was transported to the Calixto García Hospital.

> The police have arrested the shopkeeper Luis Francisco
> Achón, residing at 5428 25th Avenue, after he tried to bribe
> the commercial inspector Rogelio Rodríguez Perera, who
> discovered that hidden in his shop were sixty bags of pow-
> dered detergent.

In countries enjoying considerable freedom of the press, people at times take exception to the amount of editorial space allotted to such minor items. The accounts of these vice and crime police reports are regarded, often rightly, as an expression of unhealthy, sensationalistic voyeurism having little to do with what is in the public interest. But it is when they vanish from the news that one grasps their importance in describing and helping to understand the real world.

What started the fire at 253 Campanario Street on September 21, 2016, early in the morning? A forgotten cigarette? A pyromaniac? A gas leak? A short circuit? Was it an isolated incident or common enough that it's worth the trouble to look more closely at its cause? Should those living in the neighbourhood fear other fires of that kind? With no answers in the media, they can only resort to hearsay to gauge the gravity of the situation.

A few days ago, about a hundred metres from the site of the fire, a German friend was the target of an attempted purse snatching by some young people who had followed her from the Malecón to a quiet street. They weren't armed, they didn't hurt her, and when she cried out they fled without the purse. Amateur thieves, nothing more. But does this incident conceal others? Is there a resurgence of robberies in the streets of Havana, up to now thought to be one of the safest cities on the continent? Have the socio-economic reforms of recent years and the subsequent rise in inequality triggered an increase in petty criminality? Not having access to a wider picture of what is really happening, the citizen and visitor can only trust their personal experiences and their perception of danger to decide whether they must exercise more caution when they walk through the capital's streets.

On another day, still in Centro Habana, I happened by chance on the police raid of an apartment. "It's all about drugs," whispered the neighbours. Are consumption and trafficking on the rise on the island? Have the police just locked up users, local traffickers, or was it the boss man of a network with global connections? Is Cuba's opening onto the world transforming it into a narco-state, as some people fear, given its proximity to the enormous North American market?

In February, Jean-Guy Allard told me the story of a Korean who, recently, chose death over incarceration. Rather than surrender to the police when an agent came to his hotel room in the Vedado neighbourhood with an Interpol warrant to take him into custody, he leaped from his balcony. How had Jean-Guy learned of this story, which was not covered by the Cuban press? The former news reporter simply replied, "Everything gets known." Clearly, he'd heard from his Cuban colleagues' horses' mouths what they could not write in the State media. For years Cuba has been taking in American citizens and those from elsewhere who are fleeing the justice system in their home countries. This attempt to arrest the Korean, was it the sign of a political shift on the part of the Cuban government, one that would have implications for them? Would other sought-after criminals have already been deported in secret?

Two weeks later in Santa Clara, I was told that a man who had killed his wife the day before was apparently still roaming the city. Was he still armed and dangerous? What did he look like? What should one do if he was spotted nearby? Neither the radio, nor the television, nor the newspapers breathed a word about this. Given the official non-existence of crime, hearsay was the only available source of information for fearful citizens.

Why, for decades, have the Cuban media not reported news items and other vagaries of daily life on the island? I have no idea if the practice was formally forbidden at a certain time, or if it simply stopped when the revolutionary government tightened its control over the country's media. But the motives behind their disappearance is clear: for a regime that seeks to control the present, the past, and the future, each of these "small fates,"[16] is, by its often unforeseen and unforeseeable nature, highly disturbing. Because every murder, robbery, suicide, fire, and accident is a reminder that despite all its efforts, all the repression it exercises, and all the restrictions it imposes, the regime will never have total control over reality. To limit the impact these events might have on its power if they were described and tallied, it nevertheless ensures that the knowledge of them will not go beyond the small circle of those who have been directly affected. It is easier, then, to deny certain details of these incidents or, quite simply, that they ever happened.

In Orwell's Oceania, where reality is robbed of its indisputable existence, the regime can shape it as it wishes, and force its citizens to believe its own version. In Cuba, the Party does not have that power. Its monopoly of the media, however, makes it hard to shed light on an event or a series of events. If it's possible to deny that a fire occurred at 253 Campanario Street on September 21, 2016, at about six o'clock, how could one prove that in the end it was the authorities' negligence that was responsible?

In recent years, on blogs or news sites based offshore, or, more rarely, in Cuba, reporters and journalists have begun to expose the less glorious aspects of life on the island. Given limited access to the internet and the surveillance of the authorities, their scope, as well as their impact, have been restricted. Still, slowly but surely, stories of daily life are beginning to circulate in the Cuban world. More and more it's become possible to quantify problems, to paint a broader picture of certain situations, to correlate, to gauge tendencies, or, in the end, to identify the roles played by chance, by individuals, by the system, or by the Party, in these tragedies.

But this progress will not repair the damage already caused. The five-decade archival gap in objective reality will never be totally filled. In the absence of trustworthy data regarding many aspects of life during this period, comparisons will be hard to make. Assuming the regime will

---

16 The American writer Teju Cole's ingenious translation of the French term "faits divers."

one day lose control of the present and future, how will we be able to tell with any certainty if life was better *before* the Revolution, *under* the Revolution, or *after* the Revolution?

*

The day of the fire, in the afternoon, I spend a few hours at Daniel's, talking with him and Fabricio. It's probably the last time we'll see each other for quite a while. I'm not planning to return to Cuba before my book comes out.

As usual, Daniel is smoking one cigarette after another. And as usual, every time he lights a cigarette, he has to contend with the inferior quality of Cuban matches. Several do not contain enough sulphur to catch fire, or to burn for more than one or two seconds. On others, the frictional surface is so irregular that it makes lighting the match impossible. Some matches are even bonded at the tip, like conjoined twins attached at their heads, making them unusable.

Daniel's T-shirt also attracts my attention. It reads, in large letters, "Winston." Daniel had not even noticed. It's a clothing brand, but the fortuitous correspondence with the first name of *1984*'s protagonist makes us laugh. Especially since if there is one person in Cuba who most resembles Winston Smith, it's Daniel Díaz Mantilla. Long before I did, Daniel became interested in the archives from the time of the Revolution. He wanted to know "how things developed to be what they are today." He asked friends and acquaintances to transfer onto USB drives digitized copies of the magazines and papers of the period, he looked at the first films censored by the revolutionary government, and he read the books published during those years. "Reading those old documents, we are always surprised to see how different things were back in the early sixties, how the Party has changed through each period, how they manage to 'forget' – or make people forget – what they used to say some years earlier, and how they defend ideas they had previously considered heretical."

A few years ago, Daniel went to the corner of Luz and Compostela streets, on the Plazoleta de Belén, to see what had become of the Luz-Hilo printery. According to the colophons, it's here that between 1959 and 1961, several books that were later de facto forbidden, including Orwell's *1984*, were printed. When he passed by, there was a small plaque over a downstairs door as a reminder that the building had once housed a printing house. The second floor was uninhabited, no longer had a roof, and its walls were in ruins. When I went there myself just recently, the building was in the same condition, but I searched in vain for the plaque. "It's probably been torn off," an old woman told me, herself surprised by its disappearance. Time's wear and tear or a malicious hand had erased the last sign of Lucilo de la Peña's printing business.

Before leaving them, I share with Fabricio and Daniel an idea that has been going through my mind regarding my book, almost all of whose pages at that point are still to be written. A bit like Winston writing "DOWN WITH BIG BROTHER" in his diary, I am thinking of writing, somewhere in my book, black on white: "I HATE FIDEL CASTRO." Even if this sentence does not really reflect my feelings, I want to mark out as clearly as possible the frontier between what is acceptable and what is not in Cuba's present-day literary world. Several books published by State publishing houses now openly criticize or denounce some aspects of the Cuban system. But in 2016, it is still unthinkable to print and distribute on the island a book in which the author or one of his protagonists states plainly and unmetaphorically that he detests the historic leader of the Cuban Revolution. By deliberately ensuring my book will be banned, I could perhaps make it a bellwether of censorship for the years to come. The day when it would appear in Cuba in a Spanish version would be a clear sign that the last taboo had been lifted.

Daniel and Fabricio find the idea interesting. Or at least, they don't try to discourage me. I remind them, however, that as we agreed, I intend to quote them in the book. Some of the opinions and stories they have shared with me, without any self-censorship, might not please the Cuban authorities and some of their colleagues in the literary world. If they prefer that I omit anything that might cause them trouble, I will do so.

"I don't care," Daniel replies. "You can quote me as you wish. And you can even say that me too, I hate *him*."

I turn to Fabricio.

"I would hate *him* also, if only I could have strong enough feelings!"

All three of us burst out laughing.

I'll miss these two.

SEPTEMBER 23, 2016 TO FEBRUARY 5, 2017

BETWEEN TWO TRIPS II

THE EXPECTED AND
THE UNEXPECTED

She ought not to have lost, but she lost. He ought not to have won, but he won. Under the presidency of Hillary Clinton, American policies toward Cuba would likely have continued to follow Barack Obama's lead, easing relations. Instead of that, the White House will be led by a man with no coherent program on Cuba or most other issues.

Two weeks before the vote, in a desperate attempt to rally Cuban Americans and to win the state of Florida, Donald J. Trump visited the Bay of Pigs Museum in Miami. After having been the only candidate for the Republican nomination showing himself favourable to Obama's policies on the subject of Cuba, he promised to cancel them in their entirety if elected. This turnabout won him the official support of the Bay of Pigs Veterans Association and of its president, Félix Rodriguez.

On November 8, 2016, Trump won one hundred thousand more votes than Clinton in the "Sunshine State," picking up its twenty-nine electoral college votes.

*

Old Raúl is sitting at a desk. He is wearing his usual olive-green shirt, bedecked with medals and military insignia. On the wooden wall behind him are hung the portraits of José Martí, Antonio Maceo, and Máximo Gómez, three heroes of the War of Independence of 1895–1898. On the table below are laid out black and white photographs of other prominent figures in Cuban history and a few knick-knacks. The eighty-year-old holds in his hands a single sheet of paper. He reads its contents slowly, lifting his eyes briefly to the camera. His expression is serious, but betrays no sadness.

Dear Cuban people, it is with deep sorrow that I am here to inform our people, our friends in Our America and the world, that today, November 25, at 10:29 in the evening, the Commander-in-Chief of the Cuban Revolution, Fidel Castro Ruz, died. Following the wishes expressed by Comrade Fidel, his remains will be incinerated. In the first hour of Saturday the twenty-sixth, the commission for the organization of funerals will provide our people with detailed information regarding the organization of the posthumous tribute in honour of the founder of the Cuban Revolution.

For the last sentence of his speech, Raúl Castro lifts his chin and raises his voice, looking directly into the camera's lens.

"*¡Hasta la victoria, siempre!*"

("Ever onward to victory!")

When the news of Fidel's death turns up on my phone, I am in Bombay, 14,600 kilometres from Havana. During the hours that follow, I check out the comments on different media outlets' Facebook pages. In Europe and Canada, about half of those commenting on the internet salute this "great man who was able to stand up to the Americans." A quarter of them are ambivalent as to his legacy, while acknowledging that Fidel never left anyone indifferent. A final quarter rejoice and are happy to wish him "good riddance." In the comment section of the American mass media, praise is virtually non-existent and "good riddance" is the norm.

The disappearance of a dictator still in power is never good news. Fidel had the decency to leave power before death took it from him. He perhaps deserves no gratitude for that, but the Cuban people should be relieved. His death will not have the impact that it would have had ten years earlier. But all the same. Fidel is dead. *The* Fidel. Fidel the unkillable. He who boasted of having escaped hundreds of assassination attempts, many that the CIA acknowledge having planned. Over the years, the Americans tried to poison his cigars and his pen, to have him killed by a traitor in his entourage, to booby-trap a seashell so it would explode when he was on a dive. They thought of rendering him beardless with a chemical depilatory so as to compromise his aura of a bearded *guerrillero*. This is not to mention the many invasion plans to overthrow his regime. But nothing and no one got the better of him, and he died his good death, at the age of ninety, probably in his bed, surrounded by those close to him, like an ordinary man.

*

A week after the *Comandante*'s death, I learn that Les Offices jeunesse internationaux du Québec (LOJIQ; the International Youth Offices of Québec) are looking for five authors up to the age of thirty-five to participate in the Havana International Book Fair as part of the Canadian delegation, Canada being the invited country for the twenty-sixth edition. After having attended the launch of *1984* during the previous edition, this is my chance to return to the fair, now as a participating author. Thinking about that possibility, I get an idea for an experimental chapter written especially for the fair, but which would also have its place toward the end of my book. I apply to the organization, throw myself into the writing of that chapter, and even before getting a reply, finish the first draft of "An Anticipatory Tale." The email from LOJIQ informing me that I have received one of the grants arrives a few days later, in mid-December.

I will be going back to Havana.

*

On January 8, 2017, one month before my third trip to Cuba, a character in my book writes me to ask for "a favour that is not small." He's hoping to go to the United States to move in with a loved one who's already there. To do so, he's worked out a plan: If I can arrange for an event in

Canada to which he would be invited, he'd only have to present himself at the American border to take advantage of the policy called "Wet feet, dry feet," from the Cuban Adjustment Act of 1966, guaranteeing asylum to any Cuban who succeeds in setting foot on American soil. Would I be prepared to do him this service? I reply the same day: *What a silly question. Of course I'll help you.*

I write a few people to propose setting up a talk that would capitalize on this person's expertise. I say nothing about his true intentions.

Four days later, one week from the end of his presidency, Barack Obama announces the repeal, to take effect immediately, of the "Wet feet, dry feet" policy, which has been in force for fifty years. "By taking this step, we are treating Cuban migrants the same way we treat migrants from other countries," declares the outgoing president. The cancelling of this preferential policy is to be expected in the context of the coming together of the two countries. But for Cubans on a cobbled-together raft in the middle of the Florida Strait while the president is pronouncing these words, for those others working their way up the American continent to the Mexican–American border, and for my lovelorn character, this announcement brings a sudden end to their hopes.

*

On January 20, 2017, Donald J. Trump is sworn in as the forty-fifth president of the United States of America. Aerial images show that the crowd assembled in front of the Capitol building on that day is much smaller than the crowds during the two swearing-in ceremonies for Barack Obama. The new president's team doesn't see it that way. During his first press conference, White House press secretary Sean Spicer accuses the media of having knowingly underestimated the size of the crowd. "This was the largest audience ever to attend a swearing-in – period," he declares angrily. The next day a host on the NBC network asks the president's adviser Kellyanne Conway to justify Spicer's resorting to an "obvious falsehood." It was not a falsehood, she replies. The spokesperson was simply offering *"alternative facts."* The commentators are quick to characterize this expression as "Orwellian."

Over the following days, sales of *1984* increase 9,500 percent in the United States, propelling Orwell's dystopian novel to the top of Amazon.com's sales figures.

FEBRUARY 6 TO 16, 2017

THIRD TRIP

AFTER FIDEL

His body has been ashes for more than two months, but on the shop fronts, the billboards, and the walls of Havana, Fidel is outliving his death.

Fidel is Cuba.

Fidel is the people.

I am Fidel.

His last wishes had, however, been categorical: there was no question of promoting a cult of personality after his death. He refused to be transformed into a statue, a park, a square, a street, an institution, an honorary title, and even less an advertising or marketing product. But he had neglected to mention posters.

The taxi taking me from the airport to my *casa particular* passes through Revolution Square. That is where Fidel's funeral procession began on November 29. It's also where he pronounced several of his interminable speeches. On the front of the Ministry of the Interior, a steel-rod sculpture representing Che Guevara's face reminds the people that they must continue the battle, whatever it costs, "ever onward to victory." On the next building, housing the Ministry of Computer Science and Communications, there is the beautiful, angelic face of comrade Camilo Cienfuegos, killed in an airplane accident at the age of twenty-seven, less than a year after the triumph of the Revolution. He is giving his blessing to the *Comandante* as on the very first day: "You're doing well, Fidel," says the quote under his portrait. Death struck down Camilo and Che before the disenchantment. Despite the passing of time, the mistakes, the failures and the betrayals, their support for all that was and all that will be is there forever.

On the east side of Revolution Square is the José Martí National Library, and on the south side, a commemorative monument 109 metres high, glorifying this historical figure. Across the country, hundreds of squares, parks, and institutions bear the name of the father of the Cuban nation. His books know no shortage of ink and paper. Their printing takes priority over all others. During his entire career, Fidel Castro laid claim to the heritage of José Martí. "In Cuba, there was only one Revolution," he said: that begun by Martí in 1895, and that he, Fidel, had led to victory in 1959. Were he alive today, Castro insisted, Martí the anti-imperialist would certainly have supported the Revolution. His conviction that he was acting according to the precepts of the "prophet" was not unlike that of his predecessors and detractors. It was Fulgencio Batista who had, during his reign, raised the monument to Martí on Revolution Square, then known as Civic Square. In Florida, the dissidents have, since the beginning of their exile, named their squares, their schools, and even their gyms after José Martí. Félix Rodríguez, Che's jailer, had even tried to persuade me that if he were still alive today, the democrat Martí would never have supported Castro and his band of communists.

At the end of December, one month after Fidel's death, the Cuban parliament officially banned the appropriation of his name and his image. Unlike Che, he would never become "the man on the T-shirt." And unlike Martí, he would perhaps escape being one day transformed into a seal of approval for a regime he had never seen born, or that was an utterly distorted version of the system he'd put in place. Fidel knew better than anyone that the living have a strong tendency to manipulate the memory of the dead so that they can continue to serve their own cause even from the grave. He knew it because that's exactly, for a half-century, how he exploited his comrades Ernesto and Camilo, along with José Martí.

In making their ruling, the legislators, however, neglected to stipulate the sanctions facing those who would violate their leader's last wish. If I were an artist in Cuba these days, I would be strongly tempted to erect a statue of Fidel Castro in a public place to see if the authorities would dare to take it down in the name of law and order ...

Fidel is Cuba. Fidel is the people. I am Fidel. What the posters proclaim is that still today, to offend Fidel, dead or alive, means offending every Cuban. To offend Fidel is to betray Cuba. But if no man is an island, no island either ought to be a man.

During the year 2016 that has just ended, Cuba received four million visitors, or 11 percent more than the previous year. This increase was largely attributable to the influx of American tourists, who capitalized both on the relaxation of travel restrictions decreed by the now ex-president Obama, and the introduction of many cheap and direct flights to the island. The increase was not enough, however, to keep the Cuban economy afloat, as it shrank by 0.9 percent during the same period, primarily because of the great reduction in low-priced shipments of oil from Venezuela. Caught up in a serious political, social, and economic crisis, the Venezuelan president Nicolás Maduro could no longer permit himself the luxury of the oil in exchange for medicine formula, put in place by his predecessor, Hugo Chávez.

For Cuba, 2016 represented its first year of decline since 1993, or since the "special period in time of peace" that followed on the end of economic support from the Soviet Union – another ally that was very generous until its own internal problems caught up with it.

Despite the recession, construction sites continue to flourish in Havana, primarily in the old city. One of the most important is that of Manzana de Gómez, in front of the Parque Central, where the work proceeds twenty-four hours a day, seven days a week. By the end of the year, in this entirely restored building that, at the start of the twentieth century, housed the country's first mall, there should open the Gran Hotel Manzana Kempinski, a five-star establishment with 246 rooms. A few foreign companies, such as the Spanish brand Mango, should also be setting up shop there.

Passing near the site, I spot a few workers of Indian origin trying as best they can to communicate with their Cuban colleagues. Last summer, the disclosure of their presence on the site by the Reuters news agency caused a commotion, at least among the few Cubans who heard about it, the state media not having relayed the information.[17] In 2014, for the first time since the Revolution, a legislative change had opened the door to the hiring of foreign workers on the island. But it was specified in the law that this course ought to be taken only under "exceptional circumstances." Beyond the hiring of a hundred South Asian workers, what was most shocking in this revelation was the fact that they were being paid ten times more than their Cuban fellow workers by the French industrial giant Bouygues, in charge of the project. It took three months of marination in the regime's inner workings before an official response to the scandal emerged. Only in October was it slipped into an article on foreign investment in the tourist industry, which appeared in *Juventud Rebelde*.[18] Part way through her text, the journalist from Cuban youth's daily newspaper confessed her surprise at seeing Indian workers on the Manzana site. According to her, this feeling was "perhaps [attributable to her] lack of in-depth knowledge concerning current labour supply problems in the construction sector." Indeed, as a representative of Almest, one of the two companies controlled by the Revolutionary Armed Forces and responsible for the project, explained to her, the hiring of these foreigners was "essentially due to the need to make up for delays in the construction calendar's critical path." Since "the output of Indian workers is three to four times superior to the average within the country" and "the result of their work is of very high quality … their presence makes for an efficient workday, and enhanced productivity."

In a few lines, the *Juventud Rebelde* had not only justified in doubtful fashion a situation that was as dubious as the rationale itself, but had grossly insulted the Cuban workers on the site, implying that they were less competent and lazier than the Indians. The article obviously did not entertain the hypothesis that it was perhaps the pay gap that explained the presumed lack of enthusiasm on the part of the Cubans. Nor did it

---

17 Marc Frank, "Indians Help Build Cuba Hotels as Foreign Labor Ban Weakens," *Reuters*, July 21, 2016.

18 Marianela Martin González, "Sacudir la palanca de las inversiones turísticas," *Juventud Rebelde*, October 15, 2016.

mention that Bouygues very probably paid a sum that was equivalent to or superior to the Indians' salary for the employment of each Cuban on the site, but in conformity with the law in place the State kept almost all of it, leaving only crumbs for the workers.

In Cuba in 2017, State capitalism is on the march. The army, the extent of whose commercial activities are only vaguely known, signs large, opaque contracts with foreign investors. Meanwhile, ordinary Cubans are refused the right to negotiate directly with foreigners, on the pretext that capitalists are the enemy of the Cuban nation and the socialist dream. The highly ranked military in charge of the tourist industry's enterprises seem to be those who profit the most from this cheap workforce that has no other options.

The situation is reminiscent of the "fairy tale" written by George Orwell and published in 1945. In *Animal Farm: A Fairy Story* – the full original title – he tells of how the pigs, now the new ruling class of Animal Farm, succeeded in secretly altering one by one the seven basic commandments of the Revolution in order to better serve their own interests. At the end of the tale, though the animals are certain they've not long ago read on the barn wall that *Whatever goes upon two legs is an enemy* and *All animals are equal*, they realize that there is only one commandment remaining, and that it is curiously different from what they remember: *All animals are equal, but some animals are more equal than others.*

During the book's final drinking bout, while the pigs and the neighbouring farmers are celebrating, inside the ex-master's house, the end of their hostilities and the beginning of their partnership, the animals who are less equal than the pigs surreptitiously observe the scene through a window.

> And Mr. Pilkington once again congratulated the pigs on the low rations, the long working hours, and the general absence of pampering which he had observed on Animal Farm ...

He believed that he was right in saying that the lower animals on Animal Farm did more work and received less food than any animals in the county. ...

Between pigs and human beings there was not, and there need not be, any clash of interests whatever. Their struggles and their difficulties were one. Was not the labour problem the same everywhere? ...

Twelve voices were shouting in anger, and they were all alike. No question, now, what had happened to the faces of the pigs. The creatures outside looked from pig to man, and from man to pig, and from pig to man again; but already it was impossible to say which was which.[19]

*

These days in Havana, it's very hard to find a spot in a *colectivo*. The government has just launched an offensive against drivers who own their own vehicles, and who they suspect of enriching themselves a bit more than they should. Just a few days ago, the approximately seven thousand *boteros* in the capital were still able to decide on the price for each trip. As a general rule, they charged between ten and twenty Cuban pesos, depending on the distance, and double at night. Now, on February 8, the government has decided to impose fixed rates. A short trip could now not cost more than five pesos. Reacting to this imposition, the drivers have decided to reduce their trip distances in order to limit their gas consumption. Fewer and fewer of them are going to out-of-the-way neighbourhoods, and several are refusing to take clients whose itinerary would not be sufficiently profitable. Despite risking the loss of their licences, most drivers continue to charge the same rates. If they stage a strike, as they are threatening to do, it will

---

19 All references to *Animal Farm* are taken from the 2008 Penguin UK edition.

be the first time since the Revolution disallowed work stoppages that these will be used as a pressure tactic. For the clients, the situation has become unbearable. "I have to lie to the drivers for them to take me," says María, who lives in Vedado. "I tell them that I'm going as far as the old town, then I get off at the edge of Centro Habana, and give them only ten pesos," rather than the twenty she would have to spend if she went beyond that point. "They're mad, but there's nothing they can do."

*

One afternoon, at about 2:30, I go to the corner of O and 17th streets in Vedado. While writing the chapter "A Banal Accident" a few weeks ago, I had to ask Fabricio to describe for me the exact location of our near-disaster on the way to the launch of 1984. I now want to take some time to check out the geography of the place, in order to add details, if I need them, to my description of the scene.

Approaching the intersection, I think I'm hallucinating. An ambulance is on the shoulder, flipped onto its side, about twenty metres from a sedan with a crumpled hood. If people were hurt, they've already been taken away. All that's left are two policemen and a few onlookers.

Fabricio was right. Yet the warnings at this intersection are clear. The sign *Ceda el paso* ("yield") should have alerted the driver of the sedan, like Fabricio's father almost one year ago and at almost the same hour, that vehicles coming along O Street have priority over those on 17th.

Is this just a coincidence, or are accidents common early in the afternoon at this intersection? Might it be the shadow cast by the large residential building on the south-west side that darkens the sign at this hour, so that drivers don't see it? If the Havana papers one day resume printing news of road hazards, it will perhaps be possible to know the truth and to act in such a way as to prevent other unhappy accidents.

*

Fabricio turned forty-four yesterday. After years being afraid of "adding to the ambient noise" of bad literature, he has just started writing again. And he has realized that he's writing "not too badly." He's even thinking of leaving his publishing job to concentrate on writing essays. Just one text published on the webzine Hypermedia Magazine or another Cuban diaspora site in Florida or Spain could bring in more than his monthly salary at Letras Cubanas: thirty convertible pesos per appearance, versus the equivalent of eighteen at the publishing house where, it's true, he's not asked to do much work in exchange for his salary. "I'd like to publish two essays per month, but I'd have to do a lot of research for each one," complains Fabricio, who in an ideal world would be paid to stay home and read. Eventually, he'd like to be able to put together a collection of his essays in order to submit it for the Alejo Carpentier Prize, which amounts to three thousand CUC.

Fabricio will perhaps have competition. Daniel also wants to write enough essays to make a book. And he is further ahead than Fabricio. But Daniel doesn't think that his collection will be published in Cuba. For two reasons. First, because he has no intention of making any compromises as to the content. And second, because in any case, recurrent problems in the industry make any book's publication difficult, whatever the writer has to say. Daniel is well placed to know. None of the poetry collections he has edited in recent months will be out in time for this year's book fair. Unión Editions has run up too many debts with the printers. As long as those are not honoured, their books will not go to press. At this point, Daniel is not that concerned with what will happen to his collection. "I don't want that to affect my writing. For the moment, I'm writing, that's all."

In a few days I'll be reading the Spanish translation of "An Anticipatory Tale" at an event associated with the book fair at the Dulce María Loynaz Cultural Centre. Zurelys López Amaya, a prominent poet who works at the Centre and who is also Daniel's wife, has been able to get me what I want: a time slot that is mine alone. In the official program, my "Relato de anticipación" is described as an excerpt from the "novel [sic] *Antes del después*." During the event, it's announced, I will be introduced by Daniel, and a "conversation concerning the anticipatory tale as a narrative strategy" will follow my reading.

Neither Daniel, nor Fabricio, nor Zurelys, have read my chapter. They're intrigued but are respecting my wish to keep its contents secret until the event. In fact, only one person living on the island has read it up to now: a translator who refused to produce a Spanish version, saying she did not agree with what I had written.

QUESTIONS OF CONTEXT

Toc ... Toc Toc ... Toc

A microphone attached to a broom handle strikes a wall at irregular intervals. The movement of the microphone's pole is being generated by the motor from an old fan installed on a high shelf. Behind the wall, a loudspeaker amplifies the sound produced by each impact.

Alejandro Figueredo Díaz-Perera's installation at the Havana Hispanic American Cultural Centre is called *The Silence (...) Is Overrated.* The title refers to an older work by Joseph Beuys, *The Silence of Marcel Duchamp Is Overrated.* In 1964, the German artist wanted to denounce the decision by Duchamp, one of the most influential creators of his time, to stop producing works of art. For Beuys, art was inseparable from having one's say. To go on influencing society, an artist must continue to create. Alejandro has picked up on Beuys's words, but has given them his own meaning. For him, silence is not always a choice to be made. Sometimes circumstances prevent us from speaking out or force us to be silent. And so his installation is wilfully made up of incongruous elements that, put together, perform an action that is just as incongruous. "A fan motor is supposed to stir the air by revolving its blades," the artist reminds me. "But here the motor is the wrong way round and is trying to raise up a microphone so it will produce a sound and will talk."

I saw *The Silence (...) Is Overrated* for the first time in February 2015, in Chicago, the city where Alejandro and I both happened to be living at the time. During the exhibition's three weeks, Alejandro spent every day in silence, without reading or writing, confined in a narrow corridor behind the wall on which the microphone was knocking. The trap door through which he fed himself was his only contact with the outside world. Passing through the room you sometimes heard him coughing, sniffing, or stirring. But you never saw him. He was invisible. Invisible but distinctly present, like the immigrant he was, in an irregular situation not unlike that of millions of others on the move in American society, trying not to attract the attention of the authorities.

The previous year, Alejandro landed in the United States with an artist's visa, but determined to indefinitely prolong his stay. His loved one is American, and he wanted to pursue his career in a setting freer than that of Cuba. When his visa expired, he became an undocumented immigrant. After a year he would be able to ask for a green card, but until he was regularized it was best for him not to make any waves or hazard a wrong word. During the exhibition at the Chicago Artists Coalition, every knocking of the microphone against the wall was a reminder to the visitor that in that same room, but behind a wall, the artist, present but unseen, was not having his say.

In recreating his work in Havana, Alejandro was met with a different order of difficulties. In America, he had half-forgotten Cuba's day-to-day realities. He lost "a whole day combing through the city" in search of a wooden broom handle on which to affix the microphone. "This problem of reproducing the installation here is the metaphor that comes closest to the metaphor of the work itself," the twenty-five-year-old artist declares. Like the motor and the fan, he had the feeling he was effectuating an action that went against nature. The lack of materials on the island militates in favour of silence.

Like the right to speak out, *Silence (…) Is Overrated* is precarious. Every time Alejandro installs it, he can't be sure if it will still be working by the end of the exhibition's run. At any moment the motor might stop, or the microphone might break or damage the wall.

When he decided to go silent, Marcel Duchamp was at the height of his career and of his influence on the art world. In choosing silence at a time when people were eager for his words and his works, he turned this rare privilege to account by investing an absence of words with a power exceeding that of words themselves. "Perhaps in the arts, silence is stronger than a cry," Alejandro reflects aloud. "But in real life, you usually have to cry to get what you want. And even when fighting with all your might, it's not certain that you'll obtain it."

Technically speaking, whether it's installed in Chicago or Havana, *Silence (…) Is Overrated* is the same work. It's the context in which it is presented that moves the spectator to modify their interpretation of silence. In the United States, the First Amendment of the Constitution guarantees freedom of expression. But certain circumstances, like those in which Alejandro found himself before obtaining his green card, incite one to opt for silence. In Cuba, the constitution guarantees nothing, given the arbitrariness of the regime. The limits to freedom of expression are constantly shifting, and all those who express themselves in public must take the measure of where they are when they are speaking out. When things are not clear, self-censorship prevails.

The impact and the implications of silence vary, depending on the context. Just like with words. Saying goodbye to Alejandro, I invite him to the public reading of my "Anticipatory Tale," two days hence.

"You'll see," I tell him, "your installation and my text are not so remote from one another."

*

It's past eleven o'clock at the Havana International Book Fair. The Canadian Pavilion has just been opened. In Room K8 of la Cabaña, Margaret Atwood and her partner, Graeme Gibson, will soon be presenting the Cuban editions of their books in the company of a panel of Cuban authors, including Daniel. Meanwhile, a few metres away, in front of Room K11, the line is growing. The readers are anxious to obtain the Canadian books that will be on sale. A Canadian official is going back and forth between K8 and K11, fuming. "The Cuban employees are delaying the opening and snapping the books up for themselves!" Given the limited buying power of the Cubans, the Canadian delegation came up with the idea of purchasing the books from the publishers at cost and reselling them greatly reduced, while absorbing the difference. The three available copies of my book *Allers simples: Aventures journalistiques en Post-Soviétie* and the ten of *Ukraine à fragmentation*[20] are priced at five CUC, less than a quarter of what they sell for in Canada.

When Room K11 finally opens its doors, all the dictionaries are already gone from the shelves. The buyers hurl themselves toward the second-favourite items, the children's books in English at ten convertible centavos each. French titles like mine attract little attention.

A few minutes before the opening – I'm told this later – Cuban officials came to examine the books on the shelves to be sure that they in fact corresponded to the list submitted by the Canadian delegation. Passing in front of the stand of the Toronto publisher Between the Lines, a deputy to the Minister of Culture asked to borrow "for consultation" the only available copy of *Cuba Beyond the Beach: Stories of Life in Havana*. In this book – which, it seems, escaped the vigilance of the censors when the list was being approved – the scholar Karen Dubinsky, not without humour, sketches the portraits of various residents of the Cuban capital. When the minister's deputy returned a few minutes later, the book in hand, she declared that it would be "tolerated." On the other hand, even if she didn't dare to say so, another title by the same publisher made her ill at ease: the essay *Serial Girls: From Barbie to Pussy Riot* by Martine Delvaux. Her malaise had nothing to do with the content, but only the cover, on which one could see bare-breasted women. Discreetly, the deputy turned the book so that it faced the shelf, and then left.

A few weeks earlier, during the preliminary approval process, the Cuban authorities had demanded the removal of only one book, the erotic novel *Baiser* by Marie Gray.

Clearly, sex remains a literary matter that is more disturbing to the regime than politics.

---

20 Later published in translation as *For Want of a Fir Tree: Ukraïne Undone* (Montréal: Linda Leith Publishing, 2018).

*

In November 1949, two months before George Orwell's death, his agent Leonard Moore sent him a request from Kraft Editions in Buenos Aires. The publishing house had just completed a first translation into Spanish of *1984*, but hoped to remove 140 lines of the original version. In Juan Perón's Catholic Argentina, the publishers feared that those passages would serve as a pretext for the authorities to ban the novel. None of the problematic passages were political in nature. All described the intimate relations between Winston and Julia.

Three months later in Spain, when the Franco censors authorized the publication of another translation of *1984*, they too demanded the removal of segments dealing with the couple's sex life.[21]

*

Thursday night, at the Fábrica de Arte Cubano. The Jerry Cans (ᐸᐃ ᐃᒡᓴᐅᑎᒃᑯᑦ / *Pai Gaalaqautikkut*), originally from Iqaluit in Nunavut, are playing a few songs in front of a diverse crowd, partly Cuban and partly foreign. The musicians are part of the Canadian delegation to the book fair. Their rhythmic songs are part country and part folk, but the originality of their music is to be found above all in the Inuit throat singing (ᑲᑕᔮᖅ / *katajjaq*) that accompanies their melodies. The lead singer is in particularly good form. Toward the middle of the show, he announces that the next song, called "Kituriat," or "mosquitos" in Inuktitut, talks of an "evil man," the former Canadian prime minister Stephen Harper. Some approving applause is heard.

Like most of the people present, I don't understand their language. But I can't stop myself from showing a smile, given the irony of the

21   On this subject, see Alberto Lázaro, "La satira de George Orwell ante la censura española," *Proceedings of the XXVth AEDEAN Conference* (Granada: Universidad de Granada, 2001).

situation. A Canadian band being invited to give a show in an authoritarian regime is singing an activist song attacking the democratically elected ex-leader of their own country. Harper could have still been in power, or the song could have targeted the current Prime Minister, Justin Trudeau, and no Canadian official would ever have dared suggest to the Jerry Cans that they draw on a different part of their repertoire.

A few days later, during a cocktail party, I share my observation with a member of the band. He confesses that before their show, the musicians were advised – he didn't say by whom – to "be careful" of the words they used on stage. Not to protect the image of Canada and its leaders, but so as not to offend their Cuban hosts.

*

Esmeralda, my host in Havana, did not attend Fidel's funeral in November, although Revolution Square is not far from where she lives. "I don't go out much. I can't walk for long," she says to excuse herself, busily dusting the kitchen, while I attack the copious breakfast she has prepared for me. Something tells me that the reason for her absence from the funeral is to be found elsewhere. Fidel and his regime do not seem very dear to her heart. I let her open herself up bit by bit.

"What was your reaction when you learned of his death?"

"Everyone has to die sooner or later."

"Yes, that's true. But perhaps things are going to change now, especially after Raúl leaves in a year …"

"He's already said in the past that he would leave, so we'll have to see if it's true this time. And we don't know who will take his place."

"Miguel Díaz-Canel, no?"

"Impossible. He's not part of the family. It will have to be someone from the family. Only the family."

To justify her skepticism, Esmeralda reminds me of the fate of the former vice-president, Carlos Lage Dávila. In 2009, at the age of fifty-seven, he was seen as the successor to Raúl. Credited with the modest economic reforms that had helped the country to emerge from its "special period," he was the incarnation of a renewed regime. When the revolutionaries of the "historical generation" retired, he and a few other apparatchiks of his generation would assume their roles. That seemed to be Carlos Lage's future.

Until one day the carpet was pulled out from under him.

One Monday in March, Raúl announced that Carlos Lage was being relieved of his duties within the Council of State. The next day, in *Granma*, Fidel came out of retirement and criticized – without naming names – Lage and the Minister of Foreign Affairs, also fired. "The sweet nectar of power, for which they had made no sacrifice, awoke in them ambitions that led them to play a disgraceful role," Fidel wrote. On Wednesday, the same paper published a letter signed by Carlos Lage. He announced his retirement from all his government and Party functions. "I acknowledge the mistakes committed and take responsibility. I feel that the analysis performed at the last meeting of the Politburo was fair and thorough," Lage went on to say, without giving any hint as to the nature of the errors he had supposedly made.

"They say that during a party, he made a bad joke concerning Fidel, and that led to his removal," Esmeralda says. "Afterwards he became a simple doctor again, with no decision-making power. He worked near here. I often saw him passing in the street."

This anecdote and others make Esmeralda think that it's false to believe that Cuba is in the process of changing.

"They say there's freedom of expression, but it's not true. When I go out in the street, I say nothing suspicious, because you never know who might be listening."

"But it's better than before, no?"

"What?! Go, try speaking freely, just to see!"

"We will see," I say under my breath, without Esmeralda, still dusting away, being able to hear me.

¡LA LITERATURA ES MUY PELIGROSA!

It's Québec Day at the book fair. The ministers have not yet made their opening speeches, and I've not yet opened my mouth in public, when I find myself at the centre of a diplomatic incident.

Very late yesterday, Arnold August, an anglophone Montréaler responsible for chairing the panel on which I'm to be participating in the afternoon, sent an email to the Cuban and Canadian organizers, presenting them with an ultimatum: either I am excluded from the event, or he will refuse to moderate the discussion. To back up his demand, he drew attention to an obituary I wrote for Fidel Castro on the news site Ricochet Media in which I took a critical look at his legacy.[22] "Despite the tenacious romanticism that surrounds and will certainly continue to surround the man," I wrote, among other things, "we must recognize that in reality, Fidel Castro will have left the Cuban people with more problems than solutions."

An official with the delegation tells me he was up all night trying to devise a strategy to resolve the crisis, along with the office of the Québec Minister of International Relations Christine St-Pierre, who arrived in Cuba the previous evening. For the moment, the Cuban side has not reacted to the pro-Castro Montréaler's group email. As of now, this is only an *attempt* to create a diplomatic incident. The official also takes care to reassure me: there is no question of my being excluded from the event. August is not officially part of the delegation. He has been invited to host the panel "as a courtesy," because of his well-known interest in Cuban politics, and because he was already on the island, having self-financed his trip. Since he refuses to sit at my side, August will be replaced by another moderator.

---

22 Frédérick Lavoie, "Après Castro," Ricochet Media, November 29, 2016, ricochet.media/fr/1556/apres-castro.

Faced with a Québec official suffering from stress and sleeplessness, I still find it hard to conceal a certain satisfaction. My book is being written before my eyes. For a year I've been exploring the limits imposed on freedom of expression in Cuba, and here I am, myself the victim of an attempt at censorship, not on the part of a representative of the Cuban regime, as one might have expected, but from one of my own fellow citizens.

At about ten o'clock, under the tent set up in front of the Canadian Pavilion, Minister St-Pierre officially opens Québec Day. In her speech, she underlines "the great mutual interest" the Cuban and Québec cultural worlds have in forging bonds. The Cuban Minister of Culture, Abel Prieto, succeeds her at the microphone. "By promoting Québécois artists, we are also promoting a true culture. And that helps us to combat the dominance of American cultural imperialism," declares Prieto, considered one of the regime's powers behind the throne. At the end of his speech, all smiles, he kisses the Québec minister on the cheek and wraps her in his arms. Everyone is happy.

The ceremony ends with a performance by the acrobat Patrick Léonard from the troupe Les 7 Doigts ("the 7 fingers"). He begins by announcing in broken Spanish the theme of his performance: "*¡La literatura es muy peligrosa!*" Literature is very dangerous. To prove it, he climbs onto a table covered with books and balances a schoolroom chair on four glass bottles. He climbs onto the chair and, slowly, slides his body between the back and the chair seat, then stretches his arm out toward the piles of books, from which he pulls a copy of the Spanish translation of Gaston Miron's *L'homme rapaillé.* The master of ceremony, Québec writer Maya Ombasic, reads an excerpt.

> Y me escribo bajo la ley antimotines
> quiero sangrar sobre ustedes por todo el afecto
> escribo, escribo hasta volverme un loco
> hasta hacerme el juglar del rey de cada quien
> voluntario en la subasta de la irrisión
> mi risa en tañidos de cascabeles por sus cabezas

en zozobras de lluvia entre sus piernas
Pero no puedo desprenderme del conglomerado
soy el petirrojo de la fragua
la colilla de la sobrevivencia, el hombre agónico[23]

Soon after the end of the poem, the acrobat completes his 360-degree rotation under the seat, and sits on the chair. The amused crowd applauds. "And don't forget," Léonard reminds us, one more time. "Literature is very dangerous!"

*

During the fair, a foreign writer is awarded an honour for her last book, just translated and published in Cuba. A few chapters of the book take place on the island. The writer describes her love for the country and its people, but also includes the views of people more critical of the regime. In the Cuban version of the book, the attacks on the system expressed by a few individuals have been translated in their entirety. In fact, from all the sensitive passages, the Cuban publisher has removed only a single word: "Fidel."

*

According to the Cuban Book Institute's statistics, the bestselling book on the island during 2016 was *Raúl Castro: un hombre en Revolución* ("Raúl Castro: a man in revolution"), a biography of the president written by his old friend Nikolai S. Leonov, an ex-officer of the KGB. In second place is a new translation of an old foreign classic: *1984.*

---

23 Gaston Miron, "El hombre agonico," in *El hombre redivivo*, translated by Marco Antonio Campos and Hernán Bravo Varela (México: Universidad nacional autónoma de México; Trois-Rivières, QC: Écrits des Forges, 2001).

*

On the eve of the launch of 1984 in February 2016, Fabricio shared with me his suspicion that the Cuban authorities had perhaps permitted the reissuing of Orwell's novel because they had come to the conclusion that "literature is not dangerous, that a book will change nothing."

During the Cold War, the Soviets, like the Americans, invested heavily in the distribution across the world of novels, essays, and other works that directly or indirectly promoted their ideology and their political goals. In the mutually hostile and binary world of those years, the competing power's literature was dangerous, especially when it reached third states that each adversary wanted to absorb into its sphere of influence.

In an email exchange a few months ago, William Lenderking, an American diplomat posted in Havana between March 1959 and May 1960, told me that during that period he had been aware of the Soviet's superiority when it came to literary propaganda. During the year he spent on the island, he noticed that the Cuban bookstores and libraries were being filled with Russian works translated into Spanish by Soviet publishing houses. "In Havana, I don't remember seeing a single book whose translation was financed by the USIA or CIA," he wrote. And so he came to the conclusion that the American program "wasn't in the same league in either depth or breadth with what the Soviet Union was offering. They understood the importance of ideas and argumentation much better than we did."[24]

Since the fall of the Iron Curtain, literature is more rarely used as an ideological propaganda weapon. Still, some countries see books and other cultural products as tools of soft power. This influence is exerted most often in an indirect, even unintentional way, with no political

---

24 This last quote is taken from an interview given by Lenderking to the Association for Diplomatic Studies and Training in the context of the Foreign Affairs Oral History Project (memory.loc .gov/service/mss/mfdip/2010/2010len01/2010len01.pdf).

interference by governments in the content exported. American publishers who came to meet their equivalents during the fair last year were not trying to convert communist readers to capitalism, but to foster a new market in order to convert Cuban pesos into American dollars.

At the pace at which the country is turning toward a market economy and its dogmas are eroding, literature in Cuba is less and less seen as an ideological weapon and more and more as a simple commercial product. However, as the censoring of a first name in the foreign author's book, and that of Ionesco's *Exit the King* in its adaptation, have shown, there is a line that may still not be crossed: when it comes to Fidel, literature remains, potentially, very dangerous.

But what happens if a writer manages to cross this line without the censor having the time to act?

HIDE-AND-SEEK

Nibbling
>at the future's roots
>for want of a bone
>to gnaw

Gobbling
>raw
>what is now
>with no great faith
>in skies of blue
>mortality's ashes
>how things add up

Wary
>of the staunchest
>most reliable
>instincts
>because *what if*
>>*if on the other hand*
>>>*if there's a five-percent chance*

Reading
>in the innards of what's unsaid
>the intents
>of the docile
>>the servile
>>>the stiflers

Playing

    at hide-and-seek

    with the powerful

    most often means

    being two steps behind

    in their game

    most often

    but not forever

    but not always

AN ANTICIPATORY TALE

I'm sitting in front of an audience. I'm speaking words into a microphone. My voice resonates in the room.

Can I be heard in the back?

A few people have come to listen to me. I'm a Canadian writer invited to the twenty-sixth edition of the Havana International Book Fair. I am reading a Spanish translation of a chapter from *Avant l'après: Voyage à Cuba avec George Orwell*, still being written.

I recognize a few faces. I see Daniel and Fabricio, of course. They are two of the main characters in my book. If you've read the previous pages, you already know that. During my other visits here, I've spent hours talking with them about Cuba, *1984*, George Orwell, literature, and many other things. In September, before leaving the island, thinking I would not return before the publication of this book, I asked them if they would let me share our discussions. Up to then, their agreement had been only tacit. Daniel replied that he didn't care, that I could quote him as much as I wanted and just as I wanted. The same for Fabricio. That is what I've done.

Another person, absent today, told me that if ever she had to leave Cuba for good one day she would not want it to be because of me. It would be because she had herself chosen to do so. I could tell the story of her life, but she asked me not to reveal her name. That's what I've done. In my opinion, she's overestimated my importance and that of my writings. But she and you know it better than I do: here, even now, you never can tell.

I set my eyes once more on the people gathered before me. I recognize several faces. But not all.

Do they understand what's happening?

The future is a time that is by definition unforeseeable. The variables that must come together to transform it into the present are so many and so varied that any attempt to predict it is doomed to be inexact, at least in part.

All it would take, for example, is for one person in the room to stand up and cut me off, for the fragile control I am exerting over the immediate future between these four walls, to break down.

I look at my hands. They are trembling slightly. I'm nervous. It's that I know what's coming, if everything proceeds as planned. Still, I don't think I'll cause a huge scandal, and even less that I'll be stopped or thrown out of the country. It's just that I hate awkward situations. Especially if I'm to blame for them. And I think I'm going to create one.

Today, tomorrow, or another day, a rumour will perhaps circulate, by word of mouth or through the independent media online, that a Canadian writer pronounced words that people prefer not to say aloud, in public, in Cuba. If ever this event is discussed in *Granma* or *Juventud Rebelde*, it will be in one of two ways: either it will be said that Frédérick Lavoie, a Canadian writer, read an excerpt from his next book dealing with Cuba, without revealing the contents of this excerpt; or they will denounce the excerpt's contents without citing them and without saying who is the author and in what context he read it aloud.

On entering the country a few days ago, I read carefully the warning on the customs declaration form:

> The importation or exportation of explosives, drugs, nar-
> cotics, psychotropic substances, as well as literature, articles,
> and objects that are obscene, pornographic, or posing a
> threat to the national interest, is forbidden.

But how to know if these sheets of paper I'm holding in my hands and that I had in my baggage when coming through customs are "posing a threat to the national interest"? Who has the power and the competence to judge?

In the year 2000, during a stay in Havana, an Indian journalist I know met a Ghanaian medical student whose copy of *1984* had been confiscated on his arrival in Cuba. You have to believe that he had happened upon a customs officer who was mad about literature.

Then suddenly, in February of last year, at this same book fair, without any law or official rule being changed, the publisher Arte y Literatura made this same Orwell novel available to Cuban readers.

All that is to tell you that even if I am *nervous,* even if I tremble, I'm not really *afraid* of expressing myself before you today. More than a million of my fellow Canadian citizens come to Cuba every year and are treated like royalty by Cubans and the country's authorities. Even when they behave terribly. Why should it be any different for me?

Many people in Havana have already warned me that the book fair is one of the few events, along with the contemporary art biennial, when Cubans and invited foreigners can permit themselves to widen the scope of free speech in the country. Tania Bruguera already put this to the test with *Tatlin's Murmur #6,* in 2009. When she installed a microphone in a closed room during the biennial so that citizens could express themselves openly, she was not sanctioned by the authorities. They only denounced her action. On the other hand, when she declared five years later that she intended to repeat this performance on Revolution Square, she found herself in a lot of trouble: arrested for "resistance and public disorder," and her passport confiscated.

In *1984,* George Orwell imagined a society where a single party in power was able not only to control the present, but also the past, and even the future. I don't know if the English writer really believed in the possible advent of such a regime, one that was foolproof and indestructible. Myself, I do not believe in it.

As Daniel demonstrated in his excellent essay on *1984,* by reducing totalitarian reality purely to its political dimension, Orwell omitted other potential sources of corruption in the system that could in the long run threaten its survival.[25] Anyone who has lived through a "special period," Daniel emphasizes, knows that shortages push people to act outside the ethical and ideological norms they have up to that point respected. And that is what marks the beginning of the end of a system.

---

25   Daniel Díaz Mantilla, "1984," Hypermedia Magazine, March 30, 2016.

· Dictatorships always live on time borrowed from freedom. That is why they don't like the future. It frightens them more than anything else. Seeking absolute control over the lives of their citizens, they impose on themselves the Herculean task of having to forestall all dissent, any flaw in the system. But that is tiring, this constant vigilance and repression. It tires the people, but also the regime. All the more in that, unlike democratic regimes, dictatorships have no horizon on which to lean if they want to regenerate themselves: no election to lose, and so no time in opposition, relieved of the burden of power. Dictatorships are condemned to proclaiming themselves eternal and trying to be so. That is why they age so badly.

In his dystopia, George Orwell wanted to resolve the problem of sustainability by placing in power an immortal Big Brother. Immortal, because imaginary. Except that in the real world, as we can see clearly in our time, neither the big nor the little brothers are eternal.

In 1955, six years after the publication of *1984*, an ambitious young man who was not yet thirty years old at the time, but who was to make his mark on the history of his little country and that of the entire world, declared: "Despots disappear, the people remain." Is it this small fund of humility, well camouflaged behind an outsize ego, that pushed him to demand that no statue in his likeness be erected after he died? Or would it rather be because, all-powerful in his lifetime, he feared the day when he would have to look up from his grave and see his bronze statue being thrown to the pavement, without his being able to do anything about it?

I stop for a moment to take a sip of water. I cast my gaze over the room.

I observe that up to now I have been able to maintain control of the future.

I continue reading.

I hate Fidel Castro.
I hate Raúl Castro.

I'm the one who wrote those words, and I'm the one who's speaking them in public right now, here at the Havana International Book Fair on February 14, 2017. Fidel has been dead for two and a half months. Raúl is still in power.

I wrote those words, they are coming out of my mouth and yet they do not reflect my thinking. I do not hate either of the Castro brothers. It would be more accurate to say that I don't particularly like them, that I disapprove of the way in which they have ruled Cuba, and I believe that their policies have done more harm to the island than good. But that's only my opinion, based on observations, encounters, and readings. I don't have to live my daily life within the system they've put in place. I do not have the intention nor the desire and even less the means to overthrow the current constitutional order in Cuba. In fact, I believe that the sudden collapse of the regime installed by the Castro brothers would be a catastrophe for the country. I wish rather, for the Cubans, a gradual transition toward a system in which they would have more control over their individual and collective destinies. But that, too, is only my opinion.

I hate Fidel Castro.
I hate Raúl Castro.

This hatred is not mine. But it certainly is that of at least a few of the people in this room today. I adopt it on principle, only. It should frighten no one.

I cite Article 144 of the Cuban penal code, entitled *Desacato.* Paragraph 1:

> He who threatens, slanders, defames, insults, injures, or in
> any manner angers or offends, by his words or his writings,
> in his dignity or his modesty, an authority of the public
> service or one of his agents or auxiliaries in the exercise
> of his functions, or in other circumstances, or because of

his functions, incurs a punishment of the loss of liberty for three months to a year or a fine of one hundred to three hundred assessments or both.

Paragraph 2 stipulates that for such an offence committed against the president of the Council of State and other important figures in authority, the sanction is three years of imprisonment.

As you know – since the State media are not your only source of information – the graffiti artist Danilo Maldonado, alias El Sexto, spent nine months in prison for having wanted to release into the streets of Havana two pigs on which he had inscribed the names Fidel and Raúl. The performance was called *Rebelión en la granja*, as are all the Spanish editions of George Orwell's *Animal Farm*. The citizen Maldonado was condemned on the basis of this same article 144 of the penal code.

Have I offended, personally or legally, the President of the Council of State Raúl Castro by affirming that I hate him? If so, will he or another competent authority order my arrest in virtue of this ambiguous law?

I doubt it. In these times of state capitalism, when the regime is trying to attract foreign investors, I daresay that one would not want to alienate as loyal an ally as Canada by imprisoning one of its citizens for impoliteness. But perhaps I am wrong. We'll see. I do not control this aspect of the future.

In any case, it would be sad. For me, obviously, in my slummy prison. But for Raúl as well. Why should he need my love or even my respect? Why should someone so powerful care about my opinion or that of some ordinary Cuban citizen who has decided to take to their pen or their microphone in public?

What could he be afraid of?

The question is so naive that it merits a response. It's too bad that this microphone's wire is not long enough to reach the person most concerned.

I take another gulp of water. My hands are still trembling. At least the worst is over. I sweep my eyes across the room to get some sense of the mood. My myopia, and above all the fact that I am not Cuban, make it hard for me to see in the public's eyes just what feelings I've been able to arouse. Uneasiness? Boredom? Indifference? Satisfaction? Irritation?

At the end of January last year, learning that Arte y Literatura was preparing to publish *1984*, I launched myself into a pursuit to try and find out how this came to be. Why did a publishing house under the control of a single-party communist regime suddenly bring out one of the most notorious of anti-totalitarian novels?

I soon saw that, for the Cuban literary world, it would have been much more significant if they had announced the release of the complete works of Heberto Padilla, Reinaldo Arenas, Guillermo Cabrera Infante, or another "problematic" Cuban writer. Still, I continued to believe that this decision could not have been taken lightly. Those who authorized it must have known that it would raise questions, both in Cuba and abroad.

A year later, as I have related in the earlier chapters of this book, I don't know much more. Essentially, I've only collected rumours, speculations, deductions, half-truths, and lies. No solid facts.

Yet my questions are simple: Who, toward the beginning of the year 2014, had the idea of publishing *1984* in Cuba? Who approved the idea? And why?

Several factors come into play in a publisher's decision to publish one book rather than another. In Cuba, some titles are rejected on the pretext that they are not compatible with the Revolution. Other excellent books are turned away because they conflict with the commercial interests of the house. In the case of foreign translations, the at-times elevated copyright costs also become part of the equation. And so in Cuba a writer generally has to be dead for fifty years in order to be published. Unless he has ceded his rights at no charge during his lifetime.

Following the example of my fellow Canadian, Margaret Atwood, I am today removing the principal obstacle to an eventual publication of my writings in Cuba, if ever they were judged to be of interest:

I, Frédérick Lavoie, author of *Avant l'après: Voyage à Cuba avec George Orwell,* hereby declare that I am ceding the whole of my copyright to any publishing house that would wish to publish this book in its entirety in Spanish translation on the territory of the Republic of Cuba.

To my mind, the best way to guarantee an interest in my book on the part of Cuban readers would be to end it by revealing to them what was behind the publication of *1984* by Arte y Literatura in 2016. It would only be a simple anecdote, yes, but it would be one, I believe, that would say much about the functioning of current Cuban society and its political regime. If ever you receive any information on the subject, I would ask you to pass it on to me as soon as possible, so that I can include it in this book. I would be eternally grateful.

On this note I will conclude, and I leave this event's future in your hands.

Thank you for your attention.

BEYOND ANTICIPATION

Applause.

Daniel grabs his glass of water at the same time as the base of his microphone, which he pulls toward him while shifting in his chair. "Uh ... well." There is laughter from the audience, of relief, perhaps. A brief smile appears at the corners of Daniel's mouth. He brings his glass to his lips and swallows. "That was rather ... intense," he says, after a pause. "Frédérick has kept all this secret until now. And so it's a surprise. I'm going to try to organize my thoughts, but they might seem a bit erratic."

He doesn't say so aloud – perhaps because he is still making up his mind – but he doesn't fully agree with my approach. Each person's feelings toward certain leaders have their importance, he acknowledges that, but what Cuban society most needs at this time is a "space for dialogue," where the citizens might "express their doubts as to the rulers' decisions, and where these rulers would be led to justify their decisions and their positions and to recognize the mistakes they have made." But often it's just this voicing of over-passionate feelings with regard to the leaders, feelings running from excessive admiration to immeasurable hatred, that prevents Cubans from entering into a "serene and constructive" dialogue on the future of their society. In affirming that I hate Fidel and Raúl, I have, according to Daniel, automatically made my entire argument unacceptable in the eyes of those who support the regime. If I had chosen another approach, they might have considered certain aspects of it.

Daniel gives the public the floor. A Cuban in the first row says he's in general agreement with me as to the need for change in Cuban society. But he does not elaborate further. A Puerto Rican author – who was the only person to disturb my reading when he had a sneezing fit – asserts that for him, to wholly understand the situation in Cuba, in Puerto Rico, and elsewhere in Latin America, one must also pay attention to another form of totalitarianism, unseen and indirect: capitalist totalitarianism. The last person to speak is the Cuban writer Raúl Flores Iriarte, a friend of Daniel. I recognize him now. It was him, the previous September, putting up posters in the Alma Mater bookstore and discussing *1984* with the bookseller. "I think it's good, what you're doing with your book," he says. "It's a bit … quite provocative. On the other hand, even if you cede your copyright, I doubt that your book will be published in Cuba." The public again bursts out laughing. "But it's good. And in a way, I think that's what has merited you a room empty of Cubans."

Too intent on my text, I had not noticed that among the twenty or so people present, at least four had left the Federico García Lorca room during my reading. The Cubans represented only a fraction of the public – made up mainly of young Latin American writers invited by the Dulce María Loynaz Centre, and writers from the Québec delegation – but apparently, all those who left were Cubans. One woman had told a friend that she had to get back to work right away. A poet had justified his departure to a Québécois poet by telling her that politics didn't interest him.

Final applause. People disperse.

I approach Zurelys. I excuse myself for putting her in an awkward position as the organizer of the event. If I had not shared the contents of my chapter before, it was so that she could now plead ignorance. "Don't worry," she replies, "I'm not afraid."

In the courtyard of the cultural centre, I ask Fabricio what he thought of my reading. He says he has to reflect for a while before answering, but for the moment he has just one objection: I ought to have said "**O***dio a Fidel Castro*" and not "*Odi***o** … " I'd put the accent on the wrong syllable. And yet I had practised each word's diction in Spanish for a long time. I knew you had to say "*futuro*," "*pasado*," "*régimen*" in the singular, but "*regímenes*" in the plural. Only the pronunciation of hate had eluded me.

"And if ever you see a Lada with no licence plate coming toward you," Fabricio adds, "walk faster!"

*

The next day, I find Daniel at home. "At one point in your reading," he tells me, "I thought that people would be waiting for us at the exit to take us to Villa Marista," the general headquarters for the security services. He does not, however, remember what part of my text brought this thought to mind.

Daniel also tells me that rumours of "An Anticipatory Tale" had reached the ears of the top authorities. The director of the Dulce María Loynaz Centre, Jésus David Curbelo – whom I'd met a year ago during the visit from American publishers – had been ordered to prepare a report on what had taken place. For the moment, he had been able to reassure *them*. Daniel and Zurelys had received instructions not to spread the word about the affair any further. "They said that *they* would perhaps be in touch with us. If we're called upon, it will probably not be a pleasant meeting. But it could be instructive. In any case, what can *they* do? Fire me? Perhaps. Put me in prison? I don't think so," Daniel reflects. Despite our disagreements, he insists that he's not angry with me. If he loses his job, that will give him more time to concentrate on his essays.

A few hours later, I go to see Fabricio. I urge him to tell me more about what he thought of my reading. "Your chapter was very good, very well written." That's all I can get out of him. But coming from him, it's like getting the Nobel Prize.

*

Two days after my public reading, I'm at the José Martí Airport, about to fly off to Montréal. At passport control, I present my document to the customs officer behind the counter. In taking it, she accidentally drops it. Before leaning down to pick it up, she raises her eyes and shoots me a sardonic smile, almost seductive. "Look this way," she then says, pointing her finger at the camera that captures my face to enter it in the computer. After all the usual procedures, she stamps my passport and returns it to me. I smile, and so does she.

As predicted, nothing has happened.

EPILOGUES

SINCE THAT TIME

On March 16, a month after I left Cuba, a glowing text titled "Defying the Regime During Its Own Book Fair," and devoted in its entirety to my public reading, appears on Cubanet, one of the most popular anticastrist sites.[26] The author of the article, the writer Ernesto Santana Zaldívar, was not in the room during the event. To describe what happened, he relied on the Spanish version of "An Anticipatory Tale," which he found on the Hypermedia Magazine site a week later.[27] This version respects to the word what I said on the morning of February 14. Basing his own text on mine, Zaldívar made no mistakes. My reading unfolded as planned, which is to say that no one interrupted me, and I was able to take my drinks of water at the times indicated. And so as I read off my sentences, my anticipatory tale became a record of the event. Just as I had hoped. Still, I suspect Zaldívar of giving his imagination free rein when describing the feelings my reading aroused in the spectators, who in his view were "more surprised by each paragraph."

At the beginning of his article, Zaldívar recalls that in an interview for *Juventud Rebelde* that appeared on the day of my reading, the Minister of Culture Abel Prieto declared that the 2017 edition was much better than that of the preceding year.[28] He justified his claim by noting that this year they had given more space to arts and culture and less to the posters of sports stars and animated film heroes. The year's ten best-selling books were also a point of pride for the cultural world, since "no mediocre or superficial work" was to be found there. Abel Prieto was particularly pleased with the presence on the list of *1984*.

---

26 Ernesto Santana Zaldívar, "Desafiar al régimen en su propia Feria del Libro," Cubanet.org, March 16, 2017.

27 Frédérick Lavoie, "Relato de anticipación," Hypermedia Magazine, February 20, 2017.

28 René Camilo García Rivera, "La mercadotecnia puede convertir en caricatura del sueño de Fidel," *Juventud Rebelde*, February 14, 2017.

In concluding his article, Zaldívar used the affront to the regime that my reading, in his view, represented, to take the minister at his word. "With this explosion of energy from out of the midst of a graveyard, it's certain that this fair was superior to the preceding one. And if during the next fair, Frédérick Lavoie's finished book is presented, then without doubt [that edition] will be even better." A few comments on the article offered me more kudos. I was applauded for "having said what others keep silent."

During the days following Zaldívar's text appearing online, Daniel is uneasy. He fears it will be taken up by other dissident media outlets. If many other articles on my reading are published, the Cuban cultural institutions will have to react. And inevitably, they'll end up summoning him to explain his role in the event.

A few weeks later he writes that "fortunately, nothing has happened," adding again that "nothing much would have occurred even in the worst-case scenario." Zaldívar's article continues to entail no consequences.

In reading "An Anticipatory Tale" in public in Cuba, my aim was to defy an unwritten but obvious limit to freedom of expression on the island in order to highlight its very existence. I wanted to push the exercise far enough that the regime would have to ask itself whether to react, but not far enough to cause trouble for anyone, including myself. I had calculated that after having evaluated all the factors involved – the internal and external contexts, the gravity of the infraction, the origins of the reader, etc. – the authorities would decide that it was in their best interest to do nothing. I could have miscalculated. But it seems that I was right.

Still, there were two things I had not anticipated in giving a permanent form to "An Anticipatory Tale" a year before the book appeared. The first is that I later discovered that, contrary to what I affirmed, not all the Spanish editions of *Animal Farm* have the title *Rebelión en la granja*. In fact, even the one published by Librerías Unidas – and whose cover I had not seen at that time – was called not *Rebelión* ... but *La Rebelión en la granja*. The other thing I had not foreseen was that I would eventually decide to make the word *"voyage"* plural in the subtitle of *Avant l'après*. This minor change did not in any way alter the formal commitment I had made at the end of "An Anticipatory Tale," not to demand any copyright for the publication of this book in Cuba. If you are now reading a Cuban version of *Antes del después*, know that I am very happy.

*

At the end of March 2017, I write an email to Arnold August, the pro-regime Montréal intellectual who had tried to remove me from the panel "Intersecting Gazes: The History of Cuba as a Catalyst for Québec Writing" during Québec Day at the book fair. I share with him what I know of the incident and suggest to him that he send me his version of the facts, so that I may publish it in its entirety in my book. I also take the opportunity to confess that even if he was not successful in barring me from the panel on that day, the message he sent to the organizers still had an impact on my participation:

> Knowing that each of my words risked being analyzed by you and perhaps by others, I deliberately put the accent on my most consensual opinions, rather than those that might create discomfort among the audience ...
>
> This restraint was, however, very much in my own self-interest. I wanted to be sure not to compromise in any way the reading of my "Anticipatory Tale" (which you will find attached to this email), planned for two days later. Since the reading had been organized independent of the Canadian delegation, I knew that it would be simple for the Cuban authorities to find a pretext to cancel it without even causing a diplomatic incident.
>
> In the light of the information I later received, it seems that my precautions were justified. Immediately after the

panel, a Cuban in his mid-forties representing himself as a sociologist, approached me. He wanted to share with me his objection to the idea that Cuba would soon be entering a post-castrist period, as I had just affirmed. ... We did not agree, but our discussion ended with a cordial handshake.

A few minutes after our conversation, I saw you talking to him. Is he a friend of yours? If I ask the question, it's that it was later reported to me that this man was in fact an informer for the Cuban secret service. I would not have made much of this allegation if not for the fact that a few days later another source told me – without knowing that I had already been tipped off – that there were one or more informers in the room at the time of the panel. They were there, it seems, to evaluate the contents of my contribution. Perhaps it was your email that inspired the authorities' sudden interest in me?

In any case, exercising caution in what I said during the panel turned out to be a wise decision. Again according to the second source, the informer or informers concluded after the event that I did not represent a danger, and that there would be no point in sending observers to my public reading two days later.

If the agents had been present to hear my "Anticipatory Tale," do you think they would have deemed it necessary to interrupt me at a certain point? Also, do you know if the "sociologist" to whom we both spoke was the informer who defused the authorities' fears in my regard? And you, what did you think of my participation in the panel and of my "Anticipatory Tale"?

Five days after sending my letter, I receive a laconic message from Arnold August: "No attachment to this email."

Neither sending the documents, nor another attempt to contact him a month and a half later, resulted, unfortunately, in my obtaining a more detailed reply on his part.

PART OF THE WHOLE STORY

Santa Cruz de Rivadulla
Santiago de Compostela
La Coruña, Spain

May 28, 1961

Dear X,

It may surprise you to receive news from me from Spain. At last I had to take the road to exile: the only solution left today in our unfortunate country. Anything I may tell you about is a pale picture of the reality. I myself have suffered, and directly, the consequences of a regime where the human being has been converted into something expendable to achieve given ends.

The day of the hapless invasion, of which those of us that were in the underground had no advance notice, I was arrested in the evening together with 11 more people from our borough. The arrest was made at my bookstore. From there I was taken, together with other companions in misfortune to the Financial Bank, and from there to the moat of Morro Castle. There I was kept for 11 days. Anything I may tell you about the suffering undergone is inadequate. Imagine, we – a total of more than 7,000 men – were kept outdoors, and had to withstand during the day a scorching sun, and during the night, thanks to a late hour northern gale, an unbearable cold. As the prisoners' relatives did not know the place of detention, especially in the first days, no one had available even a miserable blanket with which to cover himself. Physiological needs had to be performed in front of others, like animals. We spent a day without water, and when water was finally provided it was by way of installing a hose hanging down the side of the moat wall, and from which the entire camp had to obtain its supply. You can readily imagine the scenes that took place to obtain the first swallow of water in over a day. We were kept without food for two days. When food was provided, the rations were so small and ridiculous – they came in little boxes – that I renounced mine. Food was organized on a little better basis later, but even then you had to stand in line more than 4 hours to obtain the miserable pittance. On the second night of our internment there, the most fantastic scene of collective panic that I have ever witnessed in my life took place. At about 8:30 that night, word spread through the internees that the sentries were going to stage a false alarm announcing the overthrow of Fidel to provoke a reaction of joy among the prisoners and massacre them. I want to tell you that the place where we found ourselves was an open ditch so that no one upon entering there could dispel from his mind that the location was the most appropriate one for a massacre that could be asked for. As you may readily gather, the stage was perfect. As it developed, at 9:00 at night, tracer bullets were fired over the open ditch, accompanied by machine gun bursts, together with commands from the sentries ordering us not to move or we would be cut down. As I told you, the panic was indescribable. I know cases of men that urinated and defecated; others, seeking refuge, threw themselves into a corner more or less protected that the people had converted into a provisional latrine, and wallowed in the feces of the whole camp. The shaking of knees could be materially heard, and everywhere could be heard voices begging for mercy. In short, something Dantesque. To summarize it, I can say that in the course of the 11 days that I was detained, six persons became insane, several had heart trouble, and a typhoid epidemic started.

I had the immense good fortune of being freed on the 27th. I had previously planned to take a trip to Spain and had a reservation for the sixth of May, so I saw an opening in the skies. I lived all those days in enormous tension. If we meet one day, I'll tell you in detail everything I went through, but to summarize it, let me tell you that the Friday before my voyage, that is to say the day before, my publishing enterprise was intervened (confiscated); they proceeded to cart away all our production.

Two or three days before sailing, I saw your mother. She beseeched me to write you and tell you, once free to do so, what was the state of the nation. I promised her and as soon as I have had an opportunity I have proceeded to inform you. First of all, let me tell you that she is in good health, although naturally, like everyone else, she is anguished by the inferno that exists in Cuba. As for the rest, you can form an idea from what I have related. Cuba is today a police state; one lives by terror and in terror. Subject to be denounced by any civic (minded) citizen (informer) member of the famous committees. I think I can thus summarize the state of our unfortunate country.

As for my future plans, I can tell you that in that respect I followed your advice and at last obtained my graduate degree. I think I have been the last to graduate from (The Catholic University of) Villanueva. I shall be in New York in the first days of September. There I shall try to find my way to see if it's possible to make headway in the field of psychology or in something else. Needless to say, I shall be very grateful for any information in this regard.

Meanwhile, I am here with my wife and my children, attempting to live a new life and to forget a little what has gone before.

I hope to be able soon to discuss things with you.

With best regards,
Adolfo Cacheiro Fernández

*

Toward the end of 1957, a new bookstore opens its doors on Obispo Street in Havana. The main commercial artery of the old town already has half a dozen, almost all of them – if not all – owned by immigrants, originally from Galicia. El Gato de Papel ("the paper cat"), the new shop, is no exception. Its owner, Adolfo Cacheiro, thirty years old, was born in Cuba, but is of Galician ancestry. His father, who bears the same name, was born in this province in Spain's north-east. He came to the island at the age of sixteen with barely a penny in his pocket. Adolfo Cacheiro the elder became a prosperous Havana businessman. At the end of the 1950s, he owns restaurants, property, and above all a licence to distribute national lottery tickets. It's to this last that he primarily owes his fortune.

Since a young age, Cacheiro the younger has worked for his father. Ethically speaking, he is, all the same, uncomfortable with the family's source of income. The national lottery is the cash cow of dictators. Fulgencio Batista, like Gerardo Machado two decades earlier, receives a percentage of the ticket sales directly, and that money helps him to sustain his regime.

The chain of lottery kiosks Cacheiro the elder owns is called El Gato Negro ("the black cat"). When his son persuades him to help him to open a bookstore, he grants him a tiny space next to a ticket outlet on Obispo Street. The two Cats are side by side, which permits the elder Cacheiro to keep an eye on his son, whose political views he considers radical.

When the bookstore opens, resistance to the Batista regime is growing across the country. In the Sierra Maestra mountains, Castro is heading up a band of insurgents. In Havana as well, there is organized dissidence. Adolfo the elder fears that his son is tempted to get involved. His fears soon prove to be founded.

To help him run the bookstore, the young Cacheiro hires some of his classmates from St. Thomas of Villanova Catholic University. Like him, these young men are leftist intellectuals, nationalists, anti-imperialists, and for the most part anti-communists. Shortly after its opening, El Gato de Papel becomes a gathering place for the members of the Civic Resistance Movement. One of its leaders, Delio Gómez Ochoa – who after the revolution's triumph was defeated trying to export the Revolution to the Dominican Republic – there holds meetings with the movement's supporters. At certain times of the day, Carlos Rodríguez Bua, the young store clerk, barely fourteen years old, is instructed not to let anyone into the shop. In the back of the store, dissidents are printing up propaganda leaflets and preparing Molotov cocktails to launch attacks on the regime. When Cacheiro the elder discovers what is going on in the locale right next to his, he demands that his son send away all his revolutionary friends. His son refuses. Their relationship will never recover from this affront.

On January 1, 1959, while the young Cacheiro is celebrating the Revolution's victory, Adolfo the elder knows that he has just lost everything. The new regime will necessarily associate him with the deposed dictator, and games of chance will soon be banned, marking an end to El Gato Negro. The following month he leaves Cuba, never to return, handing over his properties to his son.

Now out of hiding, one of the Castro brothers – Raúl, or perhaps the eldest, Ramón – becomes a regular customer at El Gato de Papel. One day, when Castro is visiting the bookstore, Adolfo Cacheiro makes him an invitation: why doesn't he come one of these days to visit his estate at Las Cuevas del Cura, on the outskirts of Havana? And while he's at it, why not bring along his brother Fidel? A short time later, the leader of the Revolution and Ramón or Raúl honour the invitation. Cacheiro proudly shows them the large natural caves that are a distinctive feature of the family property. The Castro brothers note that the site includes a hill overlooking the coast of the Florida Strait. A few days, or weeks, or months later, Adolfo Cacheiro learns that his land has been requisitioned by the State. It will be transformed into a military site. This sudden expropriation, his growing awareness of the regime's increasing authoritarianism, or probably a combination of the two, tips him into the camp of the counter-revolutionaries.

In addition to his bookstore, Adolfo Cacheiro owns a publishing house. Five and a half decades later, his wife and children will have forgotten its name, just as they will have lost the memory of his presumed partner in this venture, but they will say that they are certain of one thing: that during this tumultuous time, Adolfo Cacheiro did, among other titles, publish Eudocio Ravines's book *La Gran Estafa*. In this book, the Peruvian ex-communist denounces the tactics Moscow uses in order to try to widen its influence in Latin America and elsewhere. For Cacheiro, the publication of this book at a time when Fidel Castro is edging dangerously close to Nikita Khrushchev's Soviet Union is a way of warning his countrymen about the direction the Revolution is taking.

A Cuban edition of *La Gran Estafa* appears in August 1960, under the banner of Librerías Unidas.

Toward the end of 1960, Adolf Cacheiro sends his wife and two children to Santa Cruz de la Rivadulla, his family's ancestral village in Spain. At about the same time, El Gato de Papel becomes once again a secret meeting place. Those who not so long ago found themselves plotting there against the dictator Batista now gather to plan for the overthrow of his successor.

In February 1961, Cuban exiles, including Félix Rodríguez – who will years later participate in the capture of Che in Bolivia – secretly arrive in Havana. Their mission is to make contact with anti-revolutionary groups and to furnish them with arms. An invasion is being prepared. When it is put in motion and the revolutionary armed forces are routed, the Havana underground will assume control of the capital's key institutions.

While awaiting this imminent operation, whose exact date and place they do not know, the counter-revolutionaries are ordered to go into hiding in farms on the outskirts of the city. Some of Adolfo Cacheiro's friends take up arms, but not him. Yet in providing them with a place to meet, he is nevertheless participating in the conspiracy.

A few hours after the beginning of the Bay of Pigs invasion in April, he is arrested and held for eleven days in the Morro Castle, just beside la Cabaña.

On May 5, 1961, one week after his liberation, his publishing house is searched. The next day, the revolutionary authorities turn up at his bookstore to arrest him again. Adolfo Cacheiro is then at the José Martí Airport, waiting for a flight to Spain. It's a coincidence. His ticket was bought long before. To enable their boss to leave the country before being caught, the El Gato de Papel employees let the police cool their heels, assuring them that Cacheiro is running errands and that he'll be back soon. The ruse works. The plane takes off with Cacheiro on board. His bookstore will not long survive his departure.

From Spain he sends a letter to a Cuban friend to give him news of his mother and of the country, telling him about his difficulties and informing him of his imminent arrival in New York. A few weeks later he again crosses the Atlantic, this time on board an ocean liner with his wife and children.

During his exile in New York, Adolfo Cacheiro Fernández becomes the director of an orphanage. At the same time, he maintains a private practice as a psychologist. Both anti-imperialist and anti-communist, his feelings regarding the Revolution remain complex until the end of his life. He dies of heart disease on January 19, 1979, at the age of fifty-one, without ever again setting foot in Cuba.

*

During the mid-1940s, Rafael Fernández Villa-Urrutia is a law student at the University of Havana. Among his classmates, there is a well-built, articulate young man by the name of Fidel Castro. The two are not friends. Rafael does not like Fidel, just as he does not like law. Born into an aristocratic family in the capital, he prefers literature, language, and the arts.

A decade later, as Fidel is fighting the Batista dictatorship in the mountains, Fernández Villa-Urrutia is shuffling between Havana, where he is the assistant director of the National Museum of Fine Arts, Latin America, and Europe, where he is doing museological research thanks to a UNESCO grant.

On the night of December 31, 1958, to January 1, 1959, as Batista is fleeing and the revolutionaries are entering Havana, Rafael Fernández Villa-Urrutia is celebrating the New Year with some extravagance at the

Hotel Capri in Vedado. He does not share the widespread euphoria. Even if many of his close friends, including the bookseller Adolfo Cacheiro, are rejoicing in the triumph of the Revolution, Fernández still sees his former classmate Fidel as a brute, and does not believe a word that comes out of his mouth.

A few weeks or months later, Rafael is accused of murdering a revolutionary. But he is released before the case even goes to trial. His alibi is airtight: at the time of the crime, he was outside the country. The accusations are dropped, but he loses his job as assistant director of the museum. He suspects that the whole story was concocted to get rid of him, because he knows too much about Fidel. If he'd been found guilty of the crime, he would probably have been shot.

At the age of thirty-two, now labelled a counter-revolutionary, Rafael Fernández knows that his career on the island is over. He would like to leave to join his father in the United States, but he cannot resign himself to abandoning his sister Margarita, five years younger than he is, who has just given birth to her first child. Awaiting exile, still a bachelor, he's living with his grandmother and surviving thanks to the pension of his dead grandfather, an ex-judge of the Supreme Court.

Unlike her brother, Margarita Cano supports the Revolution. Shortly after the victory, she is hired by the José Martí National Library as an assistant to her aunt, María Teresa Freyre de Andrade, the institution's new director. The library, which had just opened its doors when the revolutionaries took power, is an institution in full flower. Thousands of books have been bought, and mobile libraries have been created to support the new government's literacy program. Margarita is swept away by it all. Working at the National Library, she is making a direct contribution to the building of a better society. And it's the Revolution that has made that possible.

Probably during the second half of 1960, Rafael Fernández is offered a small job. He is asked to translate from English the novel *Animal Farm* by George Orwell. Fernández sees in this allegory of the Russian Revolution a depiction that is also applicable to Fidel Castro's regime, which is in fact drawing ever closer to Moscow.

Five and a half decades later, Margarita will say that she does not know who asked her brother to do this translation, of which she is aware, though she has never seen a copy. She thinks, nevertheless, that it can only have been his good friend the bookseller and publisher Adolfo Cacheiro.

In January 1961, an undetermined number of copies of *La Rebelión en la granja* and of *1984* roll off the presses of the Luz-Hilo printing shop. These books were published by a house called Librerías Unidas.

The translator is not credited in either of these re-editions of Orwell's books. However, a rudimentary comparison with the existing Spanish versions shows that for *1984* the publishers reproduced the 1952 edition from the Destino publishing house in Spain. As for *La Rebelión en la granja*, the text does not correspond to either of the two translations that had previously appeared in Argentina and Mexico. It would seem that the translation published by Librerías Unidas was original. On the other hand, the drawings included in the book were taken from an English Penguin Books edition that appeared in 1954. They are by Joy Batchelor and John Halas, who the same year drew the characters for the cartoon *Animal Farm*, financed by the CIA without the artists' knowledge.

On April 17, 1961, the first day of the Bay of Pigs invasion, Rafael Fernández Villa-Urrutia is at the movies. That evening some of his friends, including Adolfo Cacheiro, are arrested. If he is aware of the imminent invasion, or if he is involved with the underground movement that is preparing an assumption of power by the Havana counter-revolutionaries, he says nothing about it to his sister. While the Year of Education is going full force, and Margarita has just given birth to her second child, she is still supporting the Revolution.

Shortly after the start of the invasion, Rafael and Margarita go onto the Malecón at nightfall. Discreetly, they toss their father's gun, which was still in the family home, into the sea.

In mid-June of the same year, at the José Marti National Library, Fidel Castro meets three times with the island's most prominent artists and intellectuals. In the course of the final meeting, he pronounces a few words that will go down in history. "Inside the Revolution, everything. Outside, nothing." The declaration is vague, but it will subsequently carry the force of law. Over the following weeks, as a consequence, the director of the Library, María Teresa Freyre de Andrade, like all highly placed cultural officials, reorganizes the functioning of the institution. Books disappear from the catalogue. To consult certain titles, users now have to obtain special permission. The same goes for American magazines and newspapers such as *Life* and the *New York Times*.

In 2017, Margarita, the assistant to the director, will recall that George Orwell's *Nineteen Eighty-Four* and *Animal Farm*, as well as Arthur Koestler's *Darkness at Noon*, were among the books that disappeared. As far as she remembers, the National Library then possessed no Spanish edition of those books, either Cuban or foreign.

This censoring of the catalogue shatters the last illusions Margarita Cano harbours regarding the blessings of the Revolution. In the months that follow, as she seeks in vain a polio vaccine for her newborn, she begins to think of exile.

On October 17, 1962, after months of preparation, Margarita, her husband, their two children, and her brother Rafael board an airplane bound for Miami. They don't know it, but this is the second-last flight before commercial air traffic will cease between Cuba and the United States, a hiatus that will last fifty-four years. A day earlier, the American president John F. Kennedy had received in his office aerial images taken from a spy plane, proving that Soviet missiles were installed in Cuba. For the following thirteen days, the entire planet is on the edge of its seat. Never has it come so close to the outbreak of nuclear war. On October 28, the First Secretary of the Central Committee of the Communist Party of the Soviet Union, Nikita Khrushchev, agrees to remove his nuclear missiles from Cuba. Some of the missiles were hidden in caves outside

Havana, on a property that until recently belonged to Adolfo Cacheiro's family.

After a long and successful museological career in Chicago and Williamstown, Rafael Fernández dies from cancer in Massachusetts on November 30, 1999.

His sister Margarita still lives in Miami's Little Havana neighbourhood, and has vivid memories of this turbulent time.

*

Some pieces of the puzzle are still missing.

Over the course of my research, I found no document and heard no testimony that would enable me to claim with complete certainty that Adolfo Cacheiro the younger owned the publishing house Librerías Unidas S.A., and was therefore the publisher of the first Cuban edition of *1984*. All indications are, however, that he was.

It took me some time to find my way to Adolfo Cacheiro and to come to this conclusion. In an earlier chapter, I referred to a Librerías Unidas ad in the April 3, 1960, edition of the conservative newspaper *Diario de la Marina*.[29] Happening on it during my research in September 2016, I had not paid it very much attention. I had been more attracted by the report in the paper a few centimetres to the left, regarding Arévalo's *Fábula del tiburón y las sardinas*. I had noted the three Havana bookstore logos below the ad, but it was only ten months later, on re-examining my photos of this newspaper page, that I realized it held the key to the solution of the first mystery: El Gato de Papel, Servi-Libros, Madiedo. These were the Librerías Unidas Editions' "united bookstores."

Entering these names one by one into a search engine, I came upon the blog of Carlos Rodríguez Bua, a retired engineer. In one of his entries, he talked of having been a clerk at the El Gato de Papel bookstore in 1958. He said he had fond memories of the then-owner, Adolfo

---

29   See pp. 165–166.

Cacheiro, a "son of a Galician who had a lot of nerve and a passion for his work," and who had "taught me a lot." Carlos Rodríguez Bua added that he had been agreeably surprised to learn more recently that one of Cacheiro's sons, Jorge Luis, had become a well-respected theatre director in the United States. In 2010, he was the first Cuban American man of the theatre in half a century to present in Havana a play written by a son of Cuban immigrants.

It was Jorge Luis who told me the story of his father. He was only four years old when, at the end of 1960, his family left Cuba for Spain, without Adolfo. And so he could only make reference to anecdotes his father later told him, along with the memories of his mother Haydee, still living, but who knew next to nothing about her husband's commercial activities at the time. Like many women in those days, she never got involved.

It was also Jorge Luis who sent me the letter Adolfo had sent to an anonymous friend in the United States soon after he fled. Luis sent the English translation of the original letter, which had been made by the friend in question and sent to an anti-communist association in Washington; the friend presented it as an "authentic narrative" by "an honourable and cultured man" of the hell Cuba had become under Castro. In the English translation of the letter, as in the few introductory paragraphs he had appended, the friend had taken care to protect his identity with an X, and to sign it with the pseudonym Pal A. Din.

While I was trying to trace the identity of this Pal A. Din, a friend of Adolfo Cacheiro put me on the trail of Rafael Fernández Villa-Urrutia, a lawyer who loved the arts, and who was also, according to him, an excellent English-to-Spanish translator. The biographical details later provided to me by Fernández's daughter and sister forced me to discard the possibility that he was behind the mysterious Pal A. Din. Rafael had, in fact, not yet left the island when Cacheiro sent his letter, and his mother had already died, while Cacheiro had testified to the good health of the recipient's mother.

In telling me that Rafael Fernández had translated Orwell around 1960, his daughter Elena and his sister Margarita did help me to come closer to solving another mystery, however: the origin of the *Animal Farm* translation used by Librerías Unidas.

All indications are that Fernández's translation is the one found in the pages of the Librerías Unidas edition. But as with the connection between Adolfo Cacheira and this publishing house, I have no direct evidence to prove it beyond any doubt. If there were documents that at one time attested to these links, they have probably disappeared, perhaps as early as May 5, 1961, the day of the raid on Adolfo Cacheiro's publishing house.

Those involved in independent publishing in Cuba in the first two years of the Revolution for the most part fled the island, taking with them only what was strictly required. Half a century later, they're almost all dead. It's possible that the proof underpinning my theories still exists somewhere, lodged in the memory of an old man or woman, or in some dusty personal archives in Cuba or elsewhere. I've perhaps just not found them. If they exist, I hope that the publication of this book will encourage those who possess them to rescue them from oblivion.

*

Trying to shed light on the circumstances surrounding the appearance of two Cuban editions of *1984*, I was aware of the futility of my quest from the start. Even if I were to end up discovering the identity of those who initiated their publication, these would constitute details of no great importance in the wider scope of what the country underwent between the release of the two editions. But I knew that along the road, I might come upon stories and anecdotes that would help me to better understand Cuba's sociopolitical context at the time of their respective publications.

What I've derived from my research is something more interesting than my discoveries themselves: despite all the obstacles the passing of time has placed in my way, I've been able to determine with what is close to certainty the identity of at least one of the people behind the first Cuban edition of *1984*, as well as the reasons that motivated him to republish this book at that precise moment in his life and in Cuban history. On the other hand, even if the players who initiated and authorized the publication of the second edition of this book with Arte y Literatura in 2016 are presumably still alive, and if I have perhaps even conversed with some of them, I have not been able to get to the bottom of the book's appearance.

Perhaps out of sheer stubbornness, I have not lost hope of one day unearthing the whole story behind this second edition. After having encountered so much resistance in the statements of those who know, I can only hope that the release of this book will help loosen some tongues.

AFTER

The present is a time so elusive that we could be excused for doubting its existence. However, it is where we are obliged to live our lives from birth until death. It is there, voluntarily or not, that we digest the past and ingest the future. The present has no duration other than what we lend to it. To try to understand it, to grasp its essence, we are constrained to impose on it arbitrary markers, to create a space between past and future.

To recount a time period when it is still passing before our eyes and when we are ignorant of what, exactly, will mark its end and even what will be considered as its beginning, is to try to draw near to our true experience of time, an experience where the muddled past and the elusive present are our only tools in confronting the murky future toward which we are steadily advancing.

In this book, I have deliberately restricted Cuba's present to somewhere between February 2016 and February 2017, the better to define it. I wanted to bear witness to this period because, as I explained from the outset, the present seemed to be leaning more toward the future than the past.

The first edition, in French, of this book, appeared in Québec in another month of February, that of 2018. For a long time, Raúl Castro had been promising that he would leave the presidency of the country on the twenty-fourth of that month. At the end of 2017, the Cuban National Assembly declared, however, a two-month prolongation of his second term, until April 19, 2018. The damage caused by Hurricane Irma in September forced a delay in the general election, and so to the Communist Party's designation of a successor to the president. In renouncing his post, Raúl, eighty-six years old, did not retire completely from politics. He said he wanted to remain General Secretary of the Party until the next Congress in 2020.

Confined to the past, I don't know if what was foreseen took place as planned. You, who are reading these lines in 2018, 2021, 2025, or perhaps even in 2059 or 2084, know better than I do at the moment of writing. A part of what was still for me the future is already for you the past.

If we cannot trace the future with absolute certainty as far as the very moment when it will be there, upon us, still it rarely manifests itself as something unexpected and inexplicable. More often than not, it results from an accumulation of pasts. It would not be surprising if between the pages of this account that are already obsolete, you may have detected certain tendencies that have become significant since this time, tendencies I was probably unaware of recording. It is my hope that these clues as to what is to come will have helped you to better connect the dots between one time period and another, between the Cuba of yesteryear and that of your own present day.

*

On each of my three visits to Havana, I went back unfailingly to the same address: 418 Concordia Street, in the neighbourhood of Centro Habana. I usually arrived shortly after 6 p.m., as the sun was beginning to descend over the city. When I crossed the threshold of this building – known as La Mansión Camagüey – the friendly doorman asked me if there was a reservation in my name at the restaurant. I replied routinely that I hoped rather to make my way to the bar on the roof, which at this hour had just opened. Ever since its beginnings in 1996, the *paladar* La Guarida had been one of the most popular spots in town. In recent years it had become a required destination for Mick Jagger, Madonna, Kim Kardashian, and the Monaco princesses of this world who come to see Havana *before it changes*. I knew that it would be hopeless for me to make an impromptu appearance early in the evening with an empty stomach, hoping to find a table. But the bar was still easily accessible. The doorman's wide smile was my green light to climb the equally wide marble, semi-circular staircase that Tomás Gutiérrez Alea's film *Fresa y chocolate* had made recognizable to all: its statue of a headless woman at the bottom of the balustrade, the faded wall running alongside it, and the lengthy quote from Fidel on the landing in which he expounds on the origins of his slogan, "Our homeland or death!" It is to here, at the beginning of Alea's classic film, that Diego, a scholarly and marginal homosexual, leads David, a member of the Young Communist League, who will become his friend rather than the lover he is hoping for. Diego calls his apartment, where he lives surrounded by books and works of art, La Guarida, "the den," a place, he says, "to which you don't just invite anyone."

At the top of the staircase was an empty floor with tablecloths and napkins drying on cords hung from pillars, pending a likely transformation of the space into another dining room for the *paladar*. A second staircase similar to the first led to the restaurant. On my final visit, however, due to ongoing renovations, you were obliged to make the climb by another route. Entering La Mansión Camagüey, you had to go to the end of the hall and climb other stairways, much narrower, that allowed you to peer into the last apartments in the building that were still occupied. There you saw residents watching television, cooking or talking, hoping either that the offers for their few square metres would continue to rise, or on the contrary, that the popularity of La Guarida would plateau and they'd be able once more to lead a quiet life.

Whichever route I took, once I arrived at the restaurant floor I climbed another staircase, this one spiral, that led me to the rooftop bar. At this hour, its few customers were sipping a beer or an early mojito, while the employees were finishing their preparations. At the back, a huge rectangle of white boards framed the landscape: bathed in the twilight glow, the breathtaking buildings of Centro Habana set against the Florida Strait always, whatever the weather, resembled a postcard come to life.

What most of the customers seemed not to know, however – since even later in the evening it remained almost deserted – was that a watchtower opened soon before my first trip offered an even more spectacular view of the capital. To get there you had to climb a second spiral staircase tucked into a corner you would have thought was reserved only for employees. Once on top you had a 360-degree view. To the north was the sea, and invisible in the distance was the Florida peninsula that so many islanders had risked their lives over the last half-century to try to reach; toward the entrance to the Bay of Havana in the east was the emblematic lighthouse of the Morro Castle, where Adolfo Cacheiro and seven thousand other counter-revolutionaries were imprisoned in April 1961; just beside it was la Cabaña, the site of summary executions in the past, and of the book fair today; a bit more to the south, at the heart of Old Havana, was the Capitol's cupola in the course of renovation; in the southwest, the José Martí monument, the reference point from on high for Revolution Square; to the west, the Habana Libre, the ex-Hilton and the capital's headquarters for the *barbudos* in January 1959, marking the beginning of the Vedado neighbourhood, and recalling the triumphant entry into history of the revolutionaries; and finally, a few blocks from La Guarida, there was the Hermanos Ameijeiras Hospital, a concrete mastodon twenty or so stories high, which the previous regime started to build and which was initially intended for bankers rather than the sick.

During the year that I made these pilgrimages to the roof of La Guarida, Havana's landscape barely changed. The restoration of Old Havana went on apace, but in Centro, just outside the Manor beneath my feet, almost no building had received a facelift. Here, as in most of the city's and the country's neighbourhoods, the real estate sector, like most of the sectors in the economy and in daily life, had remained static. Fearing that a too-abrupt loosening of restrictions would result in its losing control, and in the end, its power, the regime continued to vacillate between declared reforms and a strategic withdrawal.

In making the tour of this weary city's four cardinal points, I could not help imagining the same place in five, ten, thirty, or forty years. If it still existed, what would I have before my eyes? A landscape, largely the same, but showing its age a bit more? Or, on the contrary, an immense construction site where speculation has run riot, a past has been erased, and skyscrapers, emblematic of new disparities, tower over the ruins of historic buildings? I don't know the answer. All I know for certain is that, just as now, the landscape will mirror the society that inhabits it.

*

In 1984, George Orwell depicted the worst imaginable future for humanity: a world in which human beings, obsessed by their ever-increasing thirst for absolute power, have in the end done away with the last remnants of freedom and goodness buried in their souls. Several other writers of the twentieth and the beginning of the twenty-first centuries have turned to dystopias to comment on their times. They have done so less to *predict* the future than to *ward off* the ugliest forms it might take if certain current tendencies were maintained.

Some rarer authors have wished, on the contrary, to present a picture of the best humanity might hope for in the future. The utopias they described fed the dreams of both the masses and the elites. Some leaders were even inspired by them, including Lenin, marked in his youth by his reading of *What Is to Be Done?* by Nikolay Chernyshevsky. In this novel, written in its entirety from a Czarist jail cell fifty-five years before the Bolshevik Revolution, the heroine Vera Pavlovna sees in a dream a paradise where workers have been granted eternal joy.

The events of the twentieth century demonstrated that, in the real world, utopias on paper invariably result in dystopias when attempts are made to put them into practice.

Not being a prophet or a decision maker, I cannot hope to predict Cuba's future beyond the next sentence of a text read in public at the Havana book fair. Like the Cubans, still deprived of the right and the real power to influence the course of events in their society, I can only use my imagination.

As I said earlier, the future is most often the product of an accumulation of pasts. The *after* is a reaction to the *befores*. And so it would be naive to imagine that the period following that of the Castro brothers – should it come to an end – would represent an entirely new start. If ever another deceiver manages to persuade Cubans that this is possible, we would have to fear a new utopic cycle that would in the long run turn out badly.

There is no magic solution for a transition from authoritarianism to democracy. And in any case, democracy is far from being a cure for all ills. It is sometimes, even, part of the problem. However, as has often been repeated and proven, it remains the least bad system of government. It is so not only because it guarantees freedoms, but because it protects a bit better than the others the illusion that the *best* is possible and achievable.

Between 1989 and 1991, when most of the planet's communist regimes collapsed, Castro's system, beyond all expectations, survived. But since then, this survival has most resembled a clinical death. The system has to all intents and purposes been drained of its ideological and material substance. Beginning with the "special period in time of peace" – and even before, according to some – the realization of dreams has been a luxury that Cubans could only hope for somewhere beyond the island. Their present looked solely toward the past.

The sense of change that has appeared in recent years has had the tentative effect of turning the present's gaze to the future. But there is a good chance that this future will disappoint Cubans. The challenges are great and complex. To bond with the twenty-first century is not an easy task. Settling accounts with the past is crucial, but to dwell on it at length opens the door to a variety of vengeful acts, increasing the risk of reproducing the behaviour one wants to punish and ban.

Despite all these hazards, I still see hope for Cuba. It resides in the deferred arrival of the hoped-for transition. Unlike the Romanians, the Poles, and the Czechs in 1989, or the Soviets in 1991, the Cubans I met during my trips to the island harboured no illusions regarding what was to come. They did not imagine it to be radiant, but just less bad than the present and the past. They knew that the sudden collapse of the regime would not remedy from one day to the next all that is dysfunctional in their society. They also knew that to blindly embrace the socio-economic and political models of their great neighbour to the north, which consistently display their flaws, was not a solution either. This future of which they cautiously dreamed, without even using the word "dream," was for something *better*. Not the *best*, but *better*. Because after fifty-eight years of endless talk and disappointments they knew only too well the true nature of promising the *best*.

If ever in future years such a transition is set in motion on the island, free of grandiose illusions, a transition toward a utopia of the *better*, perhaps Cubans will succeed in drawing near to George Orwell's true dream, that which inspired all his writing as of 1936: the dream of a democratic socialism where human beings, mindful that they can never be totally *new*, will simply and humbly try to forge for themselves a society that is more just, more fair, more free, more prosperous, and in the end, happier.

AFTERWORD

I have not returned to Cuba since the last trip described in this book. A few copies of *Avant l'après: Voyages à Cuba avec George Orwell* have, however, made their way there on their own, in the baggage of vacationers or of Québécois who live on the island for part of the year. Some have told me that they experienced a certain uneasiness when they passed through customs with my book in their possession. But to my knowledge not a single one was confiscated – and such an incident would have surprised me. Its appearance in French passed unnoticed on the island. Nothing on its cover hinted that what was inside might be deemed subversive in Cuba. For the responsible authorities to have been suspicious, they would have had to read through the contents of that black and yellow, French-language brick.

My research into the many editions of *1984* published around the world has taught me that once freed from the author's control, a book can live its own life in different languages, and face adventures that may sometimes even run contrary to the author's initial intentions. As I write these lines, I can only imagine the fate reserved for the English translation of *Avant l'après*. With a bit of luck, a copy may land on the desk of a highly ranked English-speaking official in the Cuban literary world who has information regarding the publication of *1984* by Arte y Literatura in 2016. And with even more luck, this person will be kind enough to pass it on to me so that I may include it in the afterword of a subsequent edition.

From where I am now situated in time, I also have the right to dream that a reading of *Orwell in Cuba* will jog the memory of a Cuban exile who knew the Revolution's first days, and that they will be prompted to enlighten me regarding their old publisher friend's precise motivations when, early in 1961, he decided to publish a first Cuban edition of *1984*.

Without taking anything away from my immense satisfaction in seeing *Avant l'après* appear in the English language, I must admit that my fondest dream remains to be able to witness, one day, its (re)birth in Spanish. For the moment it seems unlikely that a book that includes the sentence "I hate Fidel Castro" could be published or imported and distributed on the island, at least officially.

Since my last trip to Cuba, according to what my Cuban friends report, along with the media, the sociopolitical context has barely changed. Miguel Díaz-Canel, head of state since April 2018, has been behaving like a good soldier of the Revolution under the approving gaze of Raúl Castro, who remains head of the Communist Party. On one hand, the regime made the internet accessible on cellphones in December 2018, and through home-based Wi-Fi connections in May 2019. On the other, in August 2019 it swallowed up the SNET network, up to then illegal but tolerated, and incorporated it into its official institutions, thus pronouncing the death sentence of that intranet so dear to gamers and other geeks.

The regime, however, cannot alone be blamed for the reversals of the last three years. Since occupying the White House in January 2017, Republican President Donald Trump has declared null and void almost all the measures that his predecessor, Barack Obama, put in place in order to relax the embargo imposed on Cuba in hopes of provoking change. The return of those restrictions has hurt the Cuban economy and, along with it, a majority of Cubans, without endangering the regime. Fabricio, *1984*'s translator, had begun to make some decent money from guided visits of Old Havana that he offered to tourists through the platform Airbnb Experiences – but the new restrictions imposed on American citizens travelling to Cuba deprived him of most of his clientele.

In this book I have preferred to concentrate on the present I observed rather than to speculate on events that might in future produce sudden or incremental changes in Cuba. For the purposes of this afterword, let me offer a few avenues for reflection on that subject.

It's possible that Raúl Castro's official retirement in 2021, or his death, might alter the dynamics in play at the heart of the regime. It is also possible that when the last remaining historical figure of the 1959

Revolution vacates the halls of power for good, the survival instincts of the younger Party chiefs will move them to pull together in order to ensure the survival of the system that has served them so well, at least for a few more years.

The arrival of a Democrat in the White House in 2020 or later, if it is accompanied by a majority for that party in both the House and the Senate, might at last result in the lifting of the embargo on Cuba. This decision would deprive the Cuban government of its main excuse for the pitiful state of the country's economy. More than the embargo itself, which has never ceased to demonstrate its counterproductive character over the decades, it is its removal that would pose a threat to the island's status quo, for better, but perhaps also for worse.

What I've experienced and learned in Cuba and elsewhere does not permit me to imagine the likelihood of a (new) popular uprising on the island and an overthrow of the regime. Of course, as we have been reminded by the many revolts across the world during the last decade alone – Tunisia, Syria, Egypt, Ukraine, Armenia, Algeria, etc. – it would be folly to completely exclude such a scenario, as improbable as it may seem today.

In the same way, it would also be imprudent on my part to exclude the possibility that one day, in a Castrist or post-Castrist Cuba, for reasons that I will or will not be able to understand, a Spanish edition may appear of the book you are holding in your hands.

Frédérick Lavoie
Mumbai, India, November 2019

ACKNOWLEDGMENTS

To Fabricio, Daniel, and Eric, alias George, the under-
  pinnings for this book;
to the admirable Cubans I met, often quoted under
  assumed names;
to Zeenat, the *sputnitsa*;
to Seher, the ever-encouraging;
to the Lavoies and to the Nagrees, the family;
to Juliana, Bogdan S., and S. Bogdan, the readers;
to Donald, Nancy, Diana, and Gastón, the translators;
to the CCA and to LOJIQ, the grant-givers;
to La Peuplade and Talonbooks, the publishers;
and to many more wonderful people:
my thanks.

Donald Winkler is a translator of fiction, non-fiction, and poetry. He is a three-time winner of the Governor General's Literary Award for French-to-English Translation and has been a finalist on three other occasions. He lives in Montréal.

Born in Chicoutimi in 1983, **Frédérick Lavoie** is a writer and freelance journalist. He is the author of three non-fiction books, including *For Want of a Fir Tree: Ukraine Undone* (Linda Leith Publishing, 2018). In *Avant l'après: Voyages à Cuba avec George Orwell*, winner of the 2018 Governor General's Literary Award for French-Language Non-Fiction and published in English as *Orwell in Cuba: How 1984 Came to Be Published in Castro's Twilight,* he continues his investigation of the many faces of humanity in troubled times.

As a journalist, Lavoie has contributed to many Canadian and European media outlets, reporting from more than thirty countries. Previously based in Moscow and Chicago, he now divides his time between Montréal and Mumbai. Lavoie is currently writing a book on Bangladesh.

PHOTO: JASMIN LAVOIE